WILD RUINS B.C.

The explorer's guide to Britain's ancient sites

Dave Hamilton

WILD
THINGS
PUBLISHING

Gwal y Filiast, Pembrokeshire & Mid Wales.

WILD RUINS B.C.

Bryn Cader Faner, North Wales & Anglesey

CONTENTS

———

INTRODUCTION

BEST FOR

THE RUINS

THE RUINS
— MAP —

Orkney & Shetland **28**

Northern Highlands **27**

Skye & the Western Isles **26**

Aberdeenshire **24**

Mid-Scotland **23**

West Scotland & Arran **25**

Dumfries & Galloway **22**

Northumberland & Scottish Borders **21**

Lake District **20**

Yorkshire **19**

Peak District **14**

North Wales & Anglesey **18**

Welsh Borders **15**

Pembrokeshire & Mid-Wales **17**

East Anglia **12**

The Cotswolds **11**

High Weald & Kent Downs

Central England **13**

Brecon & South-East-Wales **16**

10

Exmoor & North Devon **4**

Somerset **5**

South Downs **9**

Mid-Cornwall & Bodmin **2**

Dorset **7**

Wiltshire & Wessex **6**

Hampshire & the Isle of Wight **8**

West Penwith & the Scilly Isles **1**

Dartmoor South Devon **3**

Lligwy Burial Chamber, North Wales & Anglesey

Pike o' Stickle Cave, Lake District

FOREWORD
by Francis Pryor

---

rehistory is the story of human life before the discovery of writing. British prehistory is almost a million years long. It is extraordinarily rich and exciting and ends with the coming of the Romans in AD 43. It includes Stonehenge [p80], probably the best-known prehistoric site in the world, and a host of larger and smaller sites of equal importance. It has also been intensively studied for over a hundred years and we probably know more about life in Bronze Age Britain, say four thousand years ago, than we do about the centuries leading up to the Norman Conquest of 1066. Despite this wealth of knowledge, British prehistory was not included in the National Curriculum until very recently – and then only for primary schools. So adults have had to discover it for themselves. This book is a great way to make that journey.

This is a book about pre-Roman Britain that's aimed at people and families who like to get out and about. I have always been one of them: I would far rather get my boots muddy than sit indoors and listen to somebody droning on and on about life in Britain in 5000 BC. Somehow lectures seem so second-hand.

I prefer my information short and to the point. Even better, I like to be informed while I walk around a site. That's why I love guidebooks and this is a guidebook to the whole of prehistoric Britain – complete with a comprehensive timeline that links British prehistory with what was happening in the rest of the world. Of course I was delighted to see that Dave Hamilton mentions Flag Fen [p136] and Seahenge [p136], two sites I was closely involved with, but I was also amazed by the number of smaller sites he includes. And these are so very important because they reveal how ordinary people lived their lives and buried their dead. Inevitably the book has to be biased towards death and burial as these are the sites that still command the landscape; the farms and fields that went with them still lie hidden, just below the surface. Monuments like Stonehenge would be far less impressive if they were not surrounded by hundreds of Bronze Age barrows (burial mounds). With this book in your hand, you can discover them for yourself – just as groups of mourners did some four thousand years earlier.

Francis Pryor

Liddington Castle, Wiltshire & Wessex

WILD RUINS B.C.

*C*lose to the 709-metre summit of Pike of Stickle, high in the Lake District, I sat for a while on the safety of the mountain path, looking down over the edge at the loose scree stones below. It looked like a deadly ski slope, with rocks of all shapes and sizes tumbling down the vast mountainside. It was a clear day and the views were spectacular, much as they would have been 5,000 years ago, when this area was in the heart of the Neolithic axe industry. Precariously perched on the side of this soaring hillside, the people of the Neolithic laboriously carved stone axes from the local Langdale hornstone. Distributed far and wide across the country, they were a Neolithic status symbol, akin to Swiss watches or Italian shoes. Part of their prestige came from where they originated: a place above the clouds, as though mined from the sky itself. Looking

down, for a moment I saw with the eyes of those who had lived thousands of years before and I could understand why the provenance of these axes would have been as important as the axes themselves.

The Lake District marked the halfway point in the creation of this book. A year and a half in, I had walked alongside wild ponies at stone rows on Dartmoor, descended into a 10,000-year-old Somerset burial site, been followed by an inquisitive Orcadian seal along the shores of a 2,000-year-old broch village. I had awoken under canvas close to 5,000 year old tombs, climbed hillforts, walked ancient trackways, carried my infant son on my back to megaliths, monoliths and barrows and visited stone circles in isolated, far-flung corners all over Britain. More adventures lay ahead of me in the months to follow. I would catch sight of sea eagles swooping over an Iron Age coastal fort, watch dolphins dance in the wake of a Hebridean-bound ship, wade through rivers and be caught in a sandstorm. By the end of the three years, I had watched my six-year-old son's eyes fill with wonder at lonely tombs hidden in thick woodland, been lost in thick fog searching for the Stonehenge quarry site in the Preseli mountains and fallen knee-deep into bogs searching for lonely standing stones. Above all, I had got out from behind my desk and experienced the distant and exciting world of Britain's prehistory.

The creation of this book was not just an adventure of the body but also one of the mind. I had set out to understand the world of our ancestors, from the earliest footprints trodden on British shores over 800,000 years ago to the coming of the Romans in AD43. The more I studied, the more fascinated I became with

Nether Largie North Cairns, West Scotland & Arran

The Hurlers, Bodmin & North Cornwall

these strange, alien cultures that once shared our lands. Why did they go to so much effort to erect lonely megaliths and stone rows, and what did they use them for? Did the stone circles of Dartmoor and Bodmin have the same purpose as the recumbent stone circles of Aberdeenshire? Were the hillforts of Somerset and Dorset a meeting ground or defensive structures? Who made the engravings of cup and ring marks into the stones of Northern England and Southern Scotland, and what did they signify? The more I studied, the more I realised how little we really know for certain of these mysterious and ancient people. We can categorise them by the pots they made, by what material they mastered the use of – be it stone, bronze or iron – but we will never know what they called themselves. We can even piece together some aspects of their rituals from the ashes of fires, or from headdresses made from animal remains or even items retrieved from bogs, deliberately broken and thrown into water 3,000 years ago. However, once again we can only speculate what these ceremonies meant to them, and what went through their minds as they lit fires or discarded the items into the water. To put it into perspective, imagine future archaeologists finding a modern grave 4,000 years from now. With the inscription on the stone long eroded, the flesh, clothes and coffin rotted away, what clues would they be given to unravel the threads of a life? The may find a watch, but the strap would be long gone, or a ring and some nails from long-since-rotted shoes. Archaeologists have done an amazing job building on ideas and theories of those that came before them. They spend countless hours digging through the earth to find sometimes minute items or just marks in soil that most of us would miss, to give their best guess of what went on in these ancient times. However, as so much is still unknown, we are free to fill in the blanks, to imagine what life must have been like. I wanted this book to be about both the physical journey and the one through our own imagination. It is a chance to get out and climb those hills, walk those ancient trackways and experience the prehistoric world. So, go visit these amazing fragments of the past, breathe in their air and let your mind wander…

Dave Hamilton

Dave Hamilton

TIMELINE OF PREHISTORY

BRITAIN

800,000 years ago
Hominids leave footprints in Happisburgh (East Anglia).

700,000 years ago
Flint tools used.

500,000 years ago
Homo heidelbergensis uses hand axes, found in Boxgrove, Sussex.

410-380,000 years ago
Interglacial period: Tool use in Swanscombe (High Weald & Kent Downs).

240,000 years ago
Humans with Neanderthal characteristics in Bont-newydd cave, the oldest remains found in Wales (53.2285, -3.4859).

33,000 years ago
Modern human (Homo sapiens) ritually buried in Paviland Cave, Gower (Pembrokeshire & Mid-Wales).

14,000 years ago
First art at Creswell Crags (Peak District).

9000BC
Star Carr deer-skull ritual headdresses used (Yorkshire).

8400BC
Ritual cemetery at Aveline's Hole (Somerset).

8000BC
Hunter-gatherers visit Goldcliff (Brecon & South-East Wales).
Trees cleared (Dartmoor & South Devon).
Timber circle erected at Stonehenge site (Wiltshire & Wessex).
Lunar 'calendar' constructed at Warren Field (Aberdeenshire).

7100BC
Cheddar Man left in Mendip cave (Somerset).

6500-6200BC
Britain becomes an island.

REST OF THE WORLD

3.4 million years ago
Early hominid tool use by Kenyanthropus platyops.

3.2 million years ago
Upright ape, Australopithecus afarensis (Lucy) in Ethiopia.

2.8 million years ago
Homo erectus in Ethiopia (jawbone found in 2015).

800,000 years ago
Last time greenhouse gases were at 2017 levels.

200,000 years ago
First modern humans (Homo sapiens) found in Africa.

70,000 years ago
Toba supervolcano human population poss reduced to 15,000.

45-40,000 years ago
Modern humans arrive in Europe. Neanderthals become extinct.

8000BC
Neolithic Revolution: first farmers in the Fertile Crescent.

PALAEOLITHIC
3.4 million years ago – 11,600 years ago

Stone tools used by proto-humans. Bands of hunters camp out in caves following migratory herds. Britain occupied between ice ages.

MESOLITHIC
9600BC to 4500BC (11,600-6,500 years ago)

Hunter-gatherers, living in temporary camps. First wooden monuments built and boats made from hollowed trunks. Ceremonial burials.

4250BC
Lambourn Long Barrow built (Midlands).

4500-3500BC
Simple pottery made.

4000BC
Medway tombs e.g. Coldrum (High Weald & Kent Downs. Langdale axe factory starts (Lake District).

4000-3500BC
Clyde-type tombs built-Cairn Holy (Dumfries & Galloway), Dalineun (W Scotland & Arran).

3807BC
Sweet Track built across marshlands (Somerset).

3800-3500BC
Cotswold-Severn tombs built e.g. Stoney Littleton (Somerset).

3800BC
Windmill Hill causewayed enclosure is the first structure near Avebury (Wiltshire & Wessex).

3800-2500BC
Long barrows built in Wessex, such as Pimperne (Dorset).

4000BC
Rice farming developed in China.

3100BC
First dynasty of Egypt.

3500BC
Mid Howe Cairn built (Orkney & Shetland).

3500-2500BC
Uniquely British henge monument building begins e.g. Thornborough (Yorkshire).

3500-1600BC
Work begins on Stonehenge earthworks; added to and altered for next 1,900 years (Wiltshire & Wessex). Polished stone axes widely traded.

3200-3000BC
Castlerigg, possibly Europe's earliest stone circle, erected (Lake District).

3180-2500BC
Skara Brae settled (Orkney & Shetland).

3000-2200BC
Avebury stone circle built, then added to and altered over a long period of time.

2500BC
Ring of Brodgar built (Orkney & Shetland).

2600BC
Mayan culture Mexico, Pyramid of Djoser in Egypt.

2560BC
Great Pyramid of Giza completed.

2500-1500BC
Late Neolithic to Early Bronze Age, stone circles appear across British landscape (examples throughout).

2500-1600BC
Stonehenge reaches its present form (Wiltshire & Wessex).

2300-2000BC
Beaker culture displaces indigenous population which has been cut off from Europe and in steady decline.

2200-1100BC
Round barrows appear, e.g. Normanton Down (Wiltshire & Wessex) & Brook Down (Hampshire & Isle of Wight).

2000BC
Grime's Graves flint mines excavated (East Anglia).

2000-1900BC
Hill o' Many Stanes (Northern Highlands).

1600-1046BC
Shang dynasty in China is first to leave archaeological evidence, including writing.

1332-1323BC
Reign of Tutankhamun in Egypt.

1800BC
Copper mining at Great Orme (North Wales & Anglesey).

1500BC
Cremations become more common.

1500BC
Causeway from which objects are deposited into water built at Flag Fen (East Anglia).

1275-1140BC
Penard Period marked by more elaborate metal working influenced by European culture.

1200-800BC
Tribal kingdoms start to emerge.

1200BC
Field systems with long boundary walls (reaves) emerge; the 6¼-mile Great Western Reave passes through Merrivale (Dartmoor & South Devon).

1275-1140BC
1140BC City of Utica in Tunisia established.

800-700BC
First hillforts built.

700-500BC
Ironworking becomes more widespread.

500-100BC
Hillforts dominate the landscape Maiden Castle (Dorset), Tre'r Ceiri (North Wales & Anglesey) Castlelaw (Mid-Scotland).

400BC
Scottish brochs begin to be built: Dun Carloway (Skye & the Western Isles).

330-300BC
Greek explorer Pytheas of Massalia visits Britain, stating Britons live in thatched cottages and grow wheat, store…
…different kingdoms live in peace with each other.

483BC
Death of Buddha in India.

356-332BC
Alexander the Great.

214BC
Construction of Great Wall of China begins.

150BC
Use of metal coins starts.

55BC-54BC
Julius Caesar's failed invasions of Britain.

AD 43
Romans legions invade Britain, marking the end of prehistory and the dawn of written history.

AD 30-33
Jesus crucified.

AD 43
Claudius is Emperor in Rome AD 41-54.

NEOLITHIC
4500BC-2500BC
Britain's first farmers clear build stone monuments, chambered tombs and barrows.

BRONZE AGE
2500-800BC
First metal-working, more settled communities, climate becomes wetter and cooler. Burials of individuals in round barrows, rather than communal long barrows.

IRON AGE
800BC-AD 43
Widespread use of iron tools, building of hillforts and brochs. People live in ever-larger settlements. Romans invade in AD 43.

GLOSSARY OF TERMS

Barrow Burial mound (often marked tumulus on maps).

Bluestones Used in the context of Stonehenge for several kinds of volcanic rock, transported from quarries in Wales, smaller than the Sarsens.

Broch Iron Age dry-stone, hollow-walled round tower, mostly considered defensive. Only found in Scotland, and mostly in the Highlands and Northern Isles.

Bronze Age In Britain, the period between 2500BC and 800BC.

Cairn Pile of stones. May be piled over a burial (burial cairn) or a burial chamber (chambered cairn), or simply a pile of cleared stones in a field (clearance cairn) or to mark a boundary (boundary cairn).

Capstone Large, flat stone forming the roof of a cist or burial chamber. Most visible on top of a Dolmen.

Causewayed camp Circular enclosure built in the Neolithic. They consist of a series of ditches bisected by entrances or 'causeways', and may have served as tribal meeting places.

Chambered tomb Neolithic tomb containing one or more chambers. Normally these were covered by a mound of earth or stones (chambered Cairn).

Cist Stone coffin or pit.

Clava cairn Bronze Age circular chambered tomb covered with a cairn and surrounded by a stone cirle, found around Inverness. Entrances and stone heights are oriented south-west.

Clyde tomb Type of tomb with a semicircular forecourt and no significant passage inside, found in Western Scotland. Some of the earliest Neolithic tombs.

Cotswold–Severn barrow Chambered long barrow with a trapezoidal mound, found mostly in the South of England or Wales, in the Severn Valley and the Cotswolds.

Crannog Artificial island of wood or stone built on lakes, rivers and estuaries in the Iron Age. Known in Scotland, Wales, and Ireland.

Cromlech Welsh name for dolmen.

Cup and ring marks Strictly, a stone carving consisting of a cup-like indentation surrounded by circular grooves. The term is also used to cover other markings often found with them, with crossing or wandering lines between cups, rather than rings. See Northumberland chapter.

Cursus Ditched enclosures of uncertain purpose; sometimes miles in length, but only metres or tens of metres wide. See Stonehenge in Wiltshire & Wessex chapter.

Dolmen Table-like, single-chamber remains of Neolithic tomb, possibly once covered with earth but now bare.

Fogou Cornish term for an underground chamber or passageway, elsewhere called a souterrain. May have been used ceremonially, or to store food.

Henge A ringed bank of earth with a ditch inside it, enclosing a circular area of land. The enclosure may have contained a stone circle or timber circle.

Hillfort A settlement or stronghold on top of a hill, surrounded by rampart ditches and banks.

Hut circle Remains of a circular dwelling, usually Bronze Age.

Iron Age Period of time in Britain between 800BC and AD43. The Iron Age continued for longer in different parts of Scotland, as they were not conquered by the Romans.

Long barrow A large, elongated mound of earth constructed over a Neolithic (or sometimes Early Bronze Age) burial.

Maeshowe tomb Elaborate chambered cairn type on Orkney with a long passage to a vaulted chamber, off which are smaller compartments for burials.

Menhir French or old name for a standing stone.

Mesolithic Middle Stone Age, between 12,000BC and 4500BC.

Neolithic New Stone Age, when farming began, between 4500BC and 2500BC.

Orkney–Cromarty tomb Chambered tomb found in Scotland and Orkney, with variable external appearance but the central chamber divided into 'stalls' by dividing slabs. Similar to designs found in France and Spain.

Paleolithic Old Stone Age, between 800,000BC and 12,000BC.

Passage grave A tomb with a distinct entrance passage leading to one or more main chambers.

Promontory fort Type of hillfort on a promontory or coastal headland.

Quoit Cornish term for a dolmen.

Recumbent stone circle Circle with one large monolith laid horizontally between two tall flanking uprights, aligned with the southern moon. Found only around Aberdeen and in South-West Ireland.

Round barrow Circular burial mound, usually *Bronze Age*, but sometimes earlier (Neolithic) or later (Roman, Saxon).

Sarsen Large sandstone blocks used to make stone circles and tombs, including the distinctive trilithons of Stonehenge.

Scillonian entrance grave Mounded chambered tomb, found in Cornwall and the Isles of Scilly.

Souterrain Underground chamber or passageway, usually Iron Age. May have been used ceremonially, or to store food.

Lanyon Quoit, Penwith & Scilly Isles

FINDING YOUR WAY

CO-ORDINATES

Some of the sites in this book are remote and hard to find. At the end of each entry, after the directions, three location references have been provided: latitude and longitude, national grid reference and postcode (for example: *52.2188, -0.9202, SP738583, NN4 9UE*).

Postcodes are useful for getting to the general area if you are using a sat nav or phone. This can be all you need for sites with a car park and a well-marked footpath. However, in some sparsely populated rural areas, postcodes are very approximate. The six-figure national grid reference is a more accurate way of navigating and locates the site with 100m accuracy. These can be used with a paper map, reading the numbers across the top and along the side, and can be used on phone apps which use Ordnance Survey maps, such as Memory Map or Viewranger.

The four decimal point latitude longitude co-ordinates provide the most accurate location however. These are useful with all devices, from handheld GPS devices, to car sat navs, but especially with free online and phone mapping services such as Google or Bing maps. Do bear in mind that you are unlikely to get a phone signal at the most remote sites, so use the 'offline maps' mode to download the map areas you need before setting out or take a print-out or paper map. However, your actual location is determined by satellite GPS, which remains unaffected by lack of a network mast signal.

You can use latitude longitude to navigate using an ordinary sat nav but this may only get you to the nearest position on the road as the crow flies, and you will have to get yourself to the site on foot using paper maps. For some trickier places, the coordinates of the parking space are provided, so use these rather than the site coordinates when driving.

Whatever method you use, bring along a backup paper road map along with a local OS map and compass. Some of these sites are up mountains or on distant moors, and technology isn't infallible; phone batteries die, reflections off landscape features can affect GPS.

ACCESS TO SITES

Keep to footpaths when accessing sites. There are a handful of sites in this book on private land and some with no official footpath to them. In most cases the landowner is tolerant of visitors and it is unlikely your presence will cause any upset. Do note that trespass is a civil rather than criminal offence. This means as long as you leave if asked, the police will never be involved. However, you can be sued for damages if you have disturbed lambs with dogs or caused any damage to property. The law in Scotland is slightly different and you do have the right to be on the land for educational purposes, which includes visiting ancient monuments. However, how you use that information is entirely up to you; I personally would leave if asked to do so.

BEST PRACTICE AT SITES

All archaeological sites are protected by law and should not be tampered with in any way – which includes the practice of stacking stones. This may damage the sites so is also punishable by law, carrying a prison sentence. In addition, stone stacking has negative consequences for ground-nesting birds and rare plant life. Close gates behind you. Keep dogs on leads near livestock. Be the bigger party and reverse down country lanes if you are nearest to a passing space. Don't light fires on peat and only use designated fire areas elsewhere. Take home any waste.

Thor's Cave, Peak District

Best for Walkers

Best for Children & Families

Tre'r Ceiri, North Wales & Anglesey

Best for Pub or Café Lunch

Best for Picnics

Best for Breathtaking Views

Best for Wonderful Wildlife

Mid Howe Broch, Orkney & Shetland

Best for Wild & Adventurous

Best for Photography

Castlerigg Stone Circle, Lake District

CHAPTER I

WEST PENWITH &
THE SCILLY ISLES

*O*n days when the sun burns away the sea mist and the sky opens up to a vast, endless blue, few places compare with the very tip of Britain in West Penwith. This is an area bathed by the warm flow of the Gulf Stream, bringing with it an early spring and pushing back winter so it rarely takes a grip on the land. This balmy climate gives both the peninsula and the Scilly Isles an exotic feel, more Mediterranean than British. The region has a sparse year-round population, which swells during the summer months as holidaymakers come to the area in their thousands. However, the rich collections of ancient sites are often in wild, seldom visited parts of the region, and it is not uncommon to have them all to yourself even in peak season.

The peninsula is home to several remarkably well-preserved quoits or burial chambers – large table-like monuments, once covered in soil. These are called cromlechs in Wales and dolmens elsewhere, and some of the best examples in this part of Cornwall are Chun, Zennor and Lanyon, with Mulfra Quoit (50.1635, -5.5694) and Bosporthennis Quoit (50.1729, -5.5922) north of Penzance also worth a look.

The Scilly Isles have given their name to another kind of tomb, the Scillonian entrance tomb. Unlike chambered tombs elsewhere, the main chamber and the entrance passageway are one and the same. Porth Herrick Down Burial Chamber and Bant's Carn have been lovingly restored to look as they did back in our distant past. On the mainland other examples of entrance tombs can be found at Treen, with Pennance nearby, and Brane and Chapel Carn Brea (50.0953, -5.6563) to the west of Boscawen-ûn and Carn Euny ancient village. Although fascinating places, they have been left to the ravages of time and have suffered over the centuries.

There is no single reason for so much to exist in such a relatively small place. Some of it can be attributed to the raw material, the large granite seam which runs right down the West Country and out to the Isles of Scilly. With granite comes tin, mined for millennia for its importance in the production of bronze. Cornish tin is the oldest found in the Bronze Age, and Britain is held by some to be one of the legendary Cassiterides or Tin Islands written of by the Romans. Trading ships would have sailed around Penwith and coastal Cornwall all the way to Devon in search of this important resource, and it may also be that seafaring Neolithic and Bronze Age settlers travelled to Cornwall from the continent. Parallels have been found between many of the Cornish and Scillonian sites and those on the continent, and tantalising DNA evidence points to some very early movement here from continental Europe.

I KENIDJACK CASTLE & CAIRN CIRCLE ST JUST

From the vantage point of this cliff fort there are clear views over Cape Cornwall to where the currents of the English Channel and the untamed Atlantic meet. On a stormy day this is a truly wild place to be as the coastal winds batter the shoreline. Kenidjack is what's known as a multivallate fort, which simply means it has more than one rampart. Unfortunately, most of the southern end of the ramparts has been lost to erosion, but much of the triple northern end is still intact. There is evidence of Neolithic stone quarrying and of tin mining throughout the Bronze and Iron Ages; tin would have been a prized commodity in the Bronze Age, as it is essential to make bronze itself. This whole area must have been important to local and international trade, and its inhabitants may have adopted snippets of language or culture from beyond these Cornish shores. Remains of a cairn circle can also be found up near the ruins of the tin mine. Ballowall Barrow is just a short 1½-mile walk S, past the remains of the early Christian St Helen's Oratory and the 19th-century tin mine at Cape Cornwall.

On Cape Cornwall Road W from clock in St Just, bear L past large, white Boswedden House B&B (TR19 7NJ, 01736 788733) to coast and National Trust car park. Head N on coast path for 1¼ miles' moderate walk, passing tin mine and cairn circle (50.1332, -5.7012). Bus A17 From Penzance to Trevaylor Caravan Park Truthwall stop, or St Just.

50.1345, -5.7027, SW355326, TR19 7PU ☁🐦🚶

2 BALLOWALL BARROW ST JUST

In days gone by local miners believed this barrow, also called Carn Gloose or Gluze, to be bewitched, and claimed to see the lights of fairies dancing in rings as they returned from work. One of the first things that strikes you about the barrow is the sheer scale of it. It must have been a tremendous effort to build this with only simple tools made from stone, wood, bone and antler. However, we shouldn't be fooled into thinking that the barrow was built at one single time. It is a unique site, in that construction began in the Neolithic with a pit and cists, stone-lined and lidded 'coffins'. Further cists and stonework followed in the Bronze Age. Then, in an arguably misguided act of restoration,

much of the outer wall of the barrow was rebuilt in the Victoria era. Rather than enhance the structure, this has hidden many of the original features, making the barrow much harder to interpret. Ballowall Barrow is a site not to be missed in the area.

On Cape Cornwall Road W from clock in St Just, take L signed to Carn Gloose opposite the Bryan Warren Pavilion; it is only a mile from the town and a pleasant walk. Or stay on Cape Cornwall Road to park at National Trust car park at Cape Cornwall and follow the coast path S. Also a very pleasant walk N along the coast from the nearby Land's End Youth Hostel (TR19 7NT, 0345 371 9643). Bus A17 from Penzance to St Just.

50.1222, -5.7015, SW355312, TR19 7NP ☁🐦🚶

3 BOSCAWEN-ÛN STONE CIRCLE ST BURYAN

A carpet of bluebells sways in a light spring breeze and the morning dew evaporates, surrounding the stones with an ethereal mist. Situated on the southern slopes of Creeg Tol, there really is no other place like Boscawen-ûn on a spring morning. Its name means 'Farmstead of the Elder Tree', and it consists of 19 granite stones, including the central stone and a large quartz stone to the west-south-west. This number is in keeping with most of the circles in the Land's End area and is thought to be important in the lunar cycle. The quartz stone is said to symbolise the feminine, and it marks the position of the rising of the moon during the summer solstice. The other notable stone of course is the large, tilted, phallic stone positioned slightly off-centre. It has been suggested this symbolises an axe striking the earth, a strong masculine symbol. Many believe the presence of a quartz stone and belief in the coming together of the feminine and masculine make this an important site in Early Bronze Age ritual. However, notable archaeologist Aubrey Burl puts something of a kibosh on this theory by suggesting the central stone was originally upright and only leans thanks to over-zealous treasure hunters.

Head 4m S from Penzance on A30. 1½ miles after turning to Porthcurno and the Minack, park in the layby on L (50.0928, -5.6227). Through kissing gate, follow path ½-mile moderate walk to stones. Bus A1 from Penzance to Catchall stop and walk on along A30. A short walk NW, over the A30, is the chambered cairn at Brane (50.0969, -5.6354) with its wind-ravaged gorse headpiece. Around ¾ mile beyond, if you wind your way through fields and along a track to the N of Brane, you will come across the Bronze and Iron Age settlement of Carn Euny with its associated fogou (50.1028, -5.6339).

50.0899, -5.6192, SW412273, TR19 6EJ

4 MERRY MAIDENS
BOLEIGH

One of the best-known of all the stone circles in Cornwall, the Merry Maidens is an enchanting place. It is a near-perfect circle of 19 stones, and later Christian legends tell of dancing maidens turned to stone for the heinous crime of dancing on a Sunday. Due to its close proximity to the road the circle can get busy, so an early morning visit is perhaps the best way to avoid the hordes of tourists. Just down the road from the circle is the less well-known Tregiffian Burial Chamber. The B3315 is practically built over the top of this entrance grave, and you can hear the trundle of traffic from inside the tomb. Tregiffian is a bit of an oddity, in that it is thought to have been built in the Neolithic but incorporated into Bronze Age worship, with cup-marked stones found dated to 1950BC. The landscape around the circle is deeply ritual, with large monoliths in the surrounding fields.

From Penzance follow New Road along the seafront through Newlyn, up Chywoone Hill, becoming the B3315. Remain on this road for 3 miles, past the turning to Boleigh Farm Camping (TR19 6BM, 01736 810305), past layby to 2nd layby and bus stop on L. Park and follow path E through field. Bus A1 from Penzance to Menwinian stop, 3 minutes' walk. Tregiffian is about 2 minutes further along the road (50.0643, -5.5918).

50.0651, -5.5887, SW432245, TR19 6BQ

5 CHÛN QUOIT & CASTLE
MADRON

Flanked by the sea and the wild moors of Cornwall, Chûn Quoit rises up from the soil like an overgrown stone mushroom. Like other quoits, it was used for communal burials during the Neolithic era; it is likely these were family tombs and some form of ancestor worship took place here. Chûn Castle hillfort was built some 2,000 years after the tomb, during the Iron Age. Quite why the two are sited so close to one another is anyone's guess, but it has been suggested the area remained one of ritual significance throughout the pre-Roman period. Indeed,

the original entrance of the fort was once in line with the quoit. Its high vantage point by the ancient Tinners Way trackway, looking out to the Atlantic, makes for an outstanding view today and would have been a site of the utmost strategic importance in the Iron Age. Those stationed at the castle would have been able to see trading ships or invaders sailing from distant lands. The site may have been reoccupied in around the 5th-6th century.

From Morvah take the B3306 E towards St Ives. Take 1st R to Madron and Penzance, after ½ mile take R signed Great Bosullow. Follow road to where it becomes a dirt track, and park (50.1554, -5.6355). Walk along track, over crossroads, until path L, follow to Quoit; castle is a little further on. Bus A17 from Penzance to Pendeen.

50.1485, -5.6376, SW402339, TR20 8PX

6 PORTHMEOR CIRCLE
TREEN COMMON

Visible from the road, Porthmeor Circle is a short walk through long grass. From the common there are great views down to the sea and over the surrounding hills. There is much debate whether this is a true stone circle or an Iron Age enclosure, a ring of stones that would have surrounded one or more huts, as marked on the OS maps. Finds dating from the Late Iron Age have been found to the south of the enclosure, leading experts to lean more towards the enclosure theory. Unlike the large, better-known sites in the area, Porthmeor feels a little lost and unloved. Just off the same road, down the hill from the circle is Treen entrance grave, one of three barrows

marked as tumuli on OS maps, a very similar site in many respects to the large Bronze Age entrance graves on the Scillies. It is likely this was a family grave on the margins of arable land. If Porthmeor is forlorn and forgotten, then Treen is downright abandoned. It is so well hidden that even when you are upon it you can still miss it. However, it is worth persevering, as a glimpse of the long inner chamber alone is reward enough for your efforts. Another example, Pennance (50.1824, -5.5761), is nearby.

Head SW from Zennor village 1½ miles on B3306. When the Gurnard's Head hotel comes into view on the coast take the Penzance road, next L. About 200 metres up this road find Treen Barrows in a field to R in a line broadly S from 50.1789, -5.5899. Layby is on L ½ mile (50.1762, -5.5838), with circle on R.

50.1747, -5.5804, SW444366, TR20 8XU

7 MÊN–AN–TOL
LITTLE BOSULLOW

After Stonehenge and Avebury, Mên-an-Tol (sometimes called the Crick Stone or Devil's Eye) is perhaps one of Britain's most iconic and enigmatic megalithic monuments. The defining Polo-mint-shaped central stone gives the site its name, as Mên-an-Tol literally translates as 'stone with a hole'. In 1982 the Cornwall archaeological unit found evidence to suggest this was once part of a stone circle, thought to date back to the Early Bronze Age; the stones have been moved over time. During the 18th century the holed stone was believed to have various healing powers, and those seeking a cure for then-common diseases such as rickets and scrofula (a form of tuberculosis) would pass their naked children through it. However, the most enduring interpretation is that of a fertility symbol, and women wanting to conceive still pass through the central stone to this day. While you are in the area, the Nine Maidens, or Boskednan, circle is not to be missed (or confused with other Nine Maidens elsewhere).

From Morvah take B3306 E towards St Ives. Take 1st R to Madron and Penzance, and park by the gated track on L after about a mile. Stones are R off track, about 10 minutes walk in all. For Nine Maidens, walk from Mên-an-Tol back to the track and follow it up to the NE for around 500 metres. Continue for 200 metres and take 1st fork on R as path splits into 5. Follow path uphill then SE to stone circle (50.1605, -5.5938).

50.1585, -5.6044, SW426349, TR20 8NX

8 LANYON QUOIT
LITTLE BOSULLOW

A stone's throw from Mên-an-tol is Lanyon Quoit, resembling an enormous kitchen table ready for Cornish giants to tuck into a Sunday roast. Little effort is needed to find this monument, as it can easily be seen from the adjacent lane. When the dolmen collapsed in a storm in 1815 local residents, realising the importance of the monument, reconstructed it almost a decade later. The area around Lanyon Quoit can easily take up a day of exploring on its own; quite apart from Mên-an-tol, the area is littered with the remains of hut circles, enclosures, quoits and standing stones. West from the monument and over the road are the two remaining stones of West Lanyon Quoit. From Lanyon itself, follow the paths heading N for around 500 metres and to the R you should stumble across the circular remains of Bosiliack Barrow (50.1521, -5.5975), a Scillonian entrance grave. If this barrow were anywhere else in the country it would be a major tourist pull rather than playing second fiddle to Lanyon Quoit and Mên-an-Tol.

Take the road heading NW from Madron towards Morvah, and after 2 miles of twisting road you will see Lanyon Quoit on the R.

50.1473, -5.5991, SW429336, TR20 8NY

9 ZENNOR QUOIT
ZENNOR

A stacked granite outcrop, characteristic of the tors further to the north in Dartmoor, lies at the top of remote Zennor Hill. Large stone slabs must have been removed from just such a stack by the Neolithic builders of Zennor Quoit. The proximity of this raw material does nothing to detract from the sheer engineering marvel of these West Penwith quoits. High on the moors, Zennor is one of the most out of the way of all the Land's End quoits, but with its view out to the swelling Atlantic it is worth the effort to find. Cremated bone and pottery dating from the Neolithic era have been found at the site along with remains from the Bronze Age. In the 19th century Zennor quoit was almost lost to the world, as a farmer proposed removing part of it and drilling the capstone to use it as a cattle shelter.

*From Zennor take B3306 E toward St Ives for ¾ mile to layby/
pull in entrance marked by stone pillars, sometimes selling ice
cream. Park here and continue on road E past houses until you
see path R marked by a number of stones opposite second house.
Follow path S to ruins then up W to quoit. ¾-mile strenuous
walk. Ruined Sperris Quoit (50.1902, -5.5446) is nearby.*

50.1879, -5.5473, SW468380, TR26 3BU

IO PORTH HELLICK DOWN ST MARY'S, SCILLY

Porth Hellick Down Burial Chamber sits in a forgotten
corner on the eastern edge of the island of St Mary's.
The nearby beach is amongst the most remote on the
island and you are likely to have it all to yourself. The
mortar inside the structure gives the game away, that this
is indeed a relatively recent reconstruction of the original
tomb rather than one which has been standing as it is
since the Late Neolithic, but this does not detract from
the sense of awe this ancient monument brings. Thought
to date back to 2000BC, it would have been built when
the Scilly Isles were mostly one larger land mass. Various
other cairns and remains are found near the tomb, and it
is easy to while away a few hours in the area.

*Take Strand then Telegraph Road E from Hugh Town. After
¾ mile turn R onto A3110 for 1 mile. As road bends sharp L
continue straight on to park in pull-in and follow the path S for
300m to site. It's a pleasant cycle along the coast from Hugh
Town. Community bus along this route stops on request.*

49.9188, -6.2805, SW468380, TR21 0NY

II BANT'S CARN
ST MARYS, SCILLY

The remains at Halangy Down mark a long period of
time in Scillonian history. The large entrance burial
tomb of Bant's Carn has been reconstructed to look as
it did in the late Neolithic or Early Bronze Age, when
it would have been inland. The inside chamber is 5
metres long, and early digs uncovered the remains of
four cremations within its dark stone walls. Just as with
Porth Hellick (see entry), it is likely the tomb was first
used in the Late Neolithic (around 2000BC) before
being reused in the Late Bronze Age (1200–500BC).
The village is a much later Iron Age construction. The
outlines of the dwellings are so well preserved you can
picture their inhabitants moving from hut to hut. It
was obviously a favourable place to live, as the village is
thought to have been occupied right up to Roman times.

From Porthmellon Beach in Hugh Town head N for 1½ miles
of easy walk along coast road and coast paths. Community bus
goes through nearby Telegraph and stops on request.

49.9313, -6.3077, SV909123, TR21 0NP

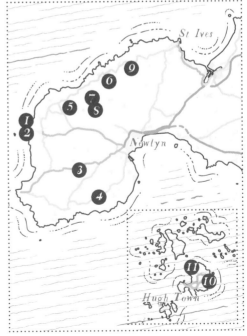

CHAPTER 2

MID–CORNWALL
& BODMIN

*I*t is all too easy to think of our prehistoric ancestors as distant and their culture as alien to ours. Yet it really only ended when the Romans arrived, some 60 generations ago, meaning the fireside tales of just 30 generations of grandparents to their grandchildren are the links in an oral chain back to the Iron Age residents of Warbstow Bury hillfort, or those who used the underground chambers of Halliggye Fogou.

Perhaps this is why stories that have roots even further back in the Bronze Age, such as Beauty and the Beast and Jack and the Beanstalk, still linger on in the popular psyche. Neil Oliver suggests other ancestral links with our forebears, postulating that the playground count of "Eeny, meeny, miny, moe" could have its roots in the ancient Celtic languages, suggested by traditional ways of counting sheep including the Cornish 'eena, mea, mona, mite'.

Just like the Welsh and Breton languages, Cornish remains close to its roots in the ancient tongue spoken in Iron Age Britain. Could this be why the Cornish name Goon Brenn hints at the wildness of the high, desolate moorland far more effectively than the English name of Bodmin Moor? Here, the Bronze Age stone circles of the Trippet Stones, Hurlers, Stannon, and Nine Stones, as well as Leaze and Louden Hill remain as clues to this mysterious past. When they were built, the climate would have supported vast farming communities. Did these circles act as solar or celestial calendars foretelling the coming of the all-important summer sun? We can only guess at their true purpose, but what is certain is they are just as atmospheric today as they would have been 3,000 years ago.

Brittany, Wales and Cornwall are linked together not only by language but also by shared myths and legends. The most enduring legend is that of King Arthur, a tale which appeared sometime around the 5th century. His story has become interwoven with that of the sites of antiquity, and many bear his name. One such is King Arthur's Hall, high on Goon Brenn in the shadow of Cornwall's tors, but it is doubtful this evocative site has anything to do with the King, as it predates him by more than 2,000 years! On the coast away from the moors, near to Arthur's supposed castle at Tintagel, we find one of the most intriguing pieces of rock art in Southern England. The labyrinth at Rocky Valley is thought to date to the Early Bronze Age. If so, as much time separates Arthur from this carving as us from the Romans.

1 CARNE BEACON OR VERYAN BARROW VERYAN

Like a mini-nature reserve set in a sea of grass, Carne Beacon is grown over with a chaotic ramble of flowering thistles, cow parsley, foxgloves, elder and hawthorn. Although the steps to the top do not cry out for the authenticity of the ancient barrow, they do make for a much easier climb to the top. From this vantage point views out to Gerrans Bay should be sufficient to delight even the coldest of souls. Legend has it that this is the last resting place of the 6th-century King Geraint, or Gerrenius, of Dumnonia, a folk saint still celebrated in the area. The story goes that his body was buried here, in a golden boat with silver oars that brought him across Gerrans Bay. The mound is considered the largest Bronze Age burial mound in England, and although there would be enough room to house a boat, when it was opened in 1855 cremated remains and a stone cist were found but sadly no gold boat. The village has a lovely old pub, the New Inn (TR2 5QA, 01872 501362), and the post office could have been plucked straight off a historical film set. From the village it is an easy stroll down to the beach and there are some fantastic walks to be had along the National Trust-owned coastline.

Park in Veryan village and follow Pendower Road SW towards sea. Enter path on L over steps just after Churchtown Farm. Keep L through field then follow sign to Cairn Beacon over stile. Bus 51 from Truro to Veryan stop.

50.2107, -4.9268, SW 9126 38, TR2 5PG

2 STANNON STONE CIRCLE ST BREWARD

Although the stones of Stannon are quite small, the ring itself is huge; originally there were 80 stones, of which 64 remain in a ring measuring over 40 metres across. The stones are said to be aligned with the summit of Rough Tor on May Day; an online sunrise calculator clearly shows the sun rises slightly to the north of Rough Tor, through a distinctive gap between its summit and neighbouring Showery Tor. Interestingly, the same online tool looking out from the centre of nearby Fernacre Stone Circle (50.5899, -4.6223) shows the sun rising up from behind Maiden Tor. Today our monuments exist in isolation and are not built to follow any seasonal patterns, so

these once-important relationships are now lost to us. However, back in the Late Neolithic and Early Bronze Age the peak of the summer day length must have been something essential to celebrate. Fernacre Stone Circle is an easy and enjoyable walk from Stannon.

Take the road N out of St Breward past the Old Inn (PL30 4PP, 01208 850711) and ½ mile after, turn R at grit bin follow the road E. Take L fork to remain on lower road, continuing N then E. Once on high moor ignore cycle path to L to remain on road until you see a small pull-in on R. Circle is 100 metres to SW. For Fernacre Stone Circle, make your way to the track to the south and follow it E for around a mile, in the direction of the comically named Brown Willy hill, passing Louden Hill Stone Circle (50.5852, -4.6399). Either side of this track you will find the remains of cairns, menhirs and three large settlements which, although undated, could be contemporary with the stone circle. Bus 55 from Bodmin or Camelford to St Breward Stores stop, about 3 miles walk.

50.5897, -4.6492, SX125800, PL32 9QA

3 HALLIGGYE FOGOU MAWGAN

Fogous are underground tunnels or chambers, but distinctly different from the souterrains found up in Scotland (see Orkney & Shetland). Halliggye comprises a central passage with a small 'creep' (a small opening which forces you to creep through it on your hands and knees) section in front and a long, winding tunnel jutting off to the right, with its own creep. A good torch is needed to fully explore this, the largest and most complete of all the fogous in Cornwall. In historical terms it is relatively modern, dating from the Iron Age and possibly still in use well after Roman occupation. It might come as no surprise to learn that the function of Cornish fogous is a bit of a mystery. Antiquarian and musician Julian Cope claims they are for ritual purposes: the worship of the gods of the earth. This is of course possible, but they may have also been used for much more secular purposes, perhaps the cool, dark storage of spoilable foods. Halligye was once part of a large Iron Age village, similar to that at Carn Euny on the Land's End peninsula, which itself has an impressive fogou. From October to April bats take precedence over human visitors, and the fogou is closed to the public. Dry Tree Menhir (see listing) is nearby.

From Helston take the A3083 S, turn L at the roundabout after the fenced airbase onto B3293 and follow 1½ miles to turn L at crossroads then R into Trelowarren Estate. Park in English Heritage lay-by on R of lane after ½ mile, walk back a few yards on same side and take road/track to the fogou. Bus 36 from Helston to Garras stop, then walk back to signed turning along lane to Trelowarren Estate.

50.0717, -5.1971, SW713239, TR12 6AH 🏊🏃🏹

4 DRY TREE MENHIR
GOONHILLY

Despite its impressive size, this large standing stone not far from the large radio-communication site of Goonhilly Earth Station is dwarfed by the satellite dishes. More than anywhere else in Britain, here we see the striking contrast between the world of archaic belief and that of modern science. The menhir is around 3 metres in height and could have only come from an area roughly 2 miles away. Transporting a stone this size would be a considerable effort today but 3,500 years ago, with nothing but brute strength and simple tools, it must have been a monumental effort. High on the downs, it would have been visible for miles around and must have been of some significance to the Bronze Age inhabitants of Goonhilly. The menhir has been a little bullied over the years: it was toppled in search of (non-existent) buried gold, and a large piece was removed from the top to build a road during the First World War. Earlier in the 18th and 19th centuries the site was a notorious hang-out for prowling highwaymen. There are a number of barrows around the area, marked as tumuli on OS maps, some of which are visible from the stone itself. Halliggye Fogou (see listing) is nearby.

Take A3083 S from Helston past the airfield, and turn L on the roundabout to follow B3293 past Goonhilly Earth Station. Look out for the NNR car park on the right just after, before the crossroads. Follow paths onto downs then along perimeter fence until you see the stone; ¾-mile moderate walk. Bus 36 from Helston to Goonhilly stop.

50.0470, -5.1781, SW725211, TR12 6LQ 🏞

5 TRIPPET STONES
BLISLAND

The stones of Trippet circle have been standing in their lonely spot in the shadow of Hawk's Tor on desolate moorland for at least four and a half thousand years. The finding of a flint blade underneath one of the stones has confirmed they date back to the Neolithic era. Although just a short drive from the A30, the moors here feel a million miles away from anywhere, and the wild ponies appear to be less acquainted with people than their friendly counterparts on Dartmoor and Exmoor. Only eight of an original 26 stones are still standing, and a further four remain but lie unceremoniously flat on the moor (the central stone is a modern boundary stone). The whereabouts of the rest are anyone's guess, but it is most likely that they were robbed for building works nearby. Around ¾ mile away, on the southern slope of Hawk's Tor, is the henge circle known as the Stripple Stones 50.5471, -4.6216, probably dating to the Late Neolithic. It is thought that these two sites are linked, as the entrance to the Stripple Stones is orientated such that the Trippet Stones can be viewed through the gap in the bank. A circular walk of just under 2 miles can be plotted, taking in the summit of Hawk's Tor, the Stripple Stones and the Trippet Stones.

Travel NE on A30 from Bodmin for 6 miles. Turn L for St Breward onto small lane, and after ¾-mile turn R at crossroads toward Hawks Tor Farm (not signed) and find somewhere to pull off. Stones are a short walk across the moor on L of road. Bus 55 from Bodmin or Camelford to St Breward Stores stop, over 3 miles' walk.

50.5448, -4.6392, SX131750, PL30 4LD 🏃🏞

6 KING ARTHUR'S HALL
ST BREWARD

In a landscape that rivals the Scottish Highlands or the peaks of Cumbria for sheer barren beauty, you'll find the enigmatic remains of King Arthur's Hall. There is very little quite like it: a henge of upright stones and a bank of earth surround a large, rectangular ditch. The centre of the henge floods regularly, and the hall supports its own marshland ecosystem. Like so many of its contemporaries, the purpose of the enclosure is

6

8

unknown, although it does bear a resemblance to a site in Brittany that was used for cremation, and sites in Wales and Ireland where corpses were left to have their flesh removed by birds and scavenger mammals prior to burial. Musician and antiquarian Julian Cope hypothesises that this may have been a meeting ground for tribal elders. Perhaps it is the remote, somewhat eerie location, but whatever it once was, King Arthur's hall does feel a very special place indeed. To the southeast of the monument are the remains of two rather neglected stone circles, the further one at Leaze (50.5655, -4.6323), whilst towards the farm and the road to the south, a burial cist with a small surrounding circle of stones can be found peeking up out of the moor (50.5627, -4.6400). In addition to these sites, single standing stones or menhirs, not marked on any OS map, can be found all over Emblance Downs.

In Churchtown/St Breward take lane E from S of the Old Inn (PL30 4PP, 01208 850711) for Casehill/Candra and after 1 mile find R, again signed Casehill/Candra. Park at the far end of road, take footpath ½ mile E. Bus 55 from Bodmin or Camelford to St Breward Stores stop, over 2 miles' walk.

50.5686, -4.6425, SX129776, PL30 4NN

7 THE HURLERS
MINIONS

Many stone circles have an enduring myth of people being turned to stone for doing something ungodly on the Sabbath. Dancing on a Sunday is usual for female petrification, but for this particular circle a group of men were turned to stone for the heinous crime of playing Cornish hurling, and from some angles they could be a crowd involved in this robust street game. However, locals report that the name may have come about from something far less supernatural: the stones are perfectly spaced for goalposts, once used in a now-lost form that was played on a pitch. Although in close enough proximity to the road to watch passing buses, the site still feels wild and remote. The large Cornish engine house and visitor centre nearby adds to the atmosphere of the place, where ancient and recent history meet. It is a unique site, as three circles were erected rather than one or two, and even more oddly they are virtually in a straight line. It has been postulated that the circles are the centre of a

wider ceremonial complex linked to Rillaton Barrow (50.5211, -4.4557) and the Stowes Hill enclosure on the Cheesewring summit beyond (50.5276, -4.4592). Two stone monoliths known as The Pipers also stand to the west of the monument; these are more likely to be boundary markers. The nearby Minions Shop and Tearoom (PL14 5LE, 01579 228652) can be a welcome escape if the Cornish weather comes in.

Park in the Hurlers car park in Minions, off the B3254 N of Liskeard. Stones are a 300-metre walk. Nearest train or bus is to Liskeard (5 miles).

50.5166, -4.4583, SX258714, PL14 5LL

8 NINE STONES
ALTARNUN

High on the barren moor, the Nine Stones of Altarnun are often surrounded by a herd of wild ponies. This might not be Cornwall's biggest stone circle but it is perhaps the most beautiful. It was restored in 1889, when only two stones remained upright. Large gaps in the formation have led archaeologists to believe at least one more stone may have existed in the ring. Evidence also points towards the central stone being added at a later date as one of a line of parish boundary markers, and it may have been taken from a fence post. This seems somewhat ironic, as more often than not stone was robbed from circles for local building projects; there are also suggestions that stone could have been moved in more contemporary history. With the rest of the moor so empty, cattle love to use the stones for a good old scratch, and after decades of this, dips have begun to form miniature reservoirs around many of the stones.

The cairn on top of Ridge Hill (50.5739, -4.4821) and the one to the east of the stones (50.5772, -4.4852) are also worth a visit; this route in from the south includes both.

From the A30 about 1 mile E of Altarnun, bear S onto B3257 for Callington. After just under 1½ miles take R and follow for 1½ miles through Trevadlock, then L down dead-end at crossroads and keep L towards Bastreet for 1½ miles. Park by side of road and walk R up hill then descend down to stone circle; ¾-mile strenuous walk. Bus 236 from Launceston or Liskeard to Trebartha opp Jubilee Cottages stop, and walk N 300 metres to take L dead-end turning to Bastreet.

50.5762, -4.4925, SX236781, PL15 7QU

9 ROCKY VALLEY LABYRINTH TINTAGEL

Rocky Valley feels like a well-kept secret. A small brook washes its way down this magical wooded valley towards the crashing Cornish coast. It is a well-trodden path, yet it is possible to walk down without passing a single soul. Behind the ruined remains of Trewethett Mill lies the best secret of all, cut into the granite rock. Sometime during the Bronze Age, someone carved two intricate labyrinths with such precision that they look as clear today as they would have done thousands of years ago; their clarity has led to suggestions that they are from the 18th century, like other carvings nearby, and possibly inspired by a fainter, original example some claim to discern above them. Carvings similar to these are found from Spain and Italy to Northern England. For some, this points to the influx of people into Britain from continental Europe, but we cannot be certain of this, as the carving is just one example in the Cornish region. Today visitors tie pieces of paper or ribbons to the nearby tree for luck, or to have their wishes granted. Sadly some also feel the need to endanger the site by hammering coins into the cracks in the rock.

Take the B3263 S from Boscastle to Tintagel. After 2 miles the road bends sharply R past a large, white house. Pull into the layby after the house next to the L hand turn. Cross road and follow signed footpath N to ruined mill buildings, 10 minutes' moderate walk. You'll see the carvings behind the buildings.

50.6735, -4.7295, SX072895, PL34 0BQ 🚶🏔️🚶

10 WARBSTOW HILLFORT WARBSTOW

Warbstow is a fine example of a multivallate hillfort (more than one rampart). Although it doesn't take long to walk around the site, it is easy to while away an afternoon up here soaking up the panoramic views. It is perhaps the largest hillfort in Cornwall and certainly one of the most intact, but despite this very little is known about the site. From the style of construction it is likely it was first in use in the Late Bronze Age. In its day it must have been an impressive sight, more so when the inner ramparts were added later, possibly lined with white quartz that would have caught the sun for miles around. Perhaps this was an ancient way of impressing the neighbours, as the fort

would have been easily spotted from Ashbury Hillfort (50.7499, -4.5132), a contemporary of Warbstow some 4½ miles away. The mound in the middle of the fort is often referred to as either The Giant's or King Arthur's Grave; in fact, no archaeological evidence supports anyone being buried in it at all, and it is thought to be a medieval rabbit warren.

Just off the road between Hallworthy and Warbstow. From Warbstow village take the road W for ⅓ of a mile to the small car park on the R and follow the footpath. Bus routes 420 and 480 from Launceston to Warbstow Bus Shelter stop.

50.6886, -4.5477, SX201907, PL15 8RH 🚶🏔️🚶

CHAPTER 3

DARTMOOR &
SOUTH DEVON

*S*ome 10,000 years ago, during the Mesolithic era, humans began to clear the vast ancient forest of Dartmoor for the first time. It is likely that fire was used to clear the trees, attracting grazing animals in to further clear the landscape. This created wide-open spaces in which the Mesolithic hunters could hunt those animals much more easily. By the Neolithic era life was changing, and the need for hunting lessened as crops were sown and people settled into small farming communities. In order to make way for crops and grazing animals, the clearings made in the Mesolithic were widened, and trees were cleared by fire and axe. Although the inhabitants did not know it at the time, the felling of the trees would bring about the bleak, barren landscape we now know as Dartmoor. Settlers of this landscape through the Neolithic and into the Bronze Age built hut circles and marked out fields in a way we may recognise today. Grimspound (50.6133, -3.8373) from the Late Bronze Age is perhaps the most famous of these settlements, but a wealth of other hut circles and enclosures can be found at Shapley Common nearby (50.6330, -3.8423), Broadun Settlement (50.6028, -3.9302), and Assycombe, Bellever and Shaugh Moor in this chapter. What is also intriguing is the way these people connected with the land during this period of change. They created large stone monuments such as the long stone rows at Merrivale, Shovel Down, Lakehead Hill (50.5832, -3.9167), and Langstone Moor (50.5913, -4.0491). The true purpose of these rows we will never know. It has been argued that they were simply trading routes or boundaries, but their purpose may have been ceremonial, as many of them are associated with stone circles and burial cists. Some even argue that they represented a walkway of the dead. The much later Medieval Lych (or Lyke) Way, which starts in Bellever, was once used for funeral processions leading to the parish church 12 miles away in Lydford, and there are many associated myths of ghosts seen walking the Lych Way. These are probably the continuation of an oral tradition that spirits walked along the length of the stone rows, which could date back to the Bronze Age.

Another prominent ancient feature of Dartmoor is its magnificent stone circles. One of the finest sites has to be the restored twin circles of Grey Wethers. The presence of two circles here has intrigued archaeologists and antiquarians for centuries. Could it be that this was part of a funeral rite where the dead would pass from the land of the living to the neighbouring circle and the land of the dead?

1 NINE STONES RING CAIRN *BELSTONE*

If travelling into the west, Nine Stones Cairn at Belstone may well be the first prehistoric monument you encounter on a trip to Dartmoor. Overlooking pastoral mid-Devon and just a short walk from the white cottages and thatched roofs of Belstone village, it may not be the most remote nor the most extensive site on Dartmoor, but there is a certain serenity about it that makes for a memorable visit. The somewhat confusing name of Nine Stones or Nine Maidens – there are 16 upright stones and others nearby – dates from early myths surrounding the site, where story has it that nine maidens were turned to stone for dancing on the Sabbath. Maybe the remaining stones were bystanders caught up in the petrification process? An alternative name of Seventeen Brothers is closer to the mark. This is often mistaken for a stone circle due to the absence of a central cist or chamber, which is thought to have been removed and robbed of all its goods centuries ago. On a fine day a route from the circle up Belstone Tor and on to Oke Tor is just challenging enough for the occasional walker.

Take the B3260/Exeter Road E from Okehampton, after the A30 and BP garage take the R at crossroads with thatched cottage, signposted Belstone. Park in car park as you enter the village and walk ½ mile S through village, past the waterworks to a gate onto moors. Follow path next to wall, as wall drops to R take grass path on L until you see the stones. Bus 670 from Okehampton to Belstone Green stop, Thursdays only; on other days 6 and 6A from Okehampton to Belstone Tongue End Cross stop, at the thatched cottage, ¾-mile walk to Belstone.

50.7186, -3.9672, SX612928, EX20 1QZ

2 SCORHILL CIRCLE *GIDLEIGH*

'What are these lonely rings? Where are we standing now? In a place of worship, where men prayed to the thunder and the sun and stars? Or a council chamber?' It is more than a century since Eden Phillpotts, author and president of the Dartmoor Preservation Association, wrote these words about Scorhill, but his questions remain unanswered. Scorhill, like so many other stone circles, is an enigma. We know that the 27-metre-wide circle is probably Bronze Age and that there were once around 70 stones at the site, of which only 34 survive and only 25 still stand. The stones are impressive, with the largest standing 2.5 metres tall. Often noted as one of the most important sites on Dartmoor, it has been a favourite for visitors to the area since Victorian times. To experience the stones at their best, pitch a tent down from the stones and visit at dawn or as the sun slowly sets over the tors. From Scorhill it's a short walk to the stone rows on Shovel Down (see next entry).

In Gidleigh head S past church and turn R at triangle by village hall and phone box, onto narrow lane signed to Scorhill. Follow lane and take dead-end on bend to car park at end. Follow path SW ½ mile. 10 minutes' moderate to strenuous walk. Bus 173 from Moretonhampstead or Exeter, or 178 from Okehampton, to Chagford Square stop, 4 miles' walk.

50.6705, -3.9052, SX654873, TQ13 8HS

3 SHOVEL DOWN & THE LONGSTONE *TEIGNCOMBE*

At least five double rows of stones, erected around 4,000 years ago, can be found in and around the slopes between Shovel Down (sometime called Shuggledown) and Chagford Common. It's thought that there may have been twice this number, or that the many rows were once one large, single network stretching across the landscape. Cairns have been found within the rows, along with the possible remains of a concentric Fourfold Circle (50.6581, -3.8985). Although they have now fallen, two stones once stood here as a portal to the ring, similar to the alternating 'male' and 'female' stone types of Kennet Avenue in Wiltshire (see Avebury entry). Although we do not know the true purpose of the site, experts believe this area must have been one of the largest and most significant ritual landscapes on Dartmoor. Evidence also shows that it was in use long before the stones were erected, as flints dating back to the Mesolithic era (10,000–8500BC) have been found here. Climbing the hill along the stone rows to the magnificent Longstone (50.6554, -3.8967) you cannot fail to be awed. From this vantage point Dartmoor stretches out before you and you get a sense of why this area was so special to those living here thousands of years ago.

From Chagford take Manor Road SW about ½ mile, then where road swings L take R after bend, signed Kestor/Thornworthy and follow road for 1½ miles through many bends, with one more sign for Kestor, R past converted wooden farm buildings and eventually the Round Pound ancient house remains (50.6660, -3.8919), to limited rough parking at end. From here follow the track/path on foot to the S to the stones for ⅓ mile. Bus 173 from Moretonhampstead or Exeter, or 178 from Okehampton, to Chagford Square stop. Train Okehampton 9 mile (cycle).

50.6572, -3.8985, SX659858, TQ13 8EU 🚗🅿🏕🚶🚴🛈

4 FERNWORTHY CIRCLE/ FROGGYMEAD HURSTONE

There is no doubt the decision to plant trees over the Fernworthy Area has irreversibly changed the landscape. However, for once it may have enhanced rather than detracted from the Bronze Age monuments there. The Forestry Commission's diligent restraint of plant growth means the stone circles and rows appear to pop up magically in woodland clearings, like something from a Tolkien film set. Fernworthy Circle sits in a large clearing in the woods to the west of the reservoir, with stone rows leading away from the circle to cairns. The charcoal remains found within the circle, following a dig in 1897, could be the remains of ritual fires from ancient gatherings, or perhaps this was a crematorium site for the cairns – much charcoal and bone were also found in one cist. The Grey Wethers stone circle lies in close proximity to the west and Scorhill to the north (see entries). So many sites in one location have led to the interpretation that the stones around Fernworthy may be just one small part of a large ceremonial landscape. Was this area a vast outdoor cathedral? A gathering place for communities across the moors, or a place to honour the dead? Elsewhere around the reservoir the Assycombe stone rows can be found by taking forestry tracks through the woods to the south (50.6275, -3.8957). A number of remarkably complete hut circles are scattered all over the forest, giving a real insight into Bronze Age life. Fernworthy is a great site for children, as they can help find the many remains as you make your way around the woods, and the long road around the reservoir means some of the site is accessible to pushchairs and wheelchair users. Take a good map or mobile app with you; it will really help locate the hidden sites.

From Chagford take Manor Road SW and follow it as it swings S. About ¾ mile after the bend, take R fork signed Fernworthy Reservoir and follow 2 miles to visitor's centre and car park with public toilet at reservoir. Park here and continue on foot or drive on for another mile (passing impressive hut circle just off the road as it bends away from the reservoir) to limited parking space at end of the road for the shortest walk along forestry track to Fernworthy Circle. Bus 173 from Moretonhampstead or Exeter, or 178 from Okehampton, to Chagford Square stop, over 4 miles' walk in all.

50.6412, -3.9036,SX654841, TQ13 8EA 🚗🏕🚶🚴🛈

5 GREY WETHERS POSTBRIDGE

In 1909, with a great deal of enthusiasm and a certain amount of guess work, Robert Burnard, secretary of the Dartmoor Preservation Association, set about restoring the Grey Wethers stone circles. To this day we do not know how accurate or true to the original he was; what we do know is that the result of his hard work is one the most remarkable ancient monuments to be found on the whole of Dartmoor. Few make it to this remote and desolate place, and the isolation of this profoundly beautiful stone monument only adds to the experience of visiting. Paths criss-cross the moor here and the circles can be approached from all directions: the most striking, but also least accessible first view has to be that of the twin circles side by side as you descend the peak of Sittaford Tor. The double circles may represent two realms, the realm of the living or newly dead and the realm of the ancestors. Parallels can also be drawn with the Bora Rings of South-Eastern Australia, used in initiation ceremonies where boys become men and move from one circle to the other.

Follow directions for Fernworthy Circle (see entry) and continue on footpath heading NW out of the forest for approximately 1 mile, then follow the footpath S for ¾ mile to the E of Sittaford Tor until you reach the stones. Ground can be boggy, and a map and compass or navigational equipment is essential.

50.6318, -3.9260, SX638831, TQ13 8EA 🅿🏕🚶🛈

6 BELLEVER COMPLEX
BELLEVER

Just as with Fernworthy (see entry), the Forestry Commission's decision to plant conifer woodland around a site of archaeological importance has met with a mixed response. Things were quite different 100 years ago; then, the area looked like any other part of Dartmoor and the many sites around Bellever would have stood out in the landscape. In the late 19th century, archaeologist Dr Arthur B Prowse visited the area. He concluded that at its peak as many as 400 people lived in 100 hut circles across the area, describing it as an 'ancient metropolis of the moor'. It is a satisfying place to visit, with the stones and earthworks suggesting a rather large village. Walking around the site today it is easy to conjour up the sights and sounds of Bronze Age village life – children running between the houses, the smells of cooking wafting through the air. It is hard to say quite where all of Prowse's circles are today, or what remains of them; some are still visible, but many must be lost under the large plantations. The oddly named Kraps Ring settlement can still be found in a clearing. Head south from the village and the remains start to show themselves a little more readily. I would suggest plotting a route through the centre of the clearing towards Bellever Tor. The twin cairn circles, complete with stone cist, to the north of the summit of the hill remain one of my favourite sites (50.5812, -3.9173).

From Postbridge head SW on B3212. Just after National Park Visitor Centre on R take 1st L over cattle grid for Bellever then park in car park on the R. Follow the track from the SW end, cross forestry road and continue SW to clearing. Bus 98 from Tavistock or Yelverton to Postbridge stop, no Sunday service.

50.5872, -3.9168, SX644781, PL20 6TU

7 MERRIVALE COMPLEX
MERRIVALE

The stone rows at Merrivale were known locally as the Plague Market or Potato Market, because in 1625 farmers left food there in exchange for money during an outbreak of the bubonic plague in Tavistock. The rows are just one small part of a complex dating back to the Bronze Age, most of which can be found a short walk from the road, in the shadow of King's Tor. The stone rows are narrow, and may have had a different purpose from other wider rows. Some have speculated that this was meant solely for the dead and not the living. Boasting several cairns – one in the middle of the southern row, with a central cist – and a stone circle, Merrivale is a rewarding place to explore. In addition to the ceremonial site you'll also find a number of Bronze Age huts dotted around the landscape. It is easy to attribute sites like this to a single short period in time, but in truth the remains may well have been built over a period of 1,500 years – roughly the same period of time that separates us today from the beginning of the Dark Ages.

Take the B3357 NW from Princetown past the prison, and turn L for Tavistock at T-junction to stay on it. After 1½ miles park in car park on L and follow footpath to S to complex. Bus 98 from Tavistock or Yelverton to Princetown stop, no Sunday service.

50.5547, -4.0439, SX553747, PL20 6ST

8 DOWN TOR STONE ROW & CIRCLE
SHEEPSTOR

Down Tor, also called Hingston Hill, is one of the most spectacular stone rows on Dartmoor, leading to a no less impressive stone circle. It feels especially remote here, even for Dartmoor. For better or worse, the row is another one of Robert Burnard's late Victorian restorations, like the Grey Wethers (see entry). Thankfully, it seems he was true to the original footings and kept much of the original stone row, including its characteristic curve. The stones vary in height, being smaller and smaller as they descend the hill. It is hard to say if this is an ancient means to trick the eye, a form of forced perspective in stone, or if it has some deeper significance. Perhaps the builders wanted to show the stones coming into being as they approach the summit – or was it the other way round, as they faded into the afterlife? The stones could have also signified the rising and setting of the sun or moon. Settlements, hut circles and enclosures surround the site, but as leading authority Aubrey Burl states, 'it is impossible to be sure that the men and women who lived in the dwellings were the people who used the rings', although he does concede: 'it is tempting to see in this settlement, so close to the row and stone circle, the homes of the people who used the ring. There is nothing to prove or disprove the thought'.

From Yelverton follow the B3212 NE to the crossroads in the centre of Dousland. There follow signs R for Burrator Reservoir/Sheepstor and then L over cattle grid at the village edge. Continue around the reservoir and park in the car park for Norsworthy Bridge. Follow path E to the summit of Down Tor then continue E to stone row. 1¼-mile strenuous walk; a map and compass or good phone app is advisable. Bus 98 from Tavistock or Yelverton to Princetown stop, no Sunday service.

50.5060, -3.9941, SX586692, PL20 6PG 🖼🏔🚶

9 SHAUGH MOOR
SHAUGH PRIOR

The clay works in the hills just beyond the Shaugh Moor have a bleak beauty about them, and if you squint, you could fool yourself into believing you are walking on snow-covered Alpine hills. This is a mixed landscape: part industrial ruin, part untouched moorland. From its highest point, vistas stretch out over lush green fields all the way down to the sea. People began living in this area around 1500BC, and there are hut circles dating to around 1700–1600BC on the N side of the summit, towards the clayworks. Nearer the road, down from the circles, are the remains of enclosures, built to keep animals away from the living area rather than impound them, and cairns. All this suggests there must have been a large organised society living here before the site was abandoned. Many large stones (masquerading as ancient sites) litter the eastern slopes of the hill. The enclosure and hut circle are just one small, easily accessible part of an ancient landscape surrounding the clayworks. You can explore for miles around this white moonscape and discover its eerie turquoise mineral lakes. Once through to the north-eastern side of the works, you'll find the remains of Trowlesworthy Warren, said to be the oldest warren on Dartmoor. During the Middle Ages rabbits were kept here in pillow mounds. Alongside these you'll find Bronze Age hut circles, lonely stone rows and the remains of stone circles (circle and row at 50.4582, -4.0068), all well worth the trek across the moor. This part of Dartmoor is a favourite amongst walkers and cyclists – be alert for the many speeding 'middle-aged men in Lycra' taking advantage of the maze of routes through the clayworks.

Park in unsigned roadside car park on SE road to Shaugh Prior (50.4452, -4.0493). Cross road and follow footpath E, cross 2nd road and follow rough footpath E up hill for about 200m before heading N for ½ mile until you see the hut circles and cairns. Bus 59 from Plymouth to Shaugh Bridge stop, no Sunday service.

50.4528, -4.0379, SX554634, PL7 5EQ 🚶

10 CHUDLEIGH ROCKS CAVE SHELTERS PIXIES HOLE & CAVES CHUDLEIGH

As you approach from the A38, it is hard to believe what primeval wilderness can lie hidden away at the back of a mid-Devon housing estate. Chudleigh Rocks is popular with climbers, especially beginners, who scale the long, straight cliff faces in organised groups. The area has attracted mankind for millennia. Flints unearthed in the caves date back as far as the Palaeolithic (40,000–12,000 years ago in Europe), and animal bones and charcoal remains show people used the caves to cook food, keep warm and perhaps shelter from cold weather. It is unfortunate for us that the caves are now locked up, but our loss is the gain of the many bats living in the caverns. At sunset they can be seen emerging in great numbers. Despite the metal gates the magnitude of the caves can still be appreciated.

On the B3344/Fore Street through Chudleigh SW towards Kingsteignton, turn L shortly after church into Lawn Drive, signed Ugbrooke House. After 250 metres park in layby on R next to dog bin. Follow path SW away from road, through park between houses. When it meets a road (Palace Meadow) dog-leg L across it to pick up path to R of yellow hydrant marker and follow out to Rock Road. Turn L to kissing gate after 20 metres on R and follow footpath through it to and around rock face to Pixies Hole. Cow Cave is beyond (50.5966 -3.6054) and Tramp's Shelter S over the brook (50.5960 -3.6035). Bus 182 from Newton Abbot to Chudleigh Memorial stop, no Sunday service.

50.5965, -3.6044, SX865786, TQ13 0JJ 🦇

9

10

II CORNWOOD MAIDENS
CORNWOOD

Quite why the Cornwood Maidens stone row is left out of so many guidebooks is a bit of a mystery. It is one of the most complete, most impressive Bronze Age sites on Dartmoor, with the largest stones standing well over 2 metres tall. It stands in splendid isolation, and the views from the top are reward enough for anyone willing to make the climb. Unlike many stone rows, it does not appear to have anything clearly marking out the beginning or the end of the row as it stands today, such as a burial cairn or a stone circle. However, there are cairns along the row, which may have been made in two phases, and as at other sites that underwent late Victorian restoration it is uncertain how authentic some of the alignments are. None of this detracts from their megalithic majesty, and if you are to visit just one stone row on Dartmoor I would suggest it should be this one! The whole area is littered with well-preserved remains, including The Dancers stone circle on Stall Moor (50.4640, -3.9243) at one end of the Upper Erme Stone Row, the longest row in Britain and maybe Europe, with its northern end 2 miles away at Green Hill (50.4941, -3.9229).

The lanes leading to Cornwood Maidens are single-track and narrow with no suitable parking. Approach by bicycle walk from Cornwood village. From the crossroads follow the lane to Torr past the school out to the NE 1 mile, over a bridge after ¾ mile. At Torr village (marked only on upright of fingerboard opp L turn) take the L then bear immediate R uphill. After 400m take L at next fork. Remain on this road to waterworks gate at end. Walk L around the works and its perimeter then NNE to summit until you see the row. 2⅓ miles total, sometimes strenuous walk. Bus 111 from Ivybridge to Cornwood Inn stop, no Sunday service.

50.4464, -3.9274, SX632625, PL21 9RB

I2 DENBURY HILLFORT
& BARROWS IPPLEPEN

Denbury Hillfort near the charming village of Ipplepen is a welcome diversion off the main road between Newton Abbot and Totnes. The path to the fort snakes through hedgerows and climbs steeply to a magical woodland, carpeted with bluebells in spring. From the top, views stretch out across Devon all the way to the expansive Dartmoor landscape. The fort itself dates from around 300BC, and was first built for pastoral communities rather than as a defensive structure. Amongst the trees at the top of the fort are two bowl barrows, burial mounds dating from the Late Bronze Age, suggesting that the site may have been in use much earlier. The name Denbury translates as 'the fort of the men of Devon' and possibly the Dumnonii tribe held out in pitched battles against the invading Saxons here. The recent finding of a Saxon wrist clasp by a metal-detectorist at least suggests a Saxon presence at the site.

Take the A381 S from Newton Abbot for Totnes, and just after the Ogwell Cross Cemetery roundabout take first R, Denbury Road, 2 miles to Denbury village. Park in village and continue on foot W from the school along Woodland Road. At the end of the village follow lane opp Denbury Down Road to top of fort. 15 minutes' strenuous walk. Bus 176 from Newton Abbot to Denbury Down Lane stop.

50.5045, -3.6700, SX816685, TQ12 6DY

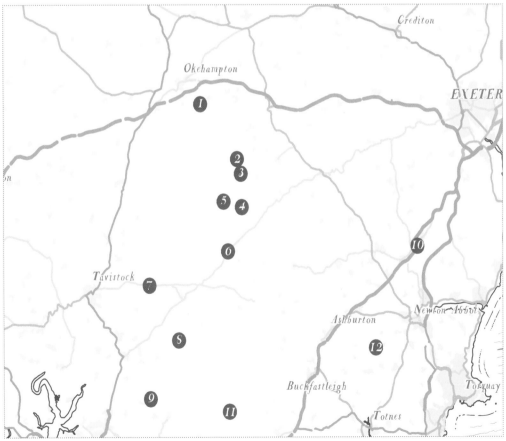

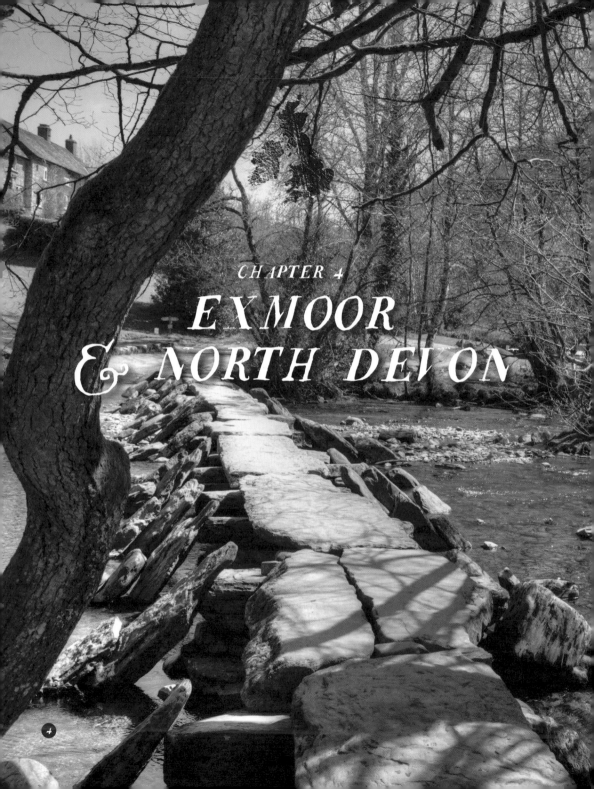

CHAPTER 4
EXMOOR
& NORTH DEVON

*T*he expansive terrain of Exmoor has England's largest population of red deer, and its highest coastal cliffs as part of the longest naturally wooded coastline in the British Isles. It boasts some of the best hillwalking in the South-West in a landscape which is no less of wilderness than the moorlands of Dartmoor and Cornwall to the south.

Down here, on the northernmost edge of the South West Peninsula, the Bristol Channel marks the transition between the Severn Estuary and the wide Atlantic. The tidal estuary changes in colour, as the waters turn from a muddy brown to a deep sea-blue, and also in nature, with sightseeing boats heading out from Ilfracombe and Lynmouth regularly reporting sightings of dolphins, seals and porpoises. All along the coastline seabirds dive from vertiginous cliffs to grab a morsel or two from the vast swell.

During the Iron Age, settlers built forts to overlook and perhaps defend the Bristol Channel coast. The most impressive of all these is just up the coast from the holiday towns of Lynton and Lynmouth. The ancient earthworks, commonly referred to as Wind Hill, command a strategic position on top of Countisbury Hill overlooking the sea to one side and the valley to the other. It is thought that one of a group of tribes known collectively as the Dumnonii once defended the hillfort; we rarely have names for these ancient people, but the lasting impact of the Dumnonii is still evident today as the basis of the name Devon. It seems at the time of Roman occupation the Dumnonii were either feared or tolerated, as the Romans had very little to do with them. Since tin was traded along the Devon and Cornwall coast from the 6th century BC, the Dumnonii would not have been an isolated tribe. Instead it is likely they were influenced by the cultures they traded with prior to the occupation, from Phoenicia, Minoa, Gaul and Rome.

The ancient remains in North Devon are more enigmatic than those anywhere else in the country. Here the branches of a vast ancient yew, a living, tangible link to our ancestors, can make for a child's den or a welcome escape from a hot summer's sun. There are woodland walks, treks across moors and jaunts up from tidal beaches to find hidden stones and ancient remains.

1 LANGRIDGE WOOD CIST
ROADWATER

Burial cists are a common occurrence on Dartmoor, but only seven have ever been discovered in the whole of the Exmoor region. These coffin-like stone structures containing the remains of the dead could be covered with a barrow, surrounded by a stone circle or topped by a stack of stones or cairn, and were a common form of burial in the Late Neolithic and Early Bronze Age. A fine example is hidden amidst the trees in Langridge Wood. Depending on the time of year, the site can be completely overgrown but it is signed from the nearby footpath, so should not be too hard to find. The woods are a little out of the way from the more tourist-friendly walks around Dunster, but this only adds to the charm of this remote site. The capstone of the cist is quite substantial, over 1.5 metres each way, and was once covered with a large barrow mound. The mound was removed around 1820, and some of the stone unearthed was sadly used for the building of a road. The cist is thought to date from a time in the Bronze Age known as the Beaker culture, 2500–1700BC in Britain, named after the many distinctively curved, bell-shaped beakers dated to this period that were used for everything from drinking to smelting.

From Roadwater village follow the road to the SW past The Valiant Soldier inn (TA23 0QZ, 01984 640223). Remain on the road for a mile, keeping R at the L fork, where the road becomes wooded, and look for L up a track signed 'Dunster Woods' up to a car park (51.1288, -3.4070). Cist is on L after ⅓ mile moderate walk SW. Bus 28 from Minehead or Taunton to Washford Shepherd's Corner stop, 2 miles' walk SW to Roadwater.

51.1273, -3.4103, ST014373, TA23 0QZ

2 ASH BRITTLE YEW
ASH BRITTLE

In the year 1000BC the Phoenicians were using the world's first alphabet, the Zhou dynasty ruled supreme in feudal China and (it is said) David was crowned the King of Israel. Meanwhile, in a remote part of Somerset a tree was growing which has lived through waves of invasions, the birth of new religions, the beginnings of new technologies, the rise of what must have seemed like unstoppable empires and then their fall. Few things are such a tangible link with our ancestors as the 3,000-year-

old Ashbrittle Yew. It is hard to fathom that something still living today has been a contemporary of the great empires of Egypt, the Iron Age, the Romans, Henry VIII and Ziggy Stardust. Local legends claim that a Bronze Age chief is buried beneath the mound at the base of the tree, and the church is also said to be built on the site of a Druidic circle. The yew may be declining in health now, so visit while you can. While in the area it is worth visiting the Stawley Village Shop and Tea Rooms (TA21 0HH, 01823 674361) for its excellent cream teas.

From Wellington follow A38 W for 2 miles from Perry Elm roundabout, then follow signs R to Ashbrittle, 3¾ miles. The tree is in the churchyard, reached by a path off the W side of the triangular green.

50.9838, -3.3519, ST052213, TA21 0LE

3 WEST ANSTEY BARROWS & LONGSTONE WEST ANSTEY

On the high hinterland of Exmoor, the barrows at West Anstey are thick with bracken and gorse, forming an island reserve for the local wildlife. The two bowl barrows (a bowl-shaped mound of earth covering a tomb) are remarkably intact, despite having been a little rough-housed over the centuries, although one of the two has a large chunk missing through being robbed or poorly excavated long ago. At the head of the coombe, 300–400 metres to the north-west of the barrows, is the Anstey Longstone (51.0526, -3.6432). Standing around 1.3 metres high, the lonely stone overlooks the wooded valley below like a farmer watching over his flock. Perhaps it is this position, looking down over the transition of moor to meadow, or perhaps it was just my isolation that day, but there did seem to be a distinctive friendliness about the Longstone. The Ridge Road south of the stone and the barrow is long and straight; excellent for cycling. The barrow and the stone are near to parking spaces and offer easy access for young and old.

In Dulverton head W over the river following the B3222 as it bends to the S. Take 1st R fork towards Oldways End, then after ⅓ mile 2nd R uphill for Hawkridge. Remain on road for 4 miles, following sign for Molland after 2 miles. Barrows will be visible on skyline to the R, pull into nearest parking spot. Longstone is at the head of the valley behind the barrows.

51.0499, -3.6352, SS849294TA22 9QT

4 TARR STEPS LISCOMBE

Tarr Steps is a 55-metre bridge made up of 17 heavy granite slabs spanning supports across the River Barle. These slab bridges are known as clapper bridges, and Tarr Steps is the longest of its kind in the country. Although the origins of the bridge are unknown it is thought a Bronze Age track may have crossed the river at this point. The trackway would have been used for trade or to move livestock between winter and summer pastures, so a bridge at this point would have been an invaluable crossing. Evidence backing this claim is rather scant, and some (including Heritage England) hold that the bridge more likely dates from the comparatively recent Middle Ages. Although it can get busy, there are so many little pools and shady pockets along the banks it is easy to find a private place to retreat to. The river is shallow enough for children, dogs and playful adults to have a paddle in its cooling waters in summer, although in recent winters it has repeatedly carried slabs many metres downstream. After a day exploring the area, there is nothing more refreshing than a pint in the Tarr Farm Inn (TA22 9PY, 01643 851507) overlooking the steps.

Head S from Royal Oak pub (TA24 7JE, 01643 851455) in Winsford. Continue over B3223 at crossroads, and 1½ miles further, bearing L over cattle grid at fork with track and past Liscombe, to park in car park on L just before river.

51.0772, -3.6176, SS867321, TA22 9PY

5 WITHYPOOL STONE CIRCLE WITHYPOOL

The enigmatic stone circle at Withypool lay concealed for thousands of years in the undergrowth until rediscovered by chance in 1898. There are 40 or so stones in a ring 36 metres across, and there may originally have been 100, but with the tallest no more than 50cm in height, it is perhaps understandable that they lay hidden away for such a length of time. Even today, they are almost completely hidden from view when the grass is long and the heather is high. The siting of this circle so close to a river may have been deliberate. This could have been a practical measure as the circle would have been easy to reach by boat, or it

could have been symbolic in nature, with the water seen as the way the souls of the dead departed or returned to this spot. What the circle lacks in height it makes up for in ambience. Set against the dramatic backdrop of the wilds of Exmoor, it is a rare joy to find. The 300-year-old Royal Oak Inn (TA24 7QP, 01643 831506) in nearby Withypool has a roaring log fire, serves hot and cold drinks and good food to windswept travellers, and has rooms for overnight stays.

From Withypool head S over river and cattle grid on Worth Lane for 1m, following signs for Hawkridge, to cattle grid and sign for 'horse-drawn vehicles and animals' L. Park on R and follow bridleway E for 900m, then head N towards summit. Map and compass or phone mapping is handy here.

51.0963, -3.6603, SS838343, TA24 7RG

6 DUNKERY BEACON CAIRNS PORLOCK

On the slopes around the modern commemorative cairn on the top of Dunkery Beacon are the remains of at least five Early Bronze Age cairns from 2000–1600BC. These would have been single or multiple burial sites topped with stone, but after a few thousand years of rain and wind on this very exposed site, along with countless tourists climbing the beacon, not all the cairns are in good shape. The largest and most visible is on the north side of the hill and appears as a large mound, around 22 metres in diameter. There are many theories as to why the cairns were made here. Was this the closest place to the gods, a fitting place to enter the afterlife? There are many paths to the top, some more challenging than others; some choose to climb up from Dunkery Bridge car park, little more than ½ mile away, while others prefer the 3½-mile challenge from the E, along Macmillan Way West from Wootton Courtenay. As the highest point in Somerset, the views from up here are unparalleled in the region.

Signed NW from Wheddon Cross on the B3224. After ¾ mile leave the B3224, taking the 2nd R turn again signed Dunkery Beacon. Remain on the road just over 1½ miles to car park R. Walk N to top of beacon on path, ¾-mile strenuous walk.

51.1627, -3.5867, SS891415, TA24 7AT

7 WIND HILL
LYNMOUTH

Wind Hill, also known as Countisbury Castle, is a hillfort high on the Countisbury headland, just off the main road into Lynmouth. It commands spectacular views down to Lynmouth to the west, across the North Devon coast of Sillery Sands to Butter Hill to the north and into the wooded river valley surrounding Watersmeet to the south. The fort is univallate, or single-walled, and dates back to the Iron Age. Although little is known about its prehistory, it is thought that it may have been the site of the legendary Battle of Cynwit in AD 878. The account says that the West Saxons under Devonian leader Odda had retreated to a hillfort with no water source as some 1,200 Vikings laid siege below. The Saxons had no choice but die or conquer, so launched a surprise attack before dawn. They were victorious, killing many of the Vikings including their leader, and ultimately turning the tide on the invasion. It is a steep but short climb to the top. Once up there, the sea seems endless, a vast swell of deep blue. This is easily one of the finest hillforts in Devon and certainly the one with the most spectacular view.

Follow A39 E from Lynmouth towards Porlock. After just over 1 mile park in small layby on R (51.2308, -3.8026). Follow the path to the top of the hillfort, 10 mins' strenuous walk. Bus 309 or 310 Barnstaple to Lynmouth, no Sunday service; on weekdays, heritage bus 300 Minehead–Lynmouth, to Countisbury stop and walk W to layby.

51.2294, -3.8052, SS740493, EX35 6NE

8 CHAPMAN LONGSTONE
CHALLACOMBE

Also called Challacombe Longstone, this is not a monument for the fair-weather walker. Although it is only a couple of miles from the nearest road, the route crosses boggy, windswept moorland. To make things even more interesting, there is no clear path directly to the stone, which sits in the centre of a large, waterlogged marsh. The reward for all this arduous exercise is a magnificent tall, thin menhir, towering up nearly 3 metres in height, the largest standing stone in Exmoor. It is surrounded by numerous Bronze Age barrows, housing the remains of people who died over

3,000 years ago, all within unspoilt, serene moorland. The large Longstone Barrow can be seen quite clearly from the stone. The landscape may have been more forgiving in the past, and what is now moorland may have once been able to support a community of subsistence farmers. Just a short walk up to the ridge above the stone takes you to the moonscape of Chapman Barrows, a splendid series of mounds, rising in a long line. Tucked away by the side of the B3358 to the south of the Longstone you will also find the Edgerley Stone, which marks the boundary between Somerset and Devon (51.1512, -3.8321).

Take the B3358 W from Simonsbath. After 3 miles, when the road swings R then bends sharply L, park in the layby at the entrance of Pinkery Centre (TA24 7LL, 01643 831437). Follow the path N to Pinkery Pond, turn L and head W for a mile over the moor to the Longstone. A map and compass or phone mapping is highly recommended.

51.1721, -3.8536, SS705430, TA24 7LL

9 DAMAGE BARTON STONES
DAMAGE BARTON

These stones are best approached by climbing the steep set of old wooden stairs that rise up the headland from the near-deserted tidal cove at Damage Hue, in Lee Bay. The shoreline here is not as explored as the Valley of the Rocks, further up the coast, yet it easily rivals its rugged charm. On a gusty day the wind funnels up the Bristol Channel to send hats flying and further ravage the headland. There are three single stones altogether dotted around the headland, all within 100-150m from each other. The stones are much too far apart to have been part of a stone circle and there has been no evidence to support a larger monument here. Many standing stones have burial remains, or they may be boundary markers between neighbouring tribes, meeting points or waymarkers for a long-forgotten route. The lovely Grampus Inn (EX34 8LR, 01271 862906) in Lee has reasonably priced food and the Smuggler's Cottage (EX34 8LR, 01271 864897) at the bay sells snacks, ice cream and hot drinks during the summer.

Check tide times before taking this route. Take the road through Lee village to the shore, park in the pay car park and at low tide

10 PORLOCK STONE CIRCLE *PORLOCK*

Almost hidden in the corner of a field, just off the meandering country lane that runs between Exford and Porlock, lies one of Exmoor's two stone circles. Like the one on Withypool Hill (see entry), this one may be associated with the watercourse below. It is thought that the 24.5-metre circle once consisted of 43 stones, but stones have been added and taken away over the years until now around 14 remain, some standing and some fallen. To the south-east of the circle is another rarity in Exmoor, a short stone row, which can be almost impossible to find due to its low stature and the surrounding grass. A lovely walk can be plotted from Porlock village through the woods at Hawk Combe.

Take the A39 W from Porlock for just over 2 miles. Take the L turn towards Exford and Cloutsham opposite car park. Remain on the road for around 1½ miles and park by a farmer's gate on the right. The stones are in this field. Bus 10 from Minehead to Porlock.

51.1895, -3.6540, SS845446, TA24 8QH 🚗🚶

walk down to the beach. Follow the shore around the rocks to the W and climb the stairs, then follow the coast path W; at high tide walk up the hill on the road W to find the coast path. Once W over the river, head inland up the hill to the first stone; the next is 150m SW (51.1957, -4.1902), and the last 120m S from that (51.1941, -4.1901). At high tide you can also approach from Mortehoe following the tracks and paths NE to the headland from the end of North Morte Road (51.1886, -4.2026). Bus 35 from Ilfracombe to Lee Beach House stop, Tuesday and Friday only.

51.1969, -4.1883, SS471464, EX34 8LR 🚗🏕🏔🍴🚶

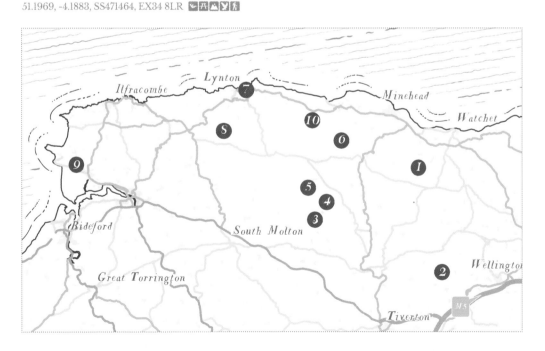

CHAPTER 5

SOMERSET

*F*rom vast, breathtaking gorges and gently rolling hills to the moors and wetlands known collectively as the Levels, Somerset is a county of varied beauty.

It is also one rich in prehistoric remains, boasting some of Britain's oldest recorded finds from human history. The first recorded human burial was at Aveline's Hole cave in the seldom visited gorge of Burrington Combe, just south of Bristol Airport. In recent years the cave also gave more glimpses into the past, as a grid of ten X's were found engraved into its solid rock walls. What this symbolised to its Mesolithic author we will never know, but to us it shows a level of sophistication among Stone Age people we didn't think existed in this country at that time. It has been suggested that these marks may be linked to the burial itself, which would make them some of the earliest grave markings in Europe. Down the road from Aveline's Hole, the body of the Cheddar man who died over 9,000 years ago was found deep within the Mendip Hills cave system. When mitochondrial DNA (that from the female line) from his tooth was analysed, it showed that he and a history teacher at Cheddar School shared a maternal ancestor. It is impressive to think someone so ancient could have a living relative still in the area, especially since these ancient Britons were almost entirely replaced by later settlers.

When Neolithic farmers replaced hunter-gatherers 3,500 years later, great tombs were built at Stoney Littleton, Rode and Orchardleigh, and their remains still stand today. So often the practices of our Neolithic predecessors seem alien and other-worldly, and we may never know why these tombs only housed selected bodyparts rather than full skeletons. It has been found that these were often removed and replaced back in the tomb, sometimes over many years. The bones would have belonged to the immediate ancestors of those who lived and farmed in the lands surrounding the tomb, but why they chose to take out and replace the bones of their great-grandparents, or more distant relations, and what they did with the bones whilst they were out of the tomb, we can only speculate.

During the Late Neolithic and Early Bronze Age, stone circles began to appear all over the country, and Somerset is also home to the vast stone circle at Stanton Drew, just off the road between Bristol and Wells. This bewitching monument rivals Avebury and Stonehenge for its sheer size. Later still, in the Iron Age, prime farming land became something of a prized commodity which needed to be defended, and we saw the rise of vast Iron Age hillforts. Somerset has some of the best examples in the country, including the coastal fort at Worlebury, the wooded beech glade of Roddenbury and the spectacular 3-mile ramparts at Hamdon Hill.

1

2

2

3

1 WORLEBURY CAMP
WESTON–SUPER–MARE

With a commanding position high above the town of Weston-super-Mare, the multiple ramparts of this multivallate Iron Age hillfort lie almost lost in a thickly wooden peninsula. From time to time volunteers come and clear away the undergrowth so the site can be seen in all its glory. Inside the fort are hut circles and 93 pits cut into the bedrock; these were mostly likely used for food storage, with the deep earth acting as a natural refrigerator, and contained remains of wheat, barley and peas. Human bones were found in some of them, many showing marks of violence, including a gashed skull. It is thought these bodies were thrown into the pits following the last great attack on the fort. The site is best reached from the end furthest away from the sea, where in summer a walk through the woods is a welcome relief not only from the sun, but also from the crowds on the beach below. The woods are full of walkers and dogs, and the long, straight paths along the centre of the peninsula make it a perfect place to zoom along on a mountain bike. Along the coast to the north, the tidal marshes at Woodspring Bay and Sand Bay are a must for birdwatchers, foragers and walkers, and an overnight stop in the shepherd's hut at Woodspring Farm (BS22 9YU, 07952 805390) perfectly rounds off a stay in this area.

From Weston-super-Mare follow the coast road N around the peninsula to Kewstoke. Just after entering Kewstoke, take hairpin L on Beach Road and park in car park L overlooking sea. Follow footpath behind up into the woods to main path, then turn R heading W towards sea. Hillfort is a mile along, easy walk. Bus 1 from Weston-super-Mare to Kewstoke Toll Gate stop.

51.357, -2.9874, ST313656, BS22 9YD

2 BURRINGTON COMBE,
BURRINGTON

Aveline's Hole, a large cave within Burrington Combe gorge, is the oldest crypt in the country. It feels as if you are entering another world when you descend into it, and it is not hard to see why Mesolithic people chose this other-worldly place, deep in the very earth itself, to honour their dead some 10,400 years ago. Today, a climb to the top of the gorge offers views to the Bristol Channel, but back in Neolithic times the seas would have been much lower and Burrington would have been considerably further inland. Despite the road running through it (popular with cyclists), the combe has very wild atmosphere, and it doesn't take long to feel like a wanderer through primeval woodland. Hidden amongst the trees up on the wooded banks of the gorge are many other caves, including Goatchurch Cavern (51.3206, -2.7536) once home to the mammoths and hyenas that wandered the area during the last ice age. Not far south from Burrington is Gough's Cave in the famous Cheddar Gorge, where Britain's oldest complete skeleton was found – his skull is now in the Natural History Museum. The museums and cave here are a more structured visit, but just as enjoyable as the wilds of Burrington.

From the A368 at Burrington, take the B3134 S about 600 metres to park at the Burrington Inn (a friendly bar and café/restaurant with a dated charm, BS40 7AT, 01761 462227) or in the free Rock of Ages car park about 150 metres further on. Aveline's Hole is by the road 100 metres to the S of the 2nd car park. For Goatchurch Cavern and the top of the gorge follow the road S and the track R up the hill along the riverside until you reach the steps. Climb here until you see the cavern. Bus 134 from Weston-super-Mare to Burrington Turn Off stop, Tuesdays only. Or Falcon coach from Bristol (for Plymouth) to Lower Langford on the A38, 2½ miles' walk.

51.3247, -2.7533, ST476586, BS40 7AT

3 MAES KNOLL
BRISTOL

This univallate, or single-rampart, hillfort with a distinctive tump lies on the outskirts of Bristol. It is close enough for you to look down on the suburbs from it, but on a clear day the sweeping panorama over the Chew Valley and beyond in all other directions makes Maes Knoll feel a million miles away from the bustle of the city. Evidence suggests the Dobunni built the fort sometime around 250BC. The Dobunni were a tribe of farmers and craftsmen who were mostly based in Gloucestershire but spread into neighbouring counties including Somerset, Worcestershire and parts of Oxfordshire. The tump is thought to be a more recent addition, built to strengthen the fort's defences around the same time as the Wansdyke or Woden's Dyke, a medieval defensive ditch that terminates here. Today it has a much more recreational purpose, as cyclists use this as a thrilling start to a long, bumping descent. Maes Knoll also makes one-third of the 17-mile Three Peaks Circular Walk, along with Knowle Hill (51.3496, -2.5983) and Blackberry Hill (51.3394, -2.5183).

Travel S out of Bristol on the A37/Wells Road for 3½ miles, at the end of Whitchurch take R turn signed Whitehall Garden Centre. Stay on road for 1½ miles, then L into Church Road towards Norton Malreward and Stanton Drew. Pull in L after 200 metres. Footpath to fort is back up to the turning and across, slightly to the L, 20 minutes' strenuous walk. Bus 376 from Bristol to Whitchurch Staunton Lane stop, 20 minutes' walk.

51.3915, -2.5774, ST600856, BS39 4EY

4 STANTON DREW
CHEW MAGNA

Likely to date from the Late Neolithic, Stanton Drew is easily Somerset's most impressive stone circle site. Its name derives from Stantune, 'the homestead by the stones', with the Drew later added for the Dreux family who owned the land. One of the largest in Western Europe, it rivals the large outer ring at Avebury (see

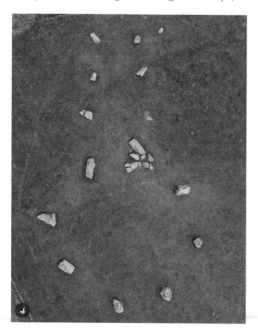

Wiltshire & Wessex). The size and layout here make it difficult for photographers to give a real sense of these megaliths, and this is one that has to be seen to be believed, because the site has not one but three circles, the large one in the centre, another smaller one in the same field and a third over the lane to the south-west. To the north of the circle, just off the B3130, the intrepid antiquarian may find the scant remains of Hautville's Quoit (51.3719, -2.5735), almost hidden in a farmer's field, but most will be more impressed by the megaliths known as the Cove, found in the garden of The Druids Arms pub (BS39 4RJ, 01275 332230) and best contemplated over a pint of ale. Recent findings point towards the cove being the remains of a chambered barrow dating some 1,000 years before the stone circle were built. Was this grouping of sites an intentional one? Perhaps the same family group who constructed the tomb went on to build the circles centuries later in homage to their ancestors? Combining this with a walk up Maes Knoll (see entry) and a good meal in the Druids Arms is a good way to spend a Sunday afternoon at any time of year.

Follow directions to Maes Knoll but continue through the village of Norton Malreward, R onto B3130 then immediate L signed Stanton Drew. Take L fork then follow the road as it doglegs L to stone circle car park in a small housing estate. There is an honesty box for the site and generous donations are always welcome. Bus 376 from Bristol or Wells to Pensford stop, 20 minutes walk.

51.3671, -2.5760, ST5999632, BA39 4EP

5 PRIDDY & ASHEN HILL BARROWS PRIDDY

The collection of Bronze Age round and bowl barrows (or burial mounds) atop North Hill have been known as Priddy Nine Barrows since the 1300s. Around 300 metres away lies another group, the Ashen Hill Barrows (51.2657, -2.6619). Archaeologists working the mounds have found grave goods, including a spear or arrowhead and amber and glass beads, along with cremated remains, giving an insight into what must have been quite a sophisticated people. Over the road to the north of the barrows are the Priddy Circles (51.2705, -2.6615, no public access), three Neolithic earthworks dating from 2700–2200BC and thought to be a ceremonial gathering place. We cannot say for certain that the

sites are linked, but their close proximity high on this picturesque Mendip hill does hint at a belief system unifying the two. This route is a short trek from Stockhill Wood, a mostly coniferous forest where you can hear the hoots of long-eared owls echoing through the trees at dusk. The woodland and surrounding area were important for lead mining from the Roman era right up until the last century; the wetlands created by the extraction are now an important home to wildlife, and during the summer you may see dragonflies darting across the water above newts and toads.

From Priddy village take Wells Road SW, after approx 1½ miles take L at crossroads with Hunter's Lodge Pub (BA5 3AR, 01749 672275) signed Harptree, after ¾ mile FC Stockhill car park is on R. Cross road and go slightly N to take Monarch's Way footpath SW nearly ½ mile; when the lake is on your L, take R to head NW on Mendip Pub Trail. Priddy Nine Barrows are through a gate on L after ½ mile. Bus 683 from Wells to Priddy opp Harptree Lodge Kennels stop and walk ¼ mile E to pick up N end of footpath, Tuesdays only.

51.2606, -2.6612, ST539520, BA5 3DB

6 EBBOR GORGE
EASTON

When a huge cavern collapsed some 200,000 years ago it left the chasm of Ebbor Gorge, a natural wonder hidden deep in the heart of Somerset's Mendip Hills. Although your calf muscles might complain about the trek to the top, the views out over the Somerset Levels and beyond will soon distract you. Finds suggest that settlement in and around the caves within Ebbor Gorge date back 12,000 years, to the Palaeolithic era. There have also been finds associated with the Neolithic and the Bronze Age Beaker people (so named for their decorated bell-shaped clay beakers). Many of the finds can be found in fascinating displays just down the road in Wookey Hole and Wells museums. Although nearby Wookey Hole has become a little dated as a tourist attraction, the caves themselves are still worth a visit. Also in the area, up the road from the gorge, in a field 100 metres to the right are two standing stones known as the Deerleap Stones (51.2345, -2.6917). They are said to mark the legendary leap of a deer, but it is unknown if they are from prehistory or boundary remains from near history.

From Wells take the A371 W towards Cheddar and Weston-super-Mare. About ⅓ mile after the B3139 fork L, take R signed to Wookey Hole. Continue past caves 1 mile, following road R at fork, to Ebbor Gorge National Trust car park R. The cycle path follows the same route. Bus 126 from Weston-super-Mare to Wookey stop on A371, 2 miles walk total, or 67 from Wells to Wookey opp church stop.

51.2337, -2.6840, ST523485, BA5 1AY

7 STONEY LITTLETON
WELLOW

The ammonite fossil at the entrance to this chambered long barrow has had archaeologists wondering what ancient people made of a prehistoric sea creature. Such an intricate pattern set in stone must have seemed remarkable – enough for them to deem it fitting to incorporate it into the entrance to their world of the dead. It has even been noted that spiral carvings at tombs such as Newgrange in Ireland and Westray, Orkney are reminiscent of this shape. In the early 19th century Reverend John Skinner entered through a hole in the roof made decades before by a farmer looking for road-building stone. He found human bones still within each chamber, along with pottery fragments. Some of the bones were separated out, such as legs and jaws; others were in a 'confused heap'. In one of the chambers, burned remains of two or three people were found in an earthen vessel. Stoney Littleton is accessible by car along its winding lanes, but arriving by bike via the Two Tunnels cycle path from Bath is far more enjoyable.

Take A367 N from Radstock towards Bath. At roundabout on Peasedown St John bypass take Wellow Lane S past hospital, and just before entering Wellow village take R signed to Long Barrow. Park in car park L on bend after ¾ mile and follow footpath ½ mile over bridge and along field edge and L to barrow. Bus 174 from Bath to Peasedown stops, 3 miles' walk.

51.3132, -2.3817, BA2 8QJ

8 ORCHARDLEIGH STONES
BUCKLAND DINHAM

The remaining stones of Murtry Hill Long Barrow rise up like two large praying hands amid long grass in the corner of a farmer's field. These uprights and a low mound are all that is left of a chambered tomb dating back to the Neolithic era. Human bones and cremation urns were found when the barrow was opened in the early 18th century, and again in the early 19th and 20th centuries. The site is easily reached from the Bell Inn (BA11 2QT, 01373 462956) at Buckland Dinham, but is best taken in as part of a longer walk. Nearby Orchardleigh Lake is worth a visit but do be warned, even in the height of summer it is muddier in places than a wet Glastonbury Festival, so a good pair of wellies are highly recommended. Longer walks can also be had along the river from the picturesque village of Mells, with its fabulous Walled Garden and café (BA11 3PN, 01373 812597).

From Frome head N on the A362 towards Buckland Dinham. After the 'Buckland Dinham' village sign take next R, single-track lane ⅓ mile to farmhouse on L. Pull off on R, keeping the lane free, enter field to R walking S for 200m. There is no official right of way here, so keep to field boundary and no dog walkers. Stones are to the L in next field on uncultivated land.

51.2546, -2.3408, ST763506, BA11 2QJ

9 THE DEVIL'S BED & BOLSTER RODE

This group of stones is a short but pleasant walk from the village of Rode on the Wiltshire-Somerset border. Like nearby Stoney Littleton (see entry) it is an example of a Cotswold-Severn tomb, a chambered burial tomb built by the Neolithic people who inhabited the region

around 3500BC. Much of the tomb is now ruined, and the large stones that would have made up the internal walls are the barrow's most prominent feature, standing proud like overgrown gravestones under a copse of trees. It is thought that tombs like this may have only been in use for as little as five generations. It is a lovely place to be, overlooking fields and the nearby St Lawrence's church, built in the 14th century when many pagan sites were said to be within the influence of the Devil, which is why so many bear his name.

Park in Church Lane in Rode village, off A361 Trowbridge to Frome. Walk back and cross A361 and follow the footpath into the field S, where you can see the copses ahead. Over the first stile, at 2nd follow the field boundary around to the R through gap in the hedge. Follow the edge of the fields back on yourself to 2nd copse of trees. 10 minutes, easy walk. Bus X34 Frome–Chippenham to Rode Hill Memorial Hall stop, or train to Trowbridge, 4 miles' walk.

51.2789, -2.2667, ST814533, BA11 6PW

10 RODDENBURY HILLFORT FROME

Cloaked under the thick cover of beech trees, Roddenbury is a hidden gem whatever the season. It is one of 47 Iron Age forts in the area; these are generally believed to have been built to defend prime farmland, such as that which still surrounds the fort today, but in more peaceful times they may also have been places where tribes or families got together at various times of the year, more like an agricultural show or summer fete today. It is not far from the town of Frome, and taking the backroads can make for a very pleasant cycle. The magnificent National Trust hillfort of Cley Hill (51.2028, -2.2325) is on the road between Frome and Warminster, visible for miles around and with panoramic views from the top that make the short but energetic climb very worthwhile.

From Frome take the B3092 S, signed Maiden Bradley, to A361 roundabout. Take 1st exit onto A361 NE, then immediate R to East Woodland. After 1¼ miles turn R at crossroads for Woodland Church and park in car park by church. Take path S, bending L and heading E over road then into woods and up hill to fort. 15 minutes' moderate to strenuous walk to top.

51.1944, -2.2897, ST798439, BA11 5LG

II *HAMDON HILL CAMP*
STOKE SUB HAMDON

This site, also called just Ham Hill, is often cited as the largest hillfort in the country. It has some 3 miles of ramparts, enclosing 210 acres – an area equivalent of 112 football pitches – in other words, huge! Findings suggest that the site was first settled in the Neolithic period, although flints have been found dating back to the Palaeolithic. Traces of hearths, field boundaries and house foundations show the site was occupied from the Late Bronze Age through the Iron Age and into the Roman period. Its history was a bloody one, as it was occupied by the Durotriges, a tribe known to have resisted the Roman occupation. Coins of the tribe have been found, along with chariot parts, currency bars, skeletons bearing marks of violent death, and Roman military equipment, all dating to the Late Iron Age. It could not hold out forever, and there is also much evidence that the Romans later used the area, including the remains of a villa. There are lovely walks all over the site, from short strolls culminating at The Prince of Wales pub (TA14 6RW, 01935 822848) to longer walks along the Monarch's Way to the National Trust property of Montacute House (50.9516, -2.7139).

Leave the A303 between Petherton and Cartgate picnic area roundabouts, just W of BP Cartgate garage, towards Stoke Sub Hamdon. Follow through village, turning L at T-junction, then R. After ½ mile take L into car parks for pub or country park. Bus 81 Yeovil to Stoke sub Hamdon Main Street stop.

50.9520, -2.7446, ST477172, TA14 6RW

12 *SWEET TRACK*
WESTHAY

Long before the Somerset Levels were drained, early settlers found ways of crossing the marsh to islands by means of wooden trackways in order to exploit food sources such as birds and fish during the winter. What is interesting about the presence of the track is the level of planning, skill and co-operation it suggests in these Neolithic farmers; it would have taken some weeks to ready the wood, and two groups of half a dozen a day to build the track. The peat-rich soil has preserved the track remarkably well, allowing tree ring dating to 3807–3806BC, and it is arguably the oldest timber trackway

still in existence. As the wood is so fragile, much has been covered back over for preservation and some is in museums. However, it is still possible to walk along its original path, and a replica of one section of the path crosses the marshes as it would have millennia ago. Mesmerising starling murmurations in the winter skies above Shapwick Heath are also a sight not to be missed!

At Glastonbury take the B3151 NW from the A39 for approx 4½ miles, then L onto Shapwick Road in Westhay and after ¾ mile Avalon Marshes Centre is on the L. Parking charges may apply. Bus 668 from Glastonbury to Westhay Post Office stop.

51.1683, -2.8215, ST426604, BA6 9TTK

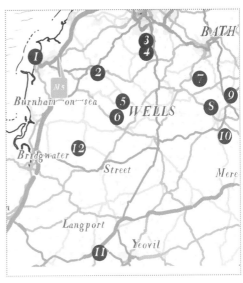

75

CHAPTER 6

WILTSHIRE & WESSEX

*T*wo world-famous sites dominate the archaeological landscape of Wiltshire; the magnificent avenue, stone circles and associated monuments of Avebury, and of course the Stonehenge landscape and circle. Both are remarkable examples of prehistoric organisation and ingenuity. With little more than hand tools made of antlers and bones, along with timbers and handmade ropes, they dug the colossal ditches and earth banks and erected the giant stones. To give you an idea of how difficult this task would have been, the large sarsen stones at Stonehenge weigh about 20 tonnes each, equivalent to about 11 large cars, or three elephants.

During the winter and summer solstices today, celebrations take place at both Stonehenge and Avebury. Stonehenge has become a huge, hedonistic explosion of neo-pagan ritual and festivity during the summer solstice. Despite the numbers, it is a peaceful place to be, with disparate groups of people coming together for a single purpose; to celebrate the dawning of the longest day. It is quite an event, and one I suggest everyone should experience at least once in their life. However, those seeking quiet contemplation to mark the passing of the year would do better visiting Avebury or a site local to them. Avebury seldom attracts anything like the numbers at Stonehenge – and it has the added advantage of having a pub within the site.

Despite their dominance, Avebury and Stonehenge are by no means the only sites worth visiting in Wiltshire. Not far from the National Trust's Stourhead House and Gardens on the western edge of the Cranborne Chase is Whitesheet Hill (51.1104, -2.2810), a Neolithic causewayed enclosure dating from 3595–3550BC. Surrounded by ditches bridged by access causeways, these spaces seem not to have been occupied, but served some ritual or social purpose. On the grounds of another National Trust property, just behind Philipps House on the Dinton Park Estate, a little-known hillfort called Wick Ball Camp (51.0872, -2.0006) is rather discreetly tucked away in the woods. Although both sites are worth visiting, I find a circular route over the three hillforts of Battlesbury, Scratchbury and Middle Hill one of the most rewarding winter rambles in all of Wiltshire.

1

2

3

4

1 FIGSBURY RING
SALISBURY

Owned by the National Trust, Figsbury Ring is a well-visited and well-looked-after Iron Age hillfort enclosing a Neolithic causewayed enclosure, or henge, close to the city of Salisbury. At any time of year a walk around the ramparts rewards you with sweeping views overlooking Salisbury Plain and out to the cathedral. During the summer, the grassland is awash with wild flowers amongst which butterflies flitter as skylarks rise into the air and let out their distinctive song. Figsbury was a small, well-defended fort, thought to have been occupied for a little over a hundred years around 500–400 BC. It may have had a strategic relationship with Old Sarum near Salisbury, another Iron Age hillfort dating to around 400BC. English Heritage has a gift shop at Old Sarum and charges an entrance fee, but Figsbury is free to enter.

Follow the A30 NE from Salisbury for 2 miles, past the village of Bracknell Croft and ½ mile after the R turn for Pitton, look for National Trust signpost to L. There is a small car park up the lane and the fort is a short walk away. Bus 87 from Salisbury to Firsdown Figsbury Ring stop.

51.1031, -1.7325, SU188337, SP4 6DT

2 SCRATCHBURY HILLFORT
WARMINSTER

The three hills of Battlesbury, Middle Hill and Scratchbury rise up at the south-eastern corner of the vast chalk plateau of Salisbury Plain. Scratchbury and Battlesbury are both hillforts dating back to the Iron Age. Scratchbury dates from around 350BC and contains seven barrows, partly excavated in the early 19th century by the antiquarian and archaeologist Sir Richard Colt Hoare. It is likely that Battlesbury was in permanent use from around 100BC to the time of Roman occupation. Finds suggest the inhabitants may have come to a bloody end when the Roman army seized control of the area, and there is possible evidence of a war cemetery outside the north-west entrance. As at many other hillforts, storage pits were found here with discarded goods such as pottery, animal bones and quern stones – large, flat stones used in conjunction with a rolling stone to grind grain for bread. With panoramic views from these hills, the inhabitants must have had a clear sight of their

attackers charging across the bare, chalky landscape of Salisbury Plain or the green fields of pastoral Wiltshire. Middle Hill may not have been of strategic importance, but the Bronze Age burial mound at the top shows it was of some spiritual significance centuries before the forts came into use. Activity in the area dates back much further than this; south-east of Battlesbury Wood, worked flints have been found dating back to the Mesolithic, around 12,000 to 6,000 years ago. The best way to visit the site is to plot a circular walk along the three hills from the Battlesbury side near the Army base.

From Warminster centre follow B3414 E past petrol station then take next L onto Imber Road. After 1½ miles, just after end of military fencing, look for footpath sign on R and pull in here (51.2154, -2.1498, no layby). Follow footpath to Battlesbury and continue on for Middle Hill (51.2034, -2.1324) and Scratchbury (51.1976, -2.1276).

51.2099, -2.1472, ST898456, BA12 0DL

3 ADAM'S GRAVE &
KNAP HILL ALTON BARNES

Causewayed enclosures like Knap Hill are amongst the oldest constructions in the British Isles, dating back to the Early Neolithic around 4000–3300BC. Knap Hill itself was the first to be identified and has been radiocarbon-dated to 3450BC. Although superficially very similar to Iron Age hillforts, it is very unlikely that they were permanent settlements or had any military or defensive purpose. Many theories for their use exist, including a meeting ground for surrounding tribes, where they would have had a chance to trade crops or animals, strengthen social bonds or take part in ceremonial worship. Much of the landscape would have been wooded during this time, and these enclosures were clearings in the trees. Just over the road from Knap Hill is Adam's Grave (51.3694, -1.8400), a long barrow which is very prominent in the landscape. The barrow is one of many in the area, and together with the causewayed enclosure shows that this was an important region during the Neolithic era. It was excavated in 1860 and fragments of four skeletons were found, along with a leaf-shaped arrowhead. Legend has it that if you run around the barrow seven times a giant will come out; on most visits you may find a photographer or two apparently testing this theory in an attempt to get the best shot.

Take the A4 W from Marlborough to Fyfield village and there take the L signed Lockeridge. Follow for 4 miles through Lockeridge towards Alton Barnes, and the summits of Adam's Grave and Knap Hill become visible in the landscape. Park at Pewsey Downs car park on L (51.3731, -1.8352) and follow footpaths to either site. Bus 101 from Pewsey to Alton Priors telephone box stop, 1-mile walk, no Sunday service.

51.3717, -1.8285, SU120636, SN8 4LD ✅🚶♿

4 LIDDINGTON CASTLE
BADBURY

Liddington Castle, known to the Anglo-Saxons as Eorthbyrig, is best approached on foot along the Ridgeway long-distance footpath. Despite its proximity to the M4 motorway it is a quiet, isolated place, so seldom visited that you are likely to have the place to yourself even in peak season. As one of the highest parts of the Ridgeway, it offers unforgettable views across the Thames Valley and Marlborough Downs. In its day this location would have made it a site of great strategic importance, and finds suggest it is likely to be one of the earliest hillforts in the country, dating to the 7th century BC and improved over a number of centuries of use. It is uncertain which tribe used the fort in the Iron Age, but digs also tell us that it was refortified during the Saxon era, and results of that excavation are on show in the Ashmolean Museum in Oxford. Although there is no physical evidence to back it up, it has been suggested this is the site of the famous 5th-century Battle of Mount Badon between the Britons, led by Arthur, and invading Saxons. While you are in the area, the large country park and Iron Age hillfort of Barbury Castle (51.4851, -1.7862) a few miles down the Ridgeway road is also worth the visit.

Leave the M4 at junction 15 taking the A346 S for 1 mile towards Marlborough. Just after a garage on R take L on Ridgeway road signed to Hinton Parva. After a mile or so there is a small pull-in R (51.5180, -1.7042). Take the track at the field edge a few metres before this, crossing L into the field with the fort at a gap and heading L near the summit to the fort, 1/3-mile strenuous walk. Alternatively, approach from Aldbourne following the B4192 for 4 miles, and pull off L just after the signed Ridgeway path and before the Ridgeway road.

51.5162, -1.7004, SU208797, SN4 0HR 🚶▶️

5 ROBIN HOOD'S BOWER
CROCKERTON

This little-known enclosure lies hidden in a dense wood, not far from Longleat Safari Park and the holiday resort of Center Parcs. It is a well-preserved, roughly rectangular earthwork enclosing around ¾ acre; there are two earth banks enclosing the space, the largest and most visible 1 metre deep and 7.2 metres wide. It may have been used to prevent grazing animals from wandering off at night or to protect them from poachers, much in the same way as a modern-day corral. It has been planted with monkey puzzle trees, and this copse within a forest is a very other-worldly, somewhat surreal place to visit.

Take the Deverill Road S from Warminster over the A36 roundabout onto A350. Take the first L after 360 metres onto Five Ash Lane; after just over ¾ mile you come to a pull-in on the R just before a main ride into the woods. Park here and follow the ride for 1/3 mile then take track R until you find the earthwork across the path.

51.1801, -2.1776, ST876423, BA12 8BB ✅🚶

6 STONEHENGE
AMESBURY

Stonehenge itself is quite unlike any other monument. Although other henges exist and there are many stone circles, Stonehenge's huge uprights topped with stone lintels are a bit of an oddity. Much of its uniqueness stems from the way it has been added to over millennia by groups of very different people. There is evidence that the site was in use in the Mesolithic, around 10,000 years ago, long before the stone circle was erected. Hunter-gatherer communities may have erected a succession of timber posts over the course of 1,000 years. Next, around 3500BC, came a Neolithic causewayed enclosure nearby known as Robin Hood's Ball (51.2128, -1.8550), along with several long barrows and two cursuses (see Stonehenge Cursus entry). Stonehenge itself was begun in 3500–2910BC with the construction of a ditch, framed by earthwork banks on either side. This kind of construction is named a henge, after Stonehenge. It may have enclosed a ring of timber posts, rather like the totem poles of native America. The sarsen (sandstone) Heel Stone to the NE was also erected at this time. The presence of thousands of cremated bones suggests this

was used as a cemetery or a place to honour the dead. The most recent work dates the fragments to 3180–2380BC, and minerals in them showed that ten of the 25 identifiable individuals analysed came from Wales. It is widely accepted that around 2600BC, at the end of the Neolithic, 82 bluestones were imported from a quarry site 140 miles to the west in the Preseli Mountains of Pembrokeshire, Wales. The circle lasted for around 100 years in this configuration before the bluestones were removed and the iconic sarsen stones erected; at this point the site began to resemble what we know today. Another 300 years later, around 2200BC, the bluestones were rearranged to form both a circle between the outer sarsen trilithons (lintel-topped uprights) and inner circle of sarsen stones, and an oval in the middle. Summer and winter, people came from far and wide on pilgrimages to the already ancient landscape, and there would have been great feasts of aurochs (an ancient cow) and pork. It must have been an awesome sight, hundreds or thousands of people gathering in this place, fires burning, the chalk-covered long barrows gleaming white as a background to the vast megaliths of the newly completed stone circle.

STONEHENGE & ITS LANDSCAPE

Theories are still emerging as to quite what Stonehenge was used for. Following digs at the site, archaeologists Tim Darvill and the late Geoffrey Wainwright interpreted it as a place of healing and pilgrimage, a Neolithic equivalent of Lourdes. Professor Mike Parker Pearson of University of Sheffield has linked it with Durrington Walls Henge, 2 miles to the north-east, arguing that they are ritually linked sites, with Durrington a place for the living and Stonehenge a place for the dead, connected by the flowing waters of the River Avon and the Stonehenge Avenue. Whatever the purpose of the site, people travelled great distances to get there; analysis of tooth isotopes and burials has found that visitors came from the Scottish Highlands, the Mediterranean and the Bavarian Alps.

Signed from the A303 3½ miles W of Amesbury or ½ miles E of Winterbourne Stoke. At roundabout, take A360 N to visitor centre. Shuttle bus to stone circle from visitor centre takes 10 mins, or you can walk. Bus Stonehenge Tour from Salisbury station; buy bus ticket only or bus and admission. Admission is by timed slots; free for National Trust and English Heritage members who book in advance.

51.1788, -1.8262, SU122421, SP4 7DE

7 NORMANTON DOWN
AMESBURY

Most of the Normanton Down Barrows were constructed between 2600BC and 1600BC, much later than the first earthworks at nearby Stonehenge. In one of the burial mounds, referred to as Bush Barrow, the remains of an adult male were found with grave goods including a flat bronze axe, three bronze daggers, one inlaid with thousands of gold pins, a rectangular gold plate, a ceremonial mace and a chest plate of gold, all dated to 2560BC and now displayed in the British Museum. Such riches indicate this man was a chieftain or important tribal leader, and date the burial to a time before Stonehenge's great sarsen stones were raised. The barrows are fenced off, but can clearly be seen even as you whizz (or crawl) past on the nearby A303, and from either of the two managed paths that run parallel either side of the barrows. During the spring and summer you can appreciate the effect of keeping people off the land here, as thousands of insects and wildflowers thrive undisturbed in this special place.

From the A303 at roundabout 3½ miles W of Amesbury or ½ mile E of Winterbourne Stoke, take the A360 S towards Salisbury. After 1⅓ miles park at -51.1515, -1.8590 in layby on L near large water tower, opposite Druids Lodge Polo Club sign. Footpath signed to the N of buildings.

51.1515, -1.8590, SU120412, SP4 6PG

8 STONEHENGE CURSUS
& BARROW AMESBURY

The cursus at Stonehenge consists of a broadly rectangular ditched and banked enclosure, 100–150 metres wide, running for nearly 2 miles across the landscape just north of the stone circle. No photo can really do the cursus justice, as the human eye is far better than any camera at picking up subtle contours. These large linear earthworks were constructed around 3500–3000BC, long before the pyramids, and some 4,500 years before the huge stone heads were carved at Easter Island. Although their function is uncertain, it is generally believed they are ceremonial processional walkways. The experience of walking between the earthen banks of the cursus with the knowledge of their antiquity is an altogether humbling experience. You can approach by following the footpath to the north-east of the circle, just up from the bus stop by the visitor centre, or for a full experience of this ancient wonder you can walk the whole length of the cursus by parking near Woodhenge (51.1894, -1.7858) and following the footpaths west. A good OS map or phone navigation comes in handy here. The group of bell barrows nearby (51.1842, -1.8315) came much later during the Bronze Age, between 2400BC and 1200BC. Grave goods such as bronze and flint daggers, awls, beakers, and amber and faience beads have all been found in the barrows. The cursus and barrows are part of the wider ceremonial Stonehenge Landscape area, which is free to walk around, but for more information you can pay the entrance fee and visit the museum at the visitor centre.

From the Countess Roundabout on A303 at Amesbury take the Countess Road/A345 N for ¾ mile, L onto Fargo Road and park in Woodhenge car park or along road after bend. Join footpath L just after Woodhenge W and follow S until you reach the path running W, follow this W for ½ a mile. The cursus begins the other side of the woods and runs W to a gap in the trees on the skyline. Bus Stonehenge Tour from Salisbury station to visitor centre.

51.1877, -1.8059, SU137431, SP4 8LL

9 THE AVENUE & AVEBURY STONE CIRCLE
AVEBURY

Avebury henge and circle were built during the Neolithic, 2850–2200BC. So huge is the circle that it surrounds the present-day village, making the Red Lion within it (SN8 1RF, 01672 539266) one of the most uniquely placed pubs in all of Britain. Away from the crowds at the main Avebury site, the huge double stone row of West Kennet Avenue still stands for over ½ mile alongside the modern B4003. Some have argued that the alternating stone shapes have a male/female symbolism, but this is only conjecture. This ceremonial walkway once ran over 1½ miles to the Sanctuary, a now-vanished stone circle indicated by concrete posts. The avenue, along with Beckhampton Avenue to the south-west, was built in 2400BC, some 200 years after the largest ring around the defensive ditch.

Park in the main Avebury car parks or find limited parking alongside the B4003 heading S from Avebury village (51.4211, -1.8460). Bus 49 Swindon to Avebury opp The Red Lion stop.

51.4237, -1.8493, SU105694, SN8 1RD

AVEBURY LANDSCAPE

It is easy to spend a day, or even a week, exploring the monuments in and around Avebury. To get some sense of the landscape, it is best to regard it chronologically. In the Early Neolithic, around 3800BC or perhaps earlier, people began to farm and settle the area near Avebury. Windmill Hill causewayed enclosure (51.4415, -1.8762) was built in around 3800BC, likely for meeting with other tribes to trade and to celebrate intertribal marriages. The people also felt a need to honour or worship their ancestors and, as a result, tombs like West Kennet Long Barrow were built around 3650BC. When Windmill Hill fell out of favour, attention was focused on Avebury itself. One, if not two, stone circles were built between 2900BC and 2600BC. Around 2600BC, earth was banked up to build the wider henge and another large stone circle was also built around the banks of the henge. It is likely, although not certain, that these were constructed on a pre-existing site. The circles may have acted like modern day churches, used for ceremonies or celebrations. Others theorise that the site was a Neolithic Lourdes, where people came to be healed. The vanished Sanctuary circle (51.4111, -1.8313), straddled this whole time period, constructed as a timber circle in 3000BC and later replaced by stone. Silbury Hill (51.4157, -1.8568), the largest prehistoric mound in Europe, was built between 2470BC and 2350BC, perhaps by subsequent generations of the same tribe. Capped in white chalk, it would have gleamed like a beacon and been a prominent feature and seen for miles around. The Sanctuary and the henge at Avebury were linked by an avenue of stones stretching 1½ miles. A second avenue was also built to the west, linking Avebury circle to the Long Stones (51.4230, -1.8726), close to Beckhampton village. The larger Long Stone was part of a cove, another type of Neolithic construction of a box-like design and unknown function; the smaller one may have been part of the avenue.

10 WEST KENNET LONG BARROW AVEBURY

The walk up through an often muddy Wiltshire field to West Kennet Long Barrow gives very little indication of just how special this monument is. Once you are in it, exploring its chambers, there is little doubt this is one of the finest reconstructed long barrows in the country. It is a Cotswold-Severn-style barrow, the largest in Southern England. It was open for about 1,000 years, although the 46 burials of adults, children and babies all seem to have died within one 30-year period. Pottery, animal bones, flints and bead ornaments have all been found there; these were either used ritualistically or left as grave goods. Bones would have been placed in the tomb, taken out and buried again a number of times. Some of these removals could have been almost contemporary with us; in the late 17th century, for example, a Dr Troope from nearby Marlborough used human bones as an ingredient in his medicines.

Take the A4 from Marlborough W for Beckhampton, just before Silbury Hill park in the layby on the L. Follow signs to barrow through fields. Bus 42 from Marlborough to West Kennet opp telephone box stop and walk ½ mile W to layby; road is very busy and not suitable for children.

51.4086, -1.8505, SU104677, SN8 1QF

11 DEVIL'S DEN FYFIELD

The remains of the Devil's Den burial chamber are largely absent from guides, perhaps because the area around Avebury is so rich in archaeological findings. But hidden in a field on Fyfield Down, between Avebury and Marlborough, this last remnant of a Neolithic passage tomb doesn't fail to impress. The 17-tonne capstone straddles two remaining uprights that marked the entrance to a long mound, ploughed away over centuries. The monument was re-erected in 1921, so there is every chance the stones are not in their original positions. Many myths surround the stones, including the story of the Devil arriving in the dead of night with eight white oxen to pull them down. Try as they might, the magical beasts could not move the cursed stones and the Devil abandoned his efforts. Another myth urges women wanting to fall pregnant to walk around the stones five

times, but with the warning that walking around them just three times will summon the Devil himself.

Take the A4 W from Marlborough and after around a mile, just at the edge of the town, take R to Manton House and Hollow. After 1 mile at end of the public road take byway L to park in Natural England car park L after 100m (51.4286, -1.7717). Walk along byway NW ⅓ mile and take L through gate follow bridleway to SW, then forking L along field boundary and through gate L to enclosure with Devil's Den.

51.4256, -1.7826, SU152696, SN8 1PN

12 GREY WETHERS & POLISHER STONE AVEBURY

The glacially deposited stones across this part of Fyfield Down were the source for the sarsens of nearby Avebury, the Devil's Den and West Kennet Long Barrow; in situ they make a unique and awe-inspiring place. The stones are so named because from a distance they resemble a flock of sheep or 'wethers'. An alternative name is Mother's Jam, as the stones are also said to resemble chunks of fruit in an oversize jam pot. For those who have the time to look, many stones strewn across the valley and hillside were marked in prehistoric times. On one hillside is the Polisher Stone, dished and grooved by the constant working of stone axes some 4,000–5,000 years ago. It is impossible not to feel compelled to rub your fingers across these marks, following the working of these ancient axes. It could have been used by those wandering the ridgeway, or by inhabitants of a settlement dating to the Late Neolithic found on the north-west side of the downs close by. The Valley of Stones below the Grey Mare barrow (see Dorset) is a very similar site to the Grey Wethers, but has nothing like the scale.

Head E from West Kennet on the A4 to park the Sanctuary car park on the L after ½ mile. Follow the Ridgeway footpath N from here for 2¼ miles. Enter field of stones through a metal gate and walk 20 metres E towards a triangular stone near a hawthorn tree. Polisher Stone is in front of these, on the hillside near a number of gorse bushes. Bus 42 from Marlborough to West Kennet opp telephone box stop and walk ½ mile E to car park; road is quite busy, but there is a hatched shoulder.

51.4423, -1.8166, SU128715, SN8 1QF

II

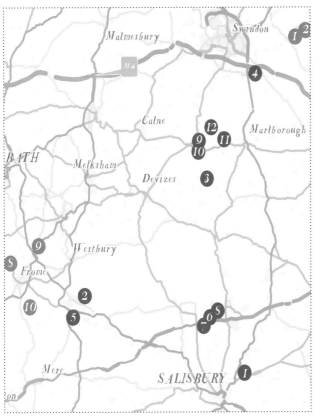

10

12

CHAPTER

DORSET

*D*orset is home to some of the earliest signs of prehistoric activity in Britain. In the years leading up to the Second World War two hand-axes, now on display at Dorset County Museum in Dorchester, were found at a quarry site near Corfe Mullen. These dated from between 474,000BC and 427,000BC, during the Lower Palaeolithic. Dorset then would have been much warmer than it is now, and elephants, rhinos and lions would have all lived alongside the very early people or proto-humans who lived here. Towards the end of the last ice age around 12,000 years ago, the climate was far cooler and more as it is today, and you could have walked from France to England, with the Solent a river valley rather than a sea. That valley would have lain below a great chalk ridge, where hunters stalked migrating deer and possibly even mammoths. Finds of tools on the hills above the large, sandy beaches of Hengistbury Head (50.7155, -1.7554) show that these hunters may have returned again and again to this area in search of food.

Dorset may have been a very important part of the country back in the Neolithic. It marked one end of the Greater Ridgeway Path, one of Britain's earliest 'roads', running from Norfolk in the east to Lyme Regis in the south. It was also home to the Dorset Cursus, often described as Britain's largest Neolithic construction. The Cursus consisted of two 6-mile-long parallel banks about ¼ mile apart, enclosing a large, linear central area of 220 acres, and it would have been a tremendous effort to build with nothing but stone and antler tools. As you may well imagine, all kinds of theories have arisen to its purpose. It is speculated that it was a ritual walkway or a long, carved path for funeral processions, or even a place where young men would prove their worth in physical challenges.

I HAMBLEDON HILL
CHILD OKEFORD

This huge Iron Age hillfort dominates the skyline above the village of Child Okeford, its impressive 1⅓ miles of inner ramparts enclosing some 31 acres. Developed in the Late Bronze Age and through the Iron Age, it would have been densely populated for the time; archaeologists have found signs of well over 350 homes throughout the interior of the fort. Its last military action was surprisingly recent, as in August of 1645, during the Civil War, local vigilantes with clubs unsuccessfully defended the fort against Cromwell's army. The area was first settled in the Neolithic, long before the hillfort was built, and to the south of the three main spurs of the hillfort are the earthworks of Hambledon Hill Neolithic camp. This causewayed enclosure predates the hillfort by at least 2,000 years and would have been a meeting place and site of celebration for surrounding tribes. For a real sense of ancient history, spend a morning walking from Child Okeford along the Stour Valley Way across the hillfort, continuing over the Neolithic Camp and onto Hod Hill to the south with the remains of a Roman hillfort.

Park by the church in Child Okeford. Follow footpath through churchyard and continue on the lane E. Where it becomes private, footpaths lead away on either side, both of which end up leading E to fort. 20 minutes' moderate to strenuous walk. Bus X10 from Blandford Forum to Child Okeford the Cross stop.

50.9135, -2.2217, ST845127, DT11 8ED

2 OAKLEY DOWN CEMETERY
SIXPENNY HADLEY

Between the modern A354 and the Roman road of Ackling Dyke lies the impressive moonscape of Oakley Down cemetery, home to 26 disc, saucer, oval and bowl barrows. Digs here in the early 19th century by Sir Richard Colt Hoare and William Cunnington showed the burials to be as diverse as the mounds above them. People were cremated or buried with grave goods, and ashes were placed in urns, stone coffins or cists. The varying mound styles and burial rites show this would have been in use throughout the Bronze Age, 2000–700BC. One of the mounds was even found to contain a secondary Saxon burial. Over the Roman road to the south is the earlier Dorset Cursus, a large Neolithic earthwork that was possibly a processional walkway. Centuries of ploughing have all but destroyed it, and it is best seen from the air. However, if you lack wings, a large part of the structure can be seen within the Salisbury Plantation (50.9510, -1.9655), an area rich with wildflowers, orchids and butterflies. Looking north from the Roman road over the modern one you can see Wor Barrow, a Neolithic long barrow that was home to Britain's earliest mummy. The body, which was interred separately from the other six burials after the barrow was built, had been wrapped and preserved for 30–130 years before being placed in the surrounding ditch. From Neolithic mummy to Saxon burial, it is clear that this area of Cranborne Chase remained significant for over 5,000 years.

Take the A354 NE from Blandford Forum. After 9 miles, at the roundabout, turn R toward Ringwood on B3081. Park ⅓ mile along in small pull-in on L (50.9460, -1.9788). Follow the path along Ackling Dyke for ½ mile to cemetery on L. Continue on path ¼ mile and follow paths to SE into Salisbury Plantation for Cursus (OS map or phone mapping is useful here). There is no public access to Wor Barrow. Bus 20 Salisbury–Blandford to Sixpenny Handley Oakley Farm stop.

50.9549, -1.9839, SU012172, BH21 5PW

3 THE NINE STONES
WINTERBOURNE ABBAS

At the edge of a little woodland just off the busy A35 stand the Nine Stones of Winterbourne Abbas. This circle is somewhat unusual in that it is tucked away in the bottom of a valley. Most other examples can be seen from a distance, often dominating the landscape (think of Stonehenge) but this one remains almost hidden, like an ancient secret. There are only four surviving stone circles in all of Dorset, and this is the most complete of them. It is likely that it was put here during the Late Neolithic or Early Bronze Age, around 2400–1000 BC, and that it was a focal point of a larger ceremonial landscape, some of which preceded and some of which came after its creation. To the west Poor Lot Barrows (50.7147, -2.5832) is a large Bronze Age cemetery visible from the A35. To the south behind Big Wood is another barrow cemetery at (50.7036, -2.5589) and another, now flattened, stone circle used to lie to the west, just off the A35.

Park at the (closed) Little Chef on the A35 at the W end of Winterbourne Abbas (DT2 9LU). Take the permissive path to the side of the building W through the fields. Bus X51 from Dorchester to Winterbourne Abbas Coach and Horses stop.

50.7121, -2.5526, SY610904, DT2 9LU 🚌🏛

4 HELL STONE & HAMPTON DOWN WADDON

The Hell Stone is the only dolmen (or cromlech) in Dorset. In the summer of 1866, local farmer Mr Mansfield took it upon himself, with no prior knowledge of Neolithic monuments, to 'restore' the dolmen. He directed eight men to straighten the supports from which the huge sarsen stone had fallen and lift and place the capstone back on them. Not everyone was happy with the result and in a letter to the editor of *The Antiquary* in 1871, an outraged correspondent complained that 'The Hellstone is now no longer an ancient erection or a lichen-clad ruined monument of the past, but a patched up structure of the present'. Before this restoration the monument would have resembled Zennor Quoit (see West Penwith) with its huge slipped capstone, but when it was built, which would have been anything up to 5,000 years ago, it would have been covered in earth and looked more like the restored barrow at Stoney Littleton (see Somerset). Shortly to the west, over the road, the Hampton Down stone circle (50.6767, -2.5731) lies forlornly by the Dorset Ridgeway footpath. There is an old Ministry of Works plaque on the fencepost next to the circle, which can become almost hidden when the grass grows long over it in the summer.

From B3159 at Winterbourne Abbas take Coombe road signed Portesham/Abbotsbury. Follow 2½ miles then ¼ mile after skewed crossroads park at gravelled pull-in L (50.6810, -2.5663). Walk E then at end of 2nd field on R head S to dolmen. For Hampton Down circle follow the Ridgeway path slightly to S on W side of road for ⅓ mile and stone circle is L by fence. Bus X51 from Dorchester to Winterbourne Abbas Coach and Horses stop and walk, or X53 from Weymouth to Portesham opp Kings Arms stop and walk 1 mile N to paths.

50.6786, -2.5592, SY605866, DT3 4EY 🚶🏛

5 THE GREY MARE & HER COLTS LITTLE BREEDY

Today we might comment that a graveyard has a fine view if it is at the top of a hill, but thousands of years ago such a position may have been of more ritual importance. The siting of the Grey Mare and her Colts barrow at the top of a dry valley must have been of some significance back in the Neolithic era. Was it that the ancestors held within the tomb looked out over and protected their descendants' land? Perhaps those working the land lived in fear of their ever-watchful elders? The mound has been reduced in size by ploughing, but it still stretches out a considerable length, 24 metres, behind the stonework. This would have once been a chambered tomb, but the capstone has fallen and lies recumbent next to the remaining uprights. Digs have found bones and pottery consistent with Neolithic burial practices. The nearby Valley of Stones (50.6828, -2.5735), a glacial deposit of sarsens, would have provided the building material for the long barrow. The valley is a natural wonder; the Grey Wethers (see entry in Wiltshire and Wessex) is similar, but these sites are rare. It is a pleasant 2-mile walk from Abbotsbury via the Macmillan Way, or for quicker route see below.

From Abbotsbury, take Hands Lane uphill to NE. After 1¼ miles take L doubling back up hill towards Gorwell Farm. Park R just after cattle grid (limited space) and follow bridleway track before cattle grid to NW. After ¼ mile go L over stile to the barrow. Bus X53 from Weymouth to Abbotsbury stops.

50.6816, -2.5903, SY583870, DT3 4JX 🚶🚌🏛⛰

6 KINGSTON RUSSELL LITTLEBREDY

Although this circle has kept its original 18 stones, they all now lie flat and may have been moved from their original position. The largest stone circle in Dorset, it is in a commanding position looking down to the sea and over the unique Dorset chalk downland. It was built much later than the nearby burial chamber of Grey Mare (see entry), but it has been speculated that the proximity of the two along the Ridgeway path had some ritual significance. The large diameter of the ring can encourage children to run around its perimeter and let off a little steam. We can only imagine how children would have reacted to these monuments when they were

constructed in the Early Bronze Age, but it is likely that tiny feet have been circling these stones for millennia. It is an enchanting area to visit; in the spring you may spot a hare running across the farmer's fields, and during the summer the area is rich with wildflowers and birdsong.

From Abbotsbury, take Hands Lane uphill to NE. After 1¼ miles take L doubling back up hill towards Gorwell Farm. Park R just after cattle grid (limited space) and follow bridleway track before cattle grid to NW for 1 mile, passing the stile L to Grey Mare barrow, until you reach a crossroads with another path; the old Ministry of Works sign here directs you R to the stone circle.

50.6886, -2.5986, SY577878, DT3 4JX 🚶🌳🏞

7 MAIDEN CASTLE
DORCHESTER

Maiden Castle is one of the most iconic hillforts in England; at 47 acres, the size of more than 50 football pitches, it is also the largest, and maybe the biggest in Europe. It was originally the site of a causewayed enclosure, a ritualistic tribal meeting ground in the Neolithic, before the site was put to use again around 600BC as a small hillfort, which was later expanded to the vast site we see today. People lived and worked here, making textiles and working metal, in roundhouses built in rows, very much like our modern streets. When they died they were buried here – 52 graves have been found at the castle, with the dead carefully interred with grave goods such as food offerings and pottery, as well as their personal effects. Some of them had suffered a violent death, and it has been debated whether this was a burial ground for those who gave up their lives fighting the Romans. It is a beautiful site to visit, with stunning views out across the Dorset countryside. Although the largest, it is not the only hillfort in Dorset: there is the tree-covered Weatherby Castle to the north-east (50.7650, -2.2750), the tumbling remains of Flower's Barrow on the coast (50.6240, -2.1922) and Woolsbarrow hidden away in Wareham Forest (50.7322, -2.1520).

From Dorchester head SW on Weymouth Ave/B3147 and take R opposite cemetery gates onto Maiden Castle Road, with EH sign for Maiden Castle. Follow for 1⅓ miles to car park at end. Steep walk up. Both Dorchester railway stations are about ⅓ mile from start of Maiden Castle Road.

50.6944, -2.4681, SY670884, DT2 9EY 🌳🏃🏔🏞

8 REMPSTONE CIRCLE
CORFE

The Rempstone stone circle is perhaps Dorset's least-explored stone circle, although it lies close to a popular tourist route, hidden in a small wood off the road between Corfe Castle and Studland Bay. Only one small arc of stones remains of this once-impressive circle, which may have measured as much as 24 metres in diameter. Investigation in the undergrowth does reveal a further pile of around nine large stones to one side of the arc, and at least two more mostly buried. There was once a stone row near the circle, which sadly has not survived, but the Nine Barrows, an impressive row of Bronze Age barrows, are nearby on a high ridge along the Purbeck Way (50.6336, -2.0081).

Take the B3351 from Corfe Castle E towards Studland Bay for 2½ miles, and after the turning for the campsite look for a pull-in on the R with a bridleway sign to Nine Barrow Way (50.6375, -2.0068). Walk back through the copse in the direction of Corfe to the NW corner. For the Nine Barrows, follow the bridleway S then SE before turning R to the join the Purbeck Way heading W.

50.6384, -2.0089, SY994820, BH20 5JQ 🏔

S

9 KNOWLTON HENGE
KNOWLTON

These three great circles have been rather mistreated down the ages. Ploughing has erased much of them, and the modern B3078 has been built right through the centre of the largest. The easiest to visit, and the most prominent, is the central henge on which the ruined Norman church now stands. It has been speculated that the henges had stone circles on top of their banks, rather like that at Arbor Low (see Peak District). In the year 2000 farmer Robert Antell rediscovered two large stones that had been ploughed out of the most southerly henge 30 years before, one of them carrying a rare example of Neolithic art, a carving of concentric rings. These are much more common in the north; in Dorset, they are almost unheard of. The many Bronze Age barrows around the henges, along with the decorated stone, suggest that the area has been one of religious importance for millennia. The church is just the latest monument on a site with a history stretching back nearly 4,000 years.

Head N on B3078 from Wimborne Minster for around 7 miles, and church is signed L on road to Brockington and Wimborne St Giles. Limited parking at the gate.

50.8919, -1.9676, SU023102, BH21 5AE

10 PIMPERNE BARROW
BLANDFORD FORUM

At over 100 metres, this is the longest long barrow in the country. The modern field boundaries and the busy A354 make it harder to imagine it would have looked 5,000 years ago, but its sheer size and placement on a rise would have ensured it dominated the Neolithic landscape. Although it has never been dug, it is likely that it contains highly venerated remains. Over 200 long barrows have survived in the Wessex region – made up of Wiltshire, Dorset and Hampshire – making it one of the most archaeologically important parts of Northern Europe. This barrow is a short diversion from the Jubilee Trail long-distance path, in a part of Dorset rich with archaeological remains.

Approaching Blandford Forum on the A354 heading SW, between Tarrant Hinton and Pimperne, look for the memorial on Blandford Camp turn-off L (Collingwood Corner). Immediately after this park in layby on R. Barrow is through field gate opposite memorial, then 300 metres to the N along footpath. Bus 20 from Salisbury to Tarrant Hinton Collingwood Corner stop.

50.8938, -2.1186, ST917104, DT11 8GY

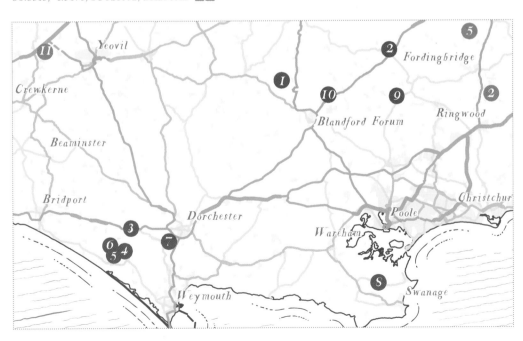

CHAPTER 5

HAMPSHIRE &
THE ISLE OF WIGHT

After a trip to find the Giant's Grave and the nearby Mizmaze at Breamore, high in the rolling, open Hampshire Downs, I noticed that my son's collection of rocks had started to favour one stone over any other. He had filled his pockets with fragments of flint and was idly chipping away at them, just as I had at his age. Something about this stone gives us a tangible, tactile link to the Neolithic and makes it utterly compelling. Flint is formed within chalk or limestone, so it is no surprise that large concentrations of early human settlements are found in areas with a chalky soil – like Breamore, Walbury and much of the Isle of Wight. During the spring these areas come alive with wildflowers that attract rare butterflies such as the distinctive Adonis Blue with its electric-blue wings. Aside from their natural beauty, the chalk lands also have a useful chemical quality that would have been exploited by Iron Age tribes such as those who lived at Danebury Hillfort. They stored their grain in large cellars dug out from the chalk, where the grain immediately in contact with the damp walls decomposed, giving off carbon dioxide that prevented the rest of the grain – the majority of the harvest – from spoiling. What is fascinating about this ancient technology is that it shows these were not barbaric, simple people living moment to moment, but civilisations that had an understanding of how to exploit the geology and chemistry of their environment.

During the Bronze Age it was common practice to bury the honoured dead, such as tribal leaders, in round barrows. These mounds of earth, sometimes huge, took many hours of labour, and it is thought whole communities would have taken part in their construction. You can still find many barrows, marked on OS maps as tumuli, in fields of grazing ponies or hidden amongst trees. Sadly many have been devastated by Victorian and Georgian 'gentlemen antiquarians' who excavated the barrows with much gusto but little sensitivity to their preservation. However, it is a real treat when you do find complete barrows, such as the pine-tree-topped tumulus at Rockford or those amongst the bracken in nearby Plumley wood.

1 *WALBURY HILL & COMBE GIBBET* INKPEN

At 297 metres, Walbury Hill is the highest point in South-East England. Part of the North Wessex Downs AONB, it is a prominent local feature, rising above the chalk landscape on the edge of West Berkshire near the Hampshire border. Although described as a hillfort, Walbury may never have been used as one. Eminent archaeologist Barry Cunliffe describes it as a hilltop enclosure used to protect cattle, which could have drunk from a dew-pond within the enclosure and grazed high on the chalk downs far from the hands of any Iron Age rustlers. Various flint instruments found at the fort can now be seen in Newbury and Reading museums. To the west, on Gallows Down, is the 65-metre Combe Gibbet Barrow (51.3578, -1.4774), a Neolithic long barrow dating to around 3500–2500BC. Atop it stands a grisly-looking gibbet, a replica of one erected in 1676 to publicly display the bodies of adulterous George Bromham and Dorothy Newman, hanged for murdering Bromham's wife and son.

On Weavers Lane in Lower Green take the road S (51.3747, -1.4841) for Combe Gibbet. Follow for 1½ miles, and on the brow of the ridge you will see the car park just off turning on the L (51.3563, -1.4700). Bus 3 from Newbury to Lower Green or Crown & Garter Inkpen (similar distance) stops.

51.3540, -1.4639, RG17 9EL

2 *PLUMLEY WOOD BARROWS* VERWOOD

The largest of the five barrows at Plumley Wood towers above the bracken and scrub in a Forestry Commission woodland clearing. Barrows in and around the New Forest have succumbed to disturbance by treasure hunters, forest planting, gravel works and wartime operations, but despite all this the barrows here have survived remarkably well. Some have been found to still contain the remains of Bronze Age cremations. Not far from the barrow cemetery to the east is Rockford Common; the large sandpit by the car park here looks like a Saharan dune, and on a hot summer's day, there really is no better place in the area to bring children. There are reportedly a number of barrows here, but most remain undetectable.

Take the B3081/Ringwood Road SE from Verwood toward Ebblake. As soon as you pass the turning for Ebblake Industrial Estate on your R at the edge of town, look for a smallish FC car park on the L at (54.8692, -1.8473). The barrows can be a little hard to find so a map or mobile mapping is recommended; look for the features marked 'tumuli' on the map around ½ mile south of Decoy Pond.

50.8884, -1.8430, SU111098, BH24 3QA

3 *BUCKLAND RINGS* LYMINGTON

In the 1st century BC the ramparts of this Iron Age hillfort were lined with timber both inside and out, and a formidable sight. Free of the trees that encroach today, it gave its inhabitants clear views of enemies approaching from any direction. Its position means it would have been one of the first to face the incoming Romans, who may have deliberately dismantled the fort following Emperor Claudius' invasion in AD 43. Today this remains one of the best-preserved examples of a multivallate hillfort (one with more than one rampart) in the whole of Dorset and Hampshire. There is a wide, flat meadow in the centre of the fort, contrasting with the wild, beech-lined ramparts to make a magical place to picnic or explore with little adventurers.

In Lymington take the A337 to the N edge of town, and before the roundabout for Wellworthy Road and hospital take Sway Road L (signed Gordleton Industrial Estate). Follow the road as it bends sharply R, then when it bends L turn R to pull in past postbox and footpath sign (50.7712, -1.5571). Space for three cars.

50.7702, -1.5530, SZ316968, SO41 8NN

4 DANEBURY HILLFORT
STOCKBRIDGE

Perched on the top of Danebury Down, a little south of Andover, are the tree-lined ramparts enclosing the wide-open centre of historic Danebury Hillfort. One of the most important hillforts in the Wessex chalklands, it has been extensively dug by archaeologists, and many of the artefacts found are on display at Andover Museum. It was first used as a burial site by the Beaker people (named for their use of pottery beakers) during the Bronze Age, around 2500–2300BC, but became more extensively settled during the Iron Age, starting in the 5th century BC. Over the course of 200 years, a small number of square dwellings grew to accommodate some 300 people. Families lived in huts of varying sizes that may have been organised into streets. In the northern sector of the fort, some 5,000 pits were dug into the chalky ground to store grain for anything up to a year after harvest. In around 400BC rectangular wooden shrines were built in the centre of the fort and, perhaps in response to an attack or a surge in population, its defences were extended. Within the hillfort you can see a replica of some roundhouse footings, giving you an idea of the confined living conditions.

Follow the High Street W out of Stockbridge, becoming the A30 with a grassed central reservation. As it starts to curve L take the R turn signed to Danebury Hillfort and Grateley (B3084). After 1¾ miles you will find the car park L with a large sign. Bus W16 from Salisbury stops at car park on weekdays. Term-time only, bus 68 Salisbury–Winchester to Broughton Road stop and walk N up Spitfire Lane (100 metres to W) to end then track slight right to road at end, turn L to find car park L after 350 metres; total 1¾ miles.

51.1374, -1.5391, SU324376, SO20 6HZ 🚌🅿🚶

5 GIANT'S GRAVE & MIZMAZE BREAMORE

The Giant's Grave long barrow would have been used as a communal burial chamber during the early to mid-Neolithic period (around 3400–2400 BC). It measures 68 metres from end to end and is one of 180 long barrows found in the Hampshire, Wiltshire and Dorset region. It has never been excavated, so this 5,000-year-

old structure still keeps its many secrets. Nearby you will find the Mizmaze, a rare turf labyrinth tucked away in a small woodland on the Breamore Estate (50.9816, -1.8001). For those who have taken the time and effort to visit the Giant's Grave, the maze is a must! Although the Mizmaze is likely to have been constructed in the 12th century, the pattern is prehistoric, and it does have some extra value as it shares the site with a Bronze Age disc barrow. You cannot walk the maze; it is fenced to protect it from wear.

Take the A338 N from Fordingbridge and follow signs L to Breamore House Museum ½ mile N of Breamore village. Park in the car park (free at time of writing) and follow bridleway NW through Breamore Wood for around a mile. Once out of the woods the Mizmaze is in a copse of trees ahead and slightly to the L, and the Giant's Grave is along a path leading L around the copse housing the Mizmaze. Bus 49 or 43 from Fordingbridge to Whitsbury Cartwheel Inn stop, 2½-mile walk to Breamore on quiet lanes, or take bridleways and footpaths NE direct to the copse – in either case have a good OS map or phone mapping.

50.9796, -1.8035, SU138200, SP6 2DE 🚶🚌

.5

6 FIVE BARROWS
BROOK DOWN

The position of the barrow cemetery at Brook Down, high in the hills, may well have been significant. Overlooking the sea, the fields and the world below, perhaps the dead were placed here to ensure the ancestors kept a watchful eye on the living. Some of the barrows were dug during the early 19th century by local rocket developer and amateur historian John Dennett, and now they have a tell-tale dip in the middle, like a loaf of bread that has collapsed in the oven. The items he found may seem rather small as a hoard, but they might have represented great wealth in the Bronze Age. From one of the barrows, he unearthed bronze weapons, a brooch and ornaments made from ivory or bone. The barrows are a good starting point on the Tennyson Trail, and it is possible to walk on 4½ miles to the Tennyson Monument or 6½ miles to The Needles. Just be mindful that you will need to walk back! There are shorter walks to the woods at Shalcombe Down or across the B road to the Long Stone at Mottistone (see entry). On Afton Down, along the Tennyson Trail, there is another barrow cemetery consisting of 14 round barrows and a long barrow (50.6703, -1.5026).

Follow the B3399 E from Afton, turning R after 3 miles R to remain on this road towards Chessell Pottery and Ventnor. After about ½ mile take the track to the R to parking, signed for the Tennyson Trail. Walk through the National Trust gate and follow the steep track. As soon as white cliffs come into view L, go R to the summit. Bus 12 from Newport to Hulverstone Brook Triangle stop, 1-mile walk.

50.6647, -1.4487, SZ390851, PO41 0UF

7 LONGSTONE
MOTTISTONE DOWN

The great twin megaliths of the Longstone are the Isle of Wight's most iconic prehistoric monument. The larger, upright stone is 4 metres in height, which is especially impressive for this part of the world, where few Neolithic monuments have lasted. Legend has it that in a supernatural wager the Devil and St Catherine held a competition to hurl the stones to their present location from a nearby hill – a story common around the country, with variations. Quite how these stones

looked when they were first erected in the Neolithic, over 6,000 years ago, is open to debate. The burial mound behind the monument has been so disturbed over the centuries that it is impossible to determine its original size. The few grave goods found around the barrow include pottery shards, a flint scraper and a hand axe. It is thought that the people of this time may have practised sky burials much like those in some regions of Tibet, laying the bodies out on platforms for birds and the elements to remove the flesh before the bones were buried within the tomb. Birds can be messy eaters at the best of times, so this must have been a rather gruesome affair, and bodyparts may have been retrieved from all over the surrounding area. During spring the woods leading up to the monument are carpeted in bluebells.

Park in the National Trust (free) car park for Mottistone Manor. The route to the Longstone is well signposted, up through the woods onto Mottistone Common. Bus 12 from Newport to Mottistone Manor stop.

50.6562, -1.4254, SZ407842, PO30 4ED

8 ASHEY DOWN BARROWS
ASHEY DOWN

Archaeologists excavating the Devil's Punch Bowl in the 19th century found a young boy buried in a crouched position along with a hammerhead made of a deer's antlers. Bowl barrows such as this are common; it is one of 10,000 that still exist in the UK. It is likely that the child was the son of an important figure in the community. Further to the west, the barrows of the impressive Bronze Age cemetery on Ashey Down are placed, like many others, just off the summit of a large hill. Within the barrows, the cremated remains of individuals were found inside pottery urns; cremations were popular during the Middle to Late Bronze Age but the practice fell out of fashion by 1800BC, as the belief system must have altered. With the discovery of a substantial Iron Age trackway to the south of here, at Alverstone Marshes (50.6672, -1.1849), it seems that this area was an important one throughout the Isle of Wight's prehistoric past. For a touch of vintage elegance close to the barrows, stay in an Airstream caravan at Vintage Vacations near Ashey (PO33 4BD, vintagevacations.co.uk).

From Brading head W on Brading Down road for about ½ mile to park in the second or third viewpoint car park. Cross the road and walk W to signed bridleway 30 metres past the third car park. Turn right inside field and walk 100 metres to barrow. It is possible to navigate a route from here to Ashey Down, or drive on W for another 1½ miles to park in a long layby on the R (50.6832, -1.1861). From the E end of the layby walk back E for around 70 metres to the footpath L over stile up onto Ashey Down (50.6861, -1.1845). Follow this NE for 100 metres then head L uphill to the barrow cemetery. 10 minutes' moderate to strenuous walk. Several bus routes serve Brading.

50.6793, -1.1565, SZ597869, PO36 0ER 🚇🚶🚴📶

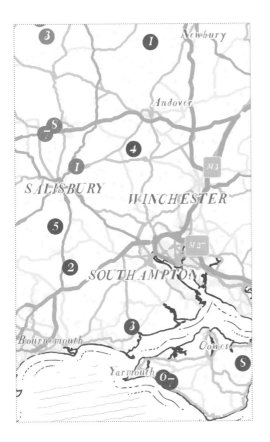

CHAPTER 9
SOUTH DOWNS

*T*he South Downs is Britain's newest National Park, but also one of the earliest inhabited landscapes in Britain. In 1993, the remains of a tibia were found in a gravel pit in the village of Boxgrove, and three years later teeth were discovered. Britain's oldest human fossils, these belonged to an early human ancestor, Homo heidelbergensis, who walked this part of Sussex nearly half a million years ago. Strongly built, in their 40s, with evidence emerging that they may have been a scavenger rather than a hunter. However, in contrast to this theory, a horse has been found with a possible puncture wound from a rudimentary spear. Given that species of now extinct bears and rhinoceroses lived in the area, however these early humans obtained their food, we know life would have been challenging, to say the least!

Pollen records have shown that parts of the downs were not the grassland we see today but covered in a vast, wild forest of predominantly yew trees, a remnant of which can still be seen at Kingley Vale. Slowly but surely, the forest was felled and animals such as wild boar and huge, cow-like aurochs were domesticated. They moved into enclosures, such as that at Belle Tout above the Seven Sisters, and would have fished and farmed along with keeping semi-domesticated animals. As settlements built up, so did the need to maintain ties with their neighbouring tribes. Causewayed enclosures, such as The Trundle and Combe Hill, would have been hilltop meeting places, high above the forest. The later Bronze Age and Iron Age inhabitants also put the rolling downs to good use by burying their dead in barrows and building hillforts on the highest land. All over the country, barrows or burial mounds seem to be situated on higher ground. Some believe this is in order for the spirit to escape, and others suggest it was so the ancestors could keep a close eye on the living as they worked in the fields below.

1

2

2

3

1 *DEVIL'S JUMPS*
TREYFORD HILL

Folklore would have it that the Devil got around a bit in days gone by, with landmarks across the country attributed to his shenanigans. He has stones, dens, punchbowls, hills, a few staircases – and in Scotland he even has his own Beef Tub. The seven mounds of the Devil's Jumps here near South Harting share the same tale as three identically named natural hills over in Churt, Surrey. It seems the Devil was having fun, jumping from one mound to the other, until Thor became angry with his antics and thrust a boulder to earth to stop him. But rather than a playground for a supernatural being, these are a line of Bronze Age bell barrows (unsurprisingly named for their bell shape) constructed sometime between 2000BC and 800BC. The formation, in a straight line north-west to south-east, is said to be aligned with the setting of the sun on Midsummer's Day. In truth, it is a little bit off, and more in line with the setting sun during late May, but considering it was constructed over 3,000 years ago, it is close enough. It's best to visit in the summer when the barrows are in full flower and the scent of wild marjoram fills the air.

From South Harting head S on the B2146 for 1/3 mile, take a L onto B2141 for 2¾ miles, then L towards Hooksway and Royal Oak pub (PO18 9JZ, 01243 535257). Walk up the restricted byway to the R of the pub heading NE up Treyford Hill for just under a mile. Towards the end of the tree line, look L and you will see the barrows and information sign. 20 minutes' strenuous walking. For a longer hike of about 3 miles, the South Downs Way over Beacon Hill from the National Trust Harting Down car park (50.9561, -0.8752) is well worth the walk.

50.9492, -0.8268, SU825172, PO18 9JZ

2 *DEVIL'S HUMPS*
KINGLEY VALE RESERVE

Conifer woodlands are dark, mysterious places. Even on a bright day the sun only ever flickers in, rarely penetrating down to the dark forest floor. Some of the twisted branches and trunks of the gnarled ancient yews at Kingley Vale NNR date back at least 2,000 years to the time of the British Iron Age. Studies of pollen in the area have shown that 4,500–6,000 years ago, during

the Mesolithic, much of the Downs would have been covered in a vast yew forest much like this. Most walks in the area naturally bring you up to the top of Bow Hill, and in the fields to the south-west of the summit, you'll find a row of four Bronze Age barrows, running north-east to south-west, known as the Devil's Humps. From here there are panoramic views across the downs, and southwards over Chichester Harbour to the distant uplands of the Isle of Wight. Earthworks or cross dykes, long mounds of earth, can be found to the north, south-west and east of the barrows, and a Neolithic flint mine was found at the south-east end of Bow Hill. These are from the same era, and the dykes may mark boundaries between tribes in the area. Further evidence of settlements can be found deep within the woods, and it is likely that people lived here in circular wattle-and-daub huts with turf roofs.

Leave the B2146 on bend at N of East Ashling towards West Stoke, and on next bend R take the L signposted to the National Nature Reserve parking (50.8731, -0.8295). It is a pleasant but strenuous 1½ mile or so walk via the yew tree grove to the Devil's Humps on the eastern summit of the hill; see information board at the site. Train to Bosham 3 miles, bus 54 from Chichester to East Ashling Horse & Groom stop, 1-mile walk.

50.8931, -0.8365, SU823102, PO18 9BS

3 *THE TRUNDLE*
GOODWOOD

The area around The Trundle was cleared of trees and first put to use around 4150BC, remaining in use until around 3600BC. It was first a causewayed enclosure, a ceremonial site often found on hills where local communities from the surrounding area may have come together. Rather than act as a defensive structure like the later hillforts, these were more likely places of celebration and ritual; perhaps a mix between a modern agricultural show, a music festival and a church fête. Pottery, animal bones, marine shells and chalk objects, including line-carved talismans, and human remains have all been found at the site. It has been suggested that it could have been the principal cult site for the western South Downs. Much later, sometime after 500BC during the Iron Age, a hillfort was constructed, with ramparts and a ditch erected in 320BC. Large timber gateways would have stood at the entrances to the north-east and the south-west, and it must have taken a number of men to open them. This remained occupied until the 1st century BC, when the Atrebates tribe settled in the area. The hill fell in and out of use across the centuries, with some evidence that it may have been used during the Roman occupation. During the 15th century, a windmill and a chapel in honour of St Roch were built here, both of which burnt down in 1773.

Take Town Lane, signed Open Air Museum and Goodwood, S from A286 in Singleton for 1⅓ miles to car park L at end of road. Follow the Monarch's Way/West Sussex Literary Trail footpath E up to the fort; 10 mins' moderate to strenuous walk. Bus 60 from Chichester to Binderton House and follow signed footpath E to join West Sussex Literary Trail, 1⅓ miles.

50.8936, -0.7544, SU877110, PO18 0PS ⛟▲☆⛟

4 CISSBURY RING
FINDON

There is no doubt that the people who ordered the construction of Cissbury Ring in the early to Mid-Iron Age in around 400BC had a tremendous amount of power and influence. Towering 184 metres above the town of Worthing, it has over 1¼ miles of ramparts enclosing an area of 15 acres. It is estimated that the timber revetment (or wall) would have needed 9,000–12,000 posts at least 5 metres long. Banks almost 4 metres high enclose a ditch over 4 metres wide, which would have been dug out with simple tools such as antler picks and shoulder blade spades. Today wild horses are the only permanent residents up here, and seem to go about their business wistfully, with very little regard for human visitors on their territory. Like many other forts, it may have begun life as more of a place for the community to meet than anything of a defensive nature. Predating the fort are the remains of Neolithic flint mines, seen as a number of ditches and depressions, some of which have been fenced off. Workers would have excavated a shaft downwards before digging horizontal galleries, possibly by the flickering glow of tallow lamps. It would have been back-breaking, claustrophobic and dangerous work, and some died on the job: the body of a woman was found deep within the shafts, buried head first, as if she had fallen.

From the A280/A24 roundabout on the NW of Findon head S towards Worthing on the A24 for just over a mile. After Findon Valley sign take the L onto May Tree Avenue, signed Cissbury Ring, then L onto Storrington Rise to the car park L on bend. Walk up the hill E. Once in the copse veer R and keep to the R of the fence to the fort. 10 minutes' moderate walk. Bus 23 from Worthing to Findon Place stop.

50.8617, -0.3808, TQ140081, BN14 0HT ⛟▲☆⛟

5 HOLLINGBURY
BRIGHTON

Part of the beauty of Hollingbury Hillfort is its proximity to the liberal metropolis of Brighton. From this vantage point at night, the city and its flickering lights are laid out before you like a vast, upturned spaceship. Hollingbury is a great example of a univallate, or single rampart, hillfort. The unusual style of the rampart, one narrow ditch with a large wooden box rampart (two parallel rows of posts, linked by beams, with rubble infill between them) behind, gave its name to the 'Hollingbury style' of fort. It was once thought that pottery found at the site suggested it was settled by immigrants from continental Europe fleeing conflict in around 400–250BC, but it could have been there as a result of trade or gifts. If we think about this in modern terms, the increase in goods from China in Europe during the late 20th and early 21st century does not suggest a Chinese invasion! A Bronze Age enclosure dating back to 1000–700BC was also discovered here, and you can still see the remains of three round barrows contemporary with it. Some of the finds, including Bronze Age axes and jewellery, are on show at the British Museum.

Traffic can be quite bad this side of Brighton, so Hollingbury is best visited by train, walking N from Moulsecoomb station, ¾ mile. Take steps up from Queensdown School Road by railway bridge, the take the path L after 50m up hill. If you must drive, avoid rush hour and head N on the Ditchling Road. Go past the entrance to Hollingbury Golf Club and after ⅓ mile take the R into the car park. Walk S across the edge of the golf course for 500m, 10 minutes' moderate walk. Several bus routes (23,24,38,50,74,78) to Wild Park stop near Moulsecoomb station.

50.8551, -0.1225, TQ322078, BN1 7HS ⛟☆⛟

6 THE CABURN
GLYNDE

As you head north from Newhaven, you can't help but be struck by the peculiar shape of Mount Caburn. Like a perfect bell curve, it looks unique amongst the downs and you get a sense of its importance in the landscape. During Neolithic times around 5,000 years ago, the area would have been covered in a dense yew forest, much like that which still exists at Kingley Vale (see Devil's Humps entry). The hill would have no doubt been visible for miles around, poking up out of the perpetual darkness of the forest. The earthworks crowning the hill come from a much later era; they are the remains of an Iron Age settlement established around 500BC, with the first defences put in place around 100BC and strengthened in AD 43 as a response to an invasion by the Romans, who may have set fire to the fort as they were marching south-west. When in use as many as 164 pits were dug at the site, much like the grain pits found in other hillforts such as those at Worlebury Camp (see Somerset). However, archaeologists found dog bones, boar tusks and coins along with broken weapons and tools. These could have been rubbish pits or middens, but it can be suggested they were ritual deposits: were these a gift to use in the underworld, or offerings to gods – a sickle to bring a good harvest, a boar's tusk to ensure a successful hunt?

From the A26/A27 Beddingham roundabout, take the A27 E for ¾ mile, then the first L to Glynde and park at the Lacys Hill free car park. Walk N away from the railway station and take Ranscombe Lane L past the post office and find the footpath after the houses R. Follow this across three fields then L to the summit. 25 mins' strenuous walk. Bus routes 124 (weekends only) and 125 Lewes–Eastbourne to Glynde Lacys Hill stop.

50.8618, 0.0512, TQ444089, BN8 6SS

7 FIRLE BEACON BARROWS
FIRLE

On the 7 miles of the South Downs Way between the Ouse and the Cuckmere rivers you come across a number of Bronze Age barrows, as well as two Neolithic long barrows. This is a vast, treeless landscape, with far-stretching views out across to the Seven Sisters, Eastbourne and the Channel. A little off the centre point, some of the most breathtaking views on the downs open up from the top of Firle Beacon. On a windy day, you can be almost blown from your feet here, and paragliders take advantage of this by launching themselves across the downs off the hilltop. During the Bronze Age, a number of round barrows were built on this windswept spot. Many of these have large depressions in the middle where treasure hunters or 'gentlemen' antiquarians unceremoniously dug into them. The oval barrow to the west of the summit was built by the first people who farmed this land over 5,000 years ago during the Neolithic. In some cases barrows like this contain whole families, in others just one or two high-status individuals. Local folklore suggests that a giant is interred in this one in a large silver coffin, the kind of legend that explains why so many round barrows have been tampered with.

At the A26/A27 Beddingham roundabout take the A27 E towards Eastbourne. After 1⅓ miles take the R towards Firle and carry straight on S up the hill past the village to car park at the road end. Follow the South Downs Way for just over 1 mile to the summit; 15 minutes' moderate to strenuous walk. Bus routes 124 (weekends only) and 125 Lewes–Eastbourne to Firle Park Gates stop, or train to Southease and walk 3 miles E along ridge on South Downs Way.

50.8338, 0.1079, TQ485058, BN8 6PA

8 LONG MAN OF WILMINGTON WILMINGTON

The figure of the Long Man has been identified as a representation of the Norse gods Odin or Thor, of Apollo and of King Harold, and even as a piece of satire dating only to the 16th or 17th century. He also bears a good resemblance to a figure holding two banners on 4th-century Roman coins. The present figure was restored in the late 19th century – it held a rake and scythe a century before – but it has been suggested he has been standing watch over this small part of the South East since pre-Roman times, and legend says a gold coffin is buried beneath him. Some even claim the figure is much older, perhaps dating to the Neolithic; historian Professor John North suggests the figure was cut into the chalk on this particular hill to mark the passing of the constellation of Orion over the ridge in that era. Even if North is wrong and the figure was cut later, the Windover Hill Long Barrow and flint mines immediately above, along with Bronze Age barrows to the east, show this area has been significant for a long, long time. Lying just off the South Downs Way, the site is very accessible and not far from the Giant's Rest pub (BN26 5SQ, 01323 870207, named for the folkloric 'crime scene outline' theory of the Long Man) in the village of Wilmington, serving beer from the excellent Long Man Brewery.

Head S out of Wilmington, past the church (with its 1,600-year-old yew) and park in the Wilmington Priory parking on the R (parking fee may apply). Continue down the road S and take the track L up to the Long Man. Paths criss-cross the area. Bus 125 Eastbourne–Lewes to Wilmington Thornwell Road stop, or nearest train Berwick 3 miles via Alfriston and South Downs Way.

50.8101, 0.1885, TQ542034, BN26 5SW

9 COMBE HILL
EASTBOURNE

Combe Hill is a causewayed enclosure dating back to around 3000–2400BC, making it contemporary with (or just before) the Pyramid of Djoser at Saqqara, Egypt (2630–2611BC). Causewayed enclosures were meeting places rather than defensive structures. This area was wooded then, and the enclosure in a newly-cleared vantage point could have had a beacon fire signalling to those below to come and visit, perhaps with animals or food and drink, to strengthen ties with neighbouring families and tribes, remember the dead or perform marriages. The find of a chalk block incised with parallel lines could be a talisman and indicate ritual activity at the site. More than a thousand years later, there must have been some pull to the area, as Bronze Age people buried their dead here in barrows. It is strange to think that as much time separated the people who built the causewayed enclosure and those who buried their dead in the barrows as separates us from the Anglo-Saxons. With no written accounts to look back on, the Neolithic inhabitants of Combe Hill would have been as much an enigma to the Bronze Age people as they are to us today. Field systems have been found on the lower slopes between the 1066 Country Walk and the South Downs Way. During the spring wild orchids are in full bloom, attracting rare visitors such as the Adonis Blue butterfly.

Take the A2270 N in Eastbourne, L on Upper King's Drive into Willingdon at large, grassy roundabout where A2021 joins. Follow to end, R onto Wish Hill and next L onto Butts Lane to car park at end (50.7934, 0.2391). Follow path to N then W for ¾ mile, moderate walk. Bus routes 1, 51 or 143 in Eastbourne to Church Street (off A2270) stop and walk W to Coopers Hill and Butts Lane.

50.7981, 0.2336, TQ575022, BN20 9EN

10 BELLE TOUT
BIRLING GAP

After the White Cliffs of Dover, the Seven Sisters are perhaps the most iconic of all the natural landmarks on the South Coast. The rolling downs and towering chalk cliffs make them a place like no other. At the time of writing, archaeologists are working hard to discover a little more about the prehistoric residents of this special area before it all falls into the sea. The outer enclosure around Belle Tout may date back to the 3rd millennium BC and could have been the largest of its kind in the country. In the mid-1970s a section of cliff fell away to reveal a circular shaft running down inside the cliffs to the beach below, which had been noted as a pit on older maps. It was wide enough for a man to fit into and had footholds running down the full 43 metres to the ground below. In the very centre of an inner enclosure thought to be Bronze Age, it has been described as a well, or possibly ritual shaft, but its use is anyone's guess. The shaft soon vanished into the sea, but in 2016 storms swept away material from the shore to expose its flat bottom end as a shallow circular pit in the base material. The outer ramparts are still very visible on the cliffs above. There is a National Trust car park and visitors centre with gift shop and café on the site. The Beehive on the Green (BN20 0BY, 01323 423631) in East Dean also sells a delicious array of local food and produce.

Birling Gap is signed from the A257 in East Dean; follow the road to car park at coast where the road turns E. Bus 13X Brighton–Eastbourne to Birling Gap or Belle Tout stops.

50.7415, 0.2046, TV556958, BN20 0AB

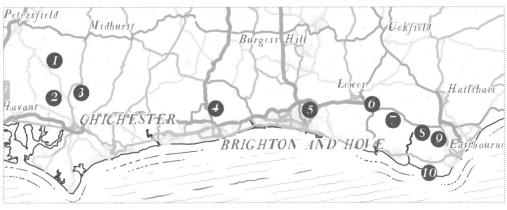

CHAPTER 10

HIGH WEALD &
KENT DOWNS

*T*he long seam of chalk that underlies south-eastern England is ideal for a series of walking tracks believed to have been used during the Neolithic, beginning at what are now Rochester and Dover then following the high ridge of chalkland through Kent into Surrey. These trails were later united and became known as the Hard Way or Harrow Way, a name derived from either herewag, the army way, or heargway, the way to the shrine. Further west the chalk ridge continued on into Salisbury Plain and eventually terminated at the mouth of the River Axe in Devon. Commodities such as cattle, tin and chert (a light-coloured flint from Portland in Dorset) would have been traded along this chalk ridge before crossing the sea into Northern France. The path may have also been important for those travelling to Stonehenge, perhaps for grand feasts during the winter solstice. Later in the Middle Ages, the eastern section of the path was kept alive by pilgrims heading to Canterbury; indeed, parts of it are still called The Pilgrims' Way.

Today, the North Downs Way long-distance footpath follows sections of this chalk ridge. All along the footpath within the Medway valley are reminders of these early wanderers, remains of chambered long barrows known collectively as the Medway Megaliths. The most famous of these are the colossal Coldrum Stones, commanding magnificent views across the countryside. Not far from Coldrum are two lesser-known barrows, both on private land. Addington (51.3071, 0.3705) has a lane through the middle, while 100 metres from it Chestnuts, deliberately laid bare back to its uprights in the 12th or 13th century, can be seen by making an appointment (Mrs J.E. Bygrave, Rose Alba, Park Road, Addington, ME19 5BQ, 01732 840220). Continuing to the east there are far more public Medway Megaliths; the two dolmens known as Kit's Coty House and Little Kit's Coty House. These are magnificent structures, rare on this side of the country, although found in larger numbers in Wales, Cornwall and North-Western France. Just off the path, we find the lesser-known Julliberrie's Grave barrow lying almost forgotten in the corner of farmer's field.

Yet further east along the North Downs Way the monuments spring forward almost to the end of our pre-historic journey, as just before the city of Canterbury you come across a section of woodland home to an Iron Age fort known as Bigbury Camp (51.2787, 1.0330). It's widely thought that the troops of Julius Caesar won the first Roman victories over the Celts here, in 54BC. After this defeat, Iron Age tribes in the region were forced to pay tribute to Rome, but it would be 100 years before the Romans took Britain as part of their empire.

1 HIGH ROCKS
TUNBRIDGE WELLS

The natural cliffs of stone at High Rocks would have looked much as they do today as when the first visitors came here during the Mesolithic (9600–4000BC) seeking shelter on seasonal hunts. Camping out in rock shelters, they shaped flint into bladed tools for everything from working animal hides and basic woodwork to butchery and hunting. Neolithic pottery has been found here, along with the remains of fires made by passing hunters, dating to 4600–4500BC. The museum in nearby Tunbridge Wells houses some of the finds. Around 100BC, during the Late Iron Age, people returned to the site but the first permanent settlement was not made here until 40–25BC, in the Late Iron Age, in the form of a promontory hillfort. This took advantage of the steep cliffs on the north-western side, while earthworks with wooden palisades would have been built at the south-east and south-west. The site is now in private ownership and there is a fee to enter, which is paid at the High Rocks pub over the road (TN3 9JJ, 01892 515532). The site is open from 10.15am Wednesday–Sunday and bank holiday Mondays, closed on other days and for functions; call the pub to check before leaving.

Heading S on the A26 through Tunbridge Wells take R at roundabout signed E. Grinstead, Groombridge and Upper Pantiles car park, onto Major Yorks Road. Turn L at next cross-roads, signposted High Rocks. Follow 1⅓ miles, High Rocks pub is on the R with free parking. Heritage train line from Tunbridge Wells West to High Rocks station. Steep walks up, with steps and boardwalks.

51.1211, 0.2291, TQ561381, TN3 9JJ

2 SWANSCOMBE SKULL
SITE SWANSCOMBE

Between 410,000 and 380,000 years ago Britain (or at least Proto-Britain) enjoyed a rather balmy climate. Taking advantage of a land no longer in the grip of an ice age, herds of animals roamed the land, travelling in from the then-adjoining mainland, now France. Following these herds came early hunters, hominids with an affinity to Neanderthals. In 1935 and 1936 fragments of a skull were found here. Miraculously,

just under 20 years later, another piece was unearthed by the archaeologist John Wymer. Judging by the size and shape of the skull, the brain of this human-like young woman would have been similar to that of modern humans. Today the site, one of very few showing Paleolithic activity, is an SSSI and NNR within Swanscombe Heritage Park. Stone axes have also been found at this former pit quarry, and towards the entrance of the country park site there is a large statue of one of these to commemorate the finds here. There is of course very little to see in terms of Lower Palaeolithic remains; however, there are many large granite blocks detailing the geology and archaeology here. There are also wide, open fields to run around and a playground for children.

Swanscombe Heritage Park is signed from A226/London Road, S on Craylands Lane ¼ mile, straight over roundabout, to free car park for Heritage Park on R before leisure centre. Train to Swanscombe station, walk SW via Alma Road across the recreation ground and along Broomfield Grove and Milton Road to Craylands Lane, turn R for park entrance opposite; ½ mile.

51.4460, 0.2977, TQ599745, DA10 0LP

3 JULLIBERRIE'S GRAVE
BAGHAM

At 45 metres, Julliberrie's Grave is a long, long barrow, and one of only three unchambered long barrows found in Kent. It was first excavated in the early 18th century by gentleman antiquarian Heneage Finch, who found 'nothing but bones'. Finch's work was followed up by William Stukeley, often referred to as one of the founding names of archaeology. Although no Neolithic burials have been found inside the barrow, a polished flint axe, thought to have been imported from Scandinavia, was discovered at its centre. This suggests the people here had trade routes linking them with those across the North Sea. It is a little unloved, lying in the corner of a field, devoid of any signs or noticeboards to alert walkers to its presence. It is not until you walk up the hill beyond the barrow and look down at it that you can fully appreciate it. The large mound is almost on the banks of the Great Stour, and views of the millhouse and river open up as you climb the field. This is an undeniably beautiful corner of Kent yet, save for a few dog walkers and locals, very few seem to visit the area. The secluded 12-pitch campsite of Sunnyside Farm (CT4 8BS, 01227 365314) is within walking distance of the barrow and a good starting point for the South Downs Way.

From A252 E of Chilham, turn S onto A28/Ashford Road into Bagham and R to park on Bagham Lane. Walk along Mill Lane (opposite Bagham Lane) SE across railway line, past no entry sign (it is a footpath) and over bridge, bear L around house, turn R at top of hill follow path around into field, and the barrow is on the R. Bus routes 1 and 1A Ashford–Canterbury to Bagham Lane stop, or train to Chilham station and walk W along A252 for 160 metres to A28.

51.2405, 0.9751, TR077532, CT4 8EE

4 COLDRUM LONG BARROW
TROTTISCLIFFE

The colossal stones that made up the burial chamber of Coldrum Long Barrow have stood looking down over the Kentish landscape since 3900BC. This was once a more extensive structure with a large capstone, which has since been lost to local building projects; the kerb stones of the mound have been so displaced that it was first thought to be a stone circle. Medway tombs such as this echo designs of tombs in North Germany and the Netherlands. This permanent stone construction was built at a time when life was fleeting, and its use could have outlived its creators by many generations. At least 17 people – adults, teenagers, and children – were buried within the barrow, with two of the skulls considered female showing unhealed fractures; cut marks on the bones indicate flesh was likely removed as part of the burial rites. Although we know little about the everyday lives of these people, bone analysis tells us that they were probably related and their diets included freshwater fish.

From Trottiscliffe village E on Church Lane ½ mile, past the village hall. R at T-junction onto Pinesfield Lane, signposted Coldrum Long Barrow. Follow L around field for two bends and past houses another ½ mile to a R turn signed to the barrow and car park. Park here and follow footpath, 10 minutes' easy walk. Bus 58 Addingstone–Maidstone to Trottiscliffe The George stop, or train to Snodland and walk W 4 miles via lanes and byways with an OS map or phone mapping.

51.3215, 0.3727, TQ654607, ME19 5EG

5 KIT'S & LITTLE KIT'S COTY HOUSE AYLESFORD

When it was constructed Kit's Coty House would have been covered in earth and perhaps 55 metres long, which is about as long as Nelson's Column is tall. It has attracted visitors for centuries; in 1669 the diarist Samuel Pepys wrote, "it is a thing of great antiquity, and I am mightily glad to see it." As you may expect, it has been the subject of many legends, including a story that circulated right into the Victorian era that the stones were brought from a distant land across the sea and placed there by a witch. 'Coty' is a word for a stone house or tomb, and some say 'Kit' is a corruption of Catigern, the son of Vortigern, who died battling the Saxons, which makes this ancient site wrongly attributed to the Saxon era. However, signs at the site suggest it means 'tomb of the forest' from the ancient British kaitom. Close by is Little Kit's Coty House (51.3160, 0.5014), a smaller structure also known as the Countless Stones, after the common folklore tale that it is impossible to count them. Both were fenced in the 1880s. Not far from these we find the Coffin Stone (51.3178, 0.4956), and the two White Horse stones (51.3150, 0.5147) on Blue Bell Hill.

Follow the A229 N From Maidstone and after passing under the M20 take the Sandling and Eccles exit. Continue over crossroads and take immediate fork R to Kit's Coty and Lower Bell Industrial Estate. Find somewhere to park along this lane. Walk N up past the cement works to lane end, cross the road and follow the footpath down the steps to the site. Continue S and over the crossroads onto lane to Little Kit's Coty House. Bus routes 142 and 185 from Chatham or 150 from Maidstone to Kit's Coty Salisbury Road stop and walk S down Chatham Road to footpath steps R. Trains Aylesford and walk NE 2½ miles on lane passing Little Kit's.

51.3199, 0.5030, TQ745608, ME20 7EG

6 OLDBURY HILLFORT & ROCK SHELTER IGHTHAM

The woods at Oldbury disguise the true size of this hillfort, with trees lining the ramparts and the central enclosure. It is hard to get a sense of the sheer scale of the construction which, with ramparts measuring over 2 miles in circumference, has been described as one of the biggest hillforts in the South East, if not the country. A spring supplied the fort with fresh water, and the central area would have been big enough to graze animals. Despite all these advantages, the invading Roman army could have overwhelmed the fort, and it is thought those who built it, apparently over a short period, never permanently occupied it and may have fled around 50BC. Human activity in this area goes back far beyond the Iron Age: in the northern part of the fort hand axes dating to the Upper Palaeolithic have been found in two rock shelters. The most visible is just off the main path (51.2850, 0.2711), and it isn't hard to imagine hunters camped out within the rocky cave.

Take the A25 E from Sevenoaks and about 2 miles after Seal take lane L signed to Oldbury Hill. Park in National Trust car park L and follow signs through Oldbury Wood to fort. Bus routes 306 and 308 Gravesend–Sevenoaks (stopping at Borough Green station) to Ightham, The George and Dragon stop and follow Sevenoaks Road and Oldbury Lane to paths in at NE corner of Oldbury Wood.

51.2814, 0.2638, TQ579560, TN15 0ET

7 AMBRESBURY BANKS EPPING

Within the confines of Epping Forest lie the hillforts of Ambresbury Banks and Loughton Camp (51.6585, 0.0502). The two may be part of a line of hillforts marking the boundary between the territory of the Trinovantes tribe, widely considered to have been the most powerful tribe in England at the time, with a capital at Colchester, and that of the Catuvellauni tribe. In 54BC Julius Caesar himself became involved in the power struggle between the Trinovantes King Imanuentius and the Catuvellauni leader Cassivellaunus during his abortive attempt at invasion. The area is now a tranquil forest thick with trees, but would have once been a wide open plain with far-reaching views. From the vantage point of Loughton, one of the highest points in the forest, the view would have been even more extensive, enabling occupants to see the Roman force long before they made it to the fort. Today these are amongst the most peaceful places for miles, and a very pleasant morning's walk can be taken between the two forts and back again, exploring the wildlife-rich forest.

Take the B1393 Epping Road SW from Epping into the forest to the Wake Arms roundabout. For Ambresbury Banks take the 1st exit onto B172 and after ½ mile park at Jack's Hill car park on L or R then walk N along Green Ride to the fort. For Loughton Camp take the 3rd exit from the roundabout onto A104 for 1 mile. Park at the Mount Pleasant car park and follow the path marked the Woodchip Ride to the fort. Bus 575 Romford–Harlow to Loughton Wake Arms stop, weekdays only.

51.6829, 0.0777, TL437002, CM16 5HN

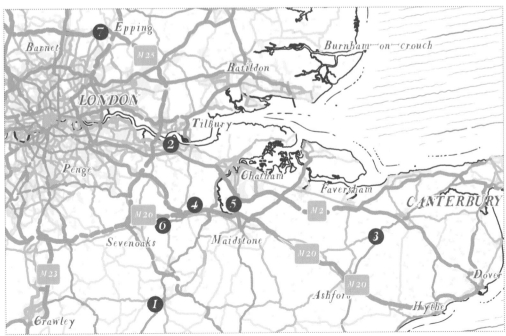

CHAPTER II
THE COTSWOLDS

O *ne* summer solstice I was offered a lift to the Rollright
Stones for what turned out to be a magical night full
of people from all walks of life. There was a coven
of witches who all worked as supply teachers, and a young
woman (whom I have sadly lost touch with) who became a
good friend and helped inspire me to write professionally.
Two of my closest friends shared a kiss for the first time that
night and years later were married. This one evening highlights how, since ancient times, people have interacted with
monuments such as the Rollrights in all kinds of ways. We
should remember this and see them not as static remnants
of history but as part of our landscape, our heritage, for us
to enjoy and live alongside.

The Cotswolds give their name to the Cotswold-Severn
barrow, an iconic type of long barrow that proliferated in this
region and into the Severn Valley in Wales. They are trapezoidal mounds of earth and stone fringed by a drystone wall.
At one end there are 'horns' enclosing a forecourt, where it
is thought fires were lit and rituals took place. Often there
is a passage behind this forecourt, leading directly into the
main chamber, which would contain the remains of up to
50 people. Could it be that the forecourt marked the fringes
of this world and the afterlife or the realm of the ancestors?
The ceremonies could have been felt as a way of existing
between the two realms for a short time. Many of the tombs
may have been in use for decades, even a century, the bones
of the long-dead being moved and replaced by those who
had passed more recently.

1 THE TOOTS LONG BARROW
SELSLEY COMMON

Measuring over 73 metres, this is not only one of the biggest long barrows in Gloucestershire, it is also one of the best preserved. Like all barrows, it would have been a communal grave for some of Britain's first farmers, living in the area around 5,000 years ago. The barrow has been dug three times but, save for part of a stone chamber and interment, there is little to say what lies inside the tomb. Looking out over to the town of Stroud and the Severn Estuary, the Toots is one of the best situated sites in the region, confirming the impression that Neolithic folk loved to be buried with a good view. It is one of many burial sites in this gently rolling, picturesque corner of England. In a wood a couple of miles to the north is the Randwick Long Barrow (51.7605, -2.2549), and on Minchinhampton Common to the south-east we find Whitefield's Tump, named after the Methodist said to have preached from the site in the 18th century (51.7138, -2.2127). Two more chambered tombs in Bown Hill (51.7145, -2.2576) and Buckholt Wood (51.7124, -2.2928) lie to the south and southwest, respectively.

Travel south from Selsley village on the B4066 for a mile until you see a car park on the R (there are four along this stretch). Walk N away from the road over the ridge and you should see the barrow in front of you; ¼ mile, 5 minutes' moderate walk. Bus 66S Gloucester–Stroud to Selsley stops, 1¼ miles' walk, or train to Stroud 2 miles, or Stonehouse 3½ miles on lanes.

51.7263, -2.2516, SO827030, GL5 5PL 🖼️

2 WINDMILL TUMP
RODMARTON

The chambered tomb we now know as Windmill Tump or Rodmarton Long Barrow was in use for two centuries during the Neolithic. To put that into perspective, 200 years is the length of time that separates us from the late Georgians. With no written culture, it is likely that burial practices changed in that time, until the point where it was felt the tombs were no longer needed and they were sealed up. This one held a mix of bones in one chamber, but 13 skeletons in another: seven men, three women and three children (ranging from about 2 to 13 years in age). We also have a hint of what went on when these bodies were interred, as traces of animal bones and ancient fires were found in the forecourt. Could these be signs of a feast to honour the dead as their bodies were placed in the tomb? A short walk off the Macmillan Way, Windmill Tump is well worth the diversion. During late summer and early autumn, the surrounding hedgerows are thick with rose hips, blackberries, sloes and elderberries. Just under a mile from the site is the notable Arts and Crafts house of Rodmarton Manor (GL7 6PF, 01285 841442).

Take the road W from Rodmarton village towards Cherington for around ⅓ mile, you should see a signpost to Rodmarton Barrow and a layby L. Follow the edge of field to the site for around 250 metres. Bus 882 Gloucester–Tetbury to Rodmarton opp St Peter's Church stop, 15 minutes' walk.

51.6744, -2.0988, ST932973, GL7 6PU 🚶🏕️

3 THE LONG STONE
MINCHINHAMPTON

Standing quietly in a corner of a field outside the village, overlooking the local rugby club, is one of the most curious ancient monuments in England. The Long Stone resembles a large piece of Swiss cheese, or the surface of the moon. In the days before immunisation, it was thought that the 'Holey Stone' had magical healing powers, and babies would be passed through the hole in an effort to cure their maladies. There are many long barrows in the area, some of which are in better condition than others. If you are in the area it is worth visiting the nearby Tingle Stone (51.6896, -2.1721) on Princess Anne's land in Gatcombe Park. Legend has it that either of these stones runs across the field when it hears the clock strike 12 times – but maybe it only works at midnight.

Follow Tetbury Street SE out of Minchinhampton a mile to park at E entrance to Gatcombe Wood (51.6973, -2.1698). Walk back along road 20 metres to gate on R. Bus 69 from Stroud to Minchinhampton before Dr Brown's Road stop.

51.6979, -2.1700, ST883999, GL6 9BA

4 ULEY LONG BARROW
DURSLEY

In an area rich in ancient remains, this beautifully restored 37-metre barrow stands out as one of the most impressive in the Cotswolds, and you can explore inside it (bring a torch). It is also known as Hetty Pegler's Tump; in the late 17th century the land was owned by Henry and Hester Pegler who had no idea the 'tump' (the contemporary name for a mound or small hill) was an ancient long barrow. Perhaps this was the spot where Henry proposed to Hetty, or maybe it was her favourite vantage point to look out across the Severn Valley. In 1821 road builders constructing what is now the B4066 destroyed one of the northern chambers in order to use the stone. Digs in both that year and 1854 explored the chambers of this Neolithic tomb, finding 15 or 20 partial and complete human skeletons. In the forecourt, two more skeletons were found, along with the tusks and jaws of several wild boars; the tusks had holes suggesting they may have been worn as jewellery. To the south of the Tump is Uley Bury hillfort which dates to the Mid-Iron Age, 300BC. To the north, linked by the Cotswolds Way, you'll find the roofless remains of Nympsfield Long Barrow (see entry).

Follow the B4066 N out of Uley for 1 mile. Just after the radio tower on R, park behind English Heritage sign on L and follow footpath – only space for one or two cars. Bus 65 Stroud–Cam & Dursley Rail to Crawley Lane stop.

51.6987, -2.3057, SO789000, GL11 5BH

5 NYMPSFIELD LONG BARROW NYMPSFIELD

Like Uley (see entry) this is one of 150 Cotswold-Severn tombs to be found in the south of Britain, ranging from Avebury (see Wiltshire & Wessex) to the Gower (see Pembroke & mid-Wales). It was built around 3800BC, and between 20 and 30 skeletons were found here along with pottery and flint weapons. Barrows of this type have a forecourt area, possibly the site of ritual behaviour. Bodies (or rather bodyparts and bones) were taken out of these tombs and later placed back in. We cannot know for certain why Neolithic people did this, but it could be that our modern boundaries between the living and the dead may not have been

so strict for them. Perhaps the ancestors in the tombs were consulted for important decisions, or their bodies removed to take part in rituals to ensure the crops for the following year – practices still seen in some cultures today. The barrow came into use again during the Middle Ages as a refuge for lepers cast out from the local villages.

Head N from Uley on the B4066 for 1¾ miles, passing Uley Barrow and L fork for Frocester, to take L at brown sign to the picnic area, viewpoint and Nympsfield Long Barrow. The barrow is just to the N of the car park. Bus 65 Stroud–Cam & Dursley Rail, to Nympsfield The Cross stop.

51.7102, -2.2998, SO793012, GL10 3TX

6 CRICKLEY HILL
BIRDLIP

It is easy to look at the past with rose-tinted glasses, to regard it as a golden age when people lived simpler, more harmonious lives. Yet mounting evidence suggests that while Neolithic people may have lived in harmony with the natural world, they certainly did not with each other. Evidence from burials shows a number of people coming to a bloody end, many of them showing fatal blows to the head or injuries from combat. At the entrance to Crickley Hill causewayed enclosure there is undeniable evidence of a large ancient battle between tribes sometime around 3600BC. Numerous flint arrowheads were found, along with evidence of the fence surrounding the site being burnt to the ground by an invading force. The site was abandoned shortly after, only being resettled in the Iron Age thousands of years later. In a strange coda over 5,000 years later, First World War poet Ivor Gurney's 'Crickley Hill' is a rapturous remembrance of his home from another battlefield.

From Gloucester junction 11a on M5 head E on A417 towards Cirencester. After 4 miles, at The Air Balloon roundabout, take A436 for Stow-on-the-Wold then immediate L signed Leckhampton and Crickley Hill Country Park, then L to car park after 140 metres. Bus 10 Gloucester–Cheltenham to Little Shurdington Whitelands Lane stop, and pick up Gloucester Way path SE with a map.

51.8457, -2.1040, SO929163, GL4 8JY

7 BELAS KNAP
WINCHCOMBE

Belas Knap is another of the region's well-restored long barrows. At least 36 individuals were buried in the various chambers here over 5,000 years ago, including men, women and children, along with animal bones and flint artefacts. The presence of fires in the larger 'false entrance' forecourt does conjure up images of night-time rituals. Some, including musician and antiquarian Julian Cope, believe the shape of the banks and the false entrance are representative of the female form and part of a goddess-based belief system; the complete picture of this theory may never fully be understood. To the west on the brow of Cleeve Cloud ridge is a hillfort (51.9276, -2.0237), still remarkable despite the presence of a golf green intruding into its ramparts.

On Gloucester Street/B4632 heading SW out of Winchcombe, Belas Knap is signposted L then L again at the edge of town, down Corndean Lane. Follow lane for just over a mile, and shortly after sharp turn L turn signposted Belas Knap park at the long pull-in L (51.9348, -1.9720). Follow the footpath opposite for ½ mile or so, moderate to strenuous walk. Bus routes W1 or 606 from Cheltenham to Winchcombe Brook Close stop.

51.9273, -1.9708, SP021254, GL54 5AL

8 ROLLRIGHT STONES
GREAT ROLLRIGHT

This is the collective name given to three ancient sites west of the village of Great Rollright, in the Oxfordshire countryside. Although at first glance the three can seem contemporary with each other, their construction spans more than two millennia. The oldest is the Whispering Knights, a portal dolmen built during the Early Neolithic over five and a half thousand years ago, around the year 3800BC. Standing alone in a field they resemble a large stone hand emerging from the soil, but folklore says the group were knights caught conspiring against the king by a witch, who turned them to stone. The largest of the three sites is the King's Men, a circle of about 70 oolitic limestone orthostats over 31 metres in diameter. It is said that it is impossible to count the same number of stones twice, a legend referenced in a 1970s episode of Doctor Who in which these stones were the 'Nine Travellers' and a fugitive alien was transformed into an extra stone. The lonely and much-chipped-away-at King Stone is the most recent of the sites, dating to around 1500BC.

Follow A44 NE from Chipping Norton to roundabout and turn L onto A3400. After 2⅓ miles turn L towards Little Rollright. After about ½ mile pull into long layby L, follow signs to stone circle; the Knights are to the E (51.9752, -1.5656) and the King Stone just across the road. Bus 488 from Banbury to Great Rollright stop and walk W on D'Arcy Dalton Way path.

51.9755, -1.5708, SP295308, OX7 5QB

9 HOAR STONE
ENSTONE

On a crossroads just off the B4022, south of the village of Enstone lies the remains of the Hoar Stone burial chamber. The monument consists of three stones, the largest of which is known as Old Soldier. Over their 5,000 years here the megaliths must have built up quite a thirst, as it is said Old Soldier wanders to the local pub for a drink each Midsummer's Eve. Perhaps this is the reason that you might not find the Hoar Stone, despite its size. Assuming that it hasn't wandered off for a pint and is just easy to miss in the shade, look for the wall surrounding the tomb. About 2½ miles to the west, north-east of Chadlington, is another Neolithic

monument known as the Hawk Stone (51.9094, -1.5083). It stands 2.6 metres high, and so many people have rubbed it for good luck that the groove at the top is now smooth to the touch.

On Oxford Road/A44 heading S through Enstone, turn R onto B4022 for Charlbury at end of village, then L at crossroads signed Fulwell and pull off. The stone is on the R by the crossroads. Bus S3 Oxford–Chipping Norton to Enstone Green stop. Trains to Charlbury 3½ miles' walk, or S3 also stops there.

51.9107, -1.4521, SP377237, OX7 4NY 🅰️

IO DEVIL'S QUOITS
STANTON HARCOURT

The Devil's Quoits lie within one of the most surreal landscapes in this book, surrounded by lakes, a reclaimed gravel pit, and a former landfill slowly healing over. Despite its location, this restored – or reconstructed – henge has an eerie beauty about it. Guidebooks of the 19th century mention only three stones standing here; the rest were put back up when the banks and stone circle were rebuilt in 2002–2008. The site was constructed in the Neolithic, some 5,000 years ago, and remarkably a Time Team dig found mammoth bones, suggesting the site was in use in the Mesolithic (9600–4000BC).

From Stanton Harcourt follow Main Road S for ½ mile on foot, take track R with the white gate/road barrier (there is limited space to pull off shortly S of this by cemetery). Follow track then permissive path W toward lake then S around lake to stone circle. Train Hanborough 7 miles, or site is 1¾ miles off the Thames Path if undertaking a longer walk.

51.7404, -1.4061, SP411048, OX29 5BB 🅰️🚶🐾

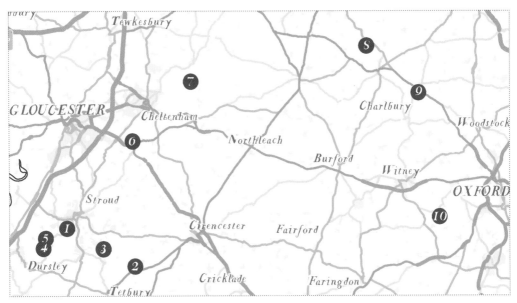

CHAPTER 12
EAST ANGLIA

*E*ast Anglia is an understated region; a flat, calm place that suits a gentler, slower pace, somewhere the traveller is encouraged to shake off the stresses of modern life. To me the placid nature of the region is reflected in the soft, rhythmic local accent. It is as if the words need time to travel to your ears, and the long vowels mirror the wide-open sky as if the words are filling up the space around them. Away from the tourist centres, the beaches of Norfolk and Suffolk are often empty, even during the height of the season. A few years ago, on one such quiet Norfolk beach, stormy seas revealed a scene from the very beginning of our human story in Britain. On a beach in Happisburgh, Norfolk, footprints were found that were left in mud a staggering 840,000 years ago. The coastline of Britain would have been very different then, with this region of the country joined to the continent. Happisburgh would have been miles inland on a combined estuary of the precursor Thames and the Bytham River, a great ancient river that flowed through Worcestershire, Oxfordshire and Derbyshire out into East Anglia and the North Sea.

Moving to a slightly more comprehensible time period, during the Neolithic the favourable climate and soils of East Anglia would have been exploited by some of Britain's first farmers. There is a rich archaeological record in this region, but a local lack of stone monuments (due to a local lack of stone!) meant there are few Neolithic traces. However, we do find the remains of barrows at Broome Heath (52.4680, 1.4478) and West Rudham (52.7952, 0.6837) and of course the crowning glory of the region, the Neolithic flint mines at Grime's Graves.

Through a changing, wetter climate, what had been favourable farmland in the Neolithic slowly became wetland during the Bronze Age. The people adapted to this, and we know a great deal about them because of many finds that were remarkably well preserved by the oxygen-free, or anaerobic, environment of the fen peat. Of course the ceremonial causeway of Flag Fen is world-famous. At nearby Must Farm (52.5551, -0.1775) an entire Late Bronze Age village of stilted roundhouses, positioned above a river, collapsed after a fire and fell into thick river silt. Food bowls and rubbish dumps were found outside the houses, and thanks to finds from the ongoing archaeological work we know they ate a mix of wild and domestic animals, along with grains such as emmer wheat and barley. At Wicken Fen another Bronze Age relic was pulled from the peat: a near-perfectly preserved fallen oak tree. This is now in pride of place outside the National Trust visitor centre (52.3106, 0.2911), and is so well preserved you can count its rings.

1 HAPPISBURGH FOOTPRINTS *HAPPISBURGH*

The Happisburgh landscape is constantly in flux. Ever-worsening winter storms aid the erosion of the shoreline, as the raging North Sea slowly but surely claims the village. It was through this process of erosion that in May 2013 a layer of sand close to the sea defences washed away to reveal footprints belonging to five adults and children of the Homo antecessor species, an archaic form of human. Laid down over 840,000 years ago, these were the oldest footprints made by a hominid species ever found outside of Africa. There isn't much to see, as the footprints washed away within two weeks of being found, but there is something very special about walking where we know our distant ancestors trod all those hundreds of thousands of years ago. It is a quiet, secluded, dog-friendly beach, and the village is home to the oldest working lighthouse in Britain.

From Happisburgh centre follow Beach Road to reasonably priced community car park. Follow the ramp to the beach and walk N around headland; the footprints were found just before the caravan site above. Bus 34 from North Walsham to Happisburgh Lighthouse Close stop; no Sunday service.

52.8254, 1.5350, TG382311, NR12 0PR

2 WARHAM CAMP *WELLS–NEXT–THE–SEA*

This perfectly circular multivallate hillfort (one surrounded by two or more ramparts) just south of the village of Warham is a rare East Anglian example of Iron Age earthworks, and is situated on an equally rare East Anglian hill, just 15 metres above sea level. Warham Camp is thought to date from between the 1st century BC and the 1st century AD. The outer ramparts only measure 215 metres in diameter, but they were once crowned by a large palisade or timber fence that protected the Icini (Boudica's tribe) defendants during the initial Roman invasion. Large amounts of Roman pottery have been found at the site, suggesting the fort was reused during the occupation – finds can be seen in Norwich Castle Museum. A short walk from the site, at a crossroads between Warham and Binham, a Neolithic long barrow lies hidden in the corner of field (52.9310, 0.9167). There are two further hillforts in the area, Holkham Camp at the coast (52.9672, 0.7899) and Bloodgate Hill at South Creake (52.8825, 0.7449).

Park in Warham and take the lane running S from the Three Horsehoes pub (NR23 1NL, 01328 710547), towards Wighton. Continue for ½ mile, over the bridge, to find a grassed footpath to the fort to your R. Bus 46 from Holt to Warham on weekdays. Wells–Walsingham Light Railway narrow-gauge steam trains stop in Warham.

52.9303, 0.8905, TF943409, NR23 1NJ

3 GRIME'S GRAVES *BRANDON*

Some 4,600 years ago, using red deer antler picks, our Neolithic ancestors dug 12-metre deep, hourglass-shaped pits into the chalky ground. From each of these ran horizontal tunnels up to nine metres long. Within these tunnels they would have had nothing but tallow lamps by which to see the seam of flints, which they sent back up to the surface using baskets and ropes. They dug hundreds of pits this way, backfilling them after, and their efforts are marked by over 360 indentations spread across the landscape, like a golf course for surrealists. During a 1939 dig overseen by A.L. Armstrong, a female figurine and male genitalia carved from chalk were found – however, these appeared freshly made and it was suspected they were planted by a prankster working on the dig. Today, you can have a small taste of what life must have been like as you descend into a restored pit via a ladder and peer into the tunnels (over-tens only at time of writing, but improvements are planned) and the area is great for walks and kite flying. The shop and information centre are open to all.

Head N from Brandon on the A1065, after 1¾ miles take R signed West Tofts and Grimes Graves. After 1⅓ miles R through English Heritage signed gate with lodge to car park at end. Train Brandon 3½ miles; if walking you can take more direct tracks through the Brecks with an OS map or phone mapping.

52.4768, 0.6763, TL818899, IP26 5DE

4 HUT HILL BARROW
KNETTISHALL HEATH

The population of the Bronze Age was very well nourished and small enough to not make demands on neighbouring lands, so unlike the Iron Age or sometimes brutal Neolithic, this was a remarkably settled time in our nation's prehistory. At this time we see lavish burials in large mounds or barrows often marked as 'tumulus' on OS maps, like the large bowl barrow on Hut Hill; 10,000 of these are recorded across the country. There is another well-preserved example, known as Brickkiln Covert, hidden in the woods just 720 metres to the east of Hut Hill (52.3851, 0.8814). Some believe these barrows were the last resting place of a warrior elite or powerful clan leaders, but we have no way of knowing the social system during this period of prehistory, and it is all too easy to project our own ways of thinking onto these ancient peoples. Knettishall Heath itself is a wonderful haven for wildlife; knocking woodpeckers can be heard, and kingfishers dart across the Little Ouse River. It also marks one end of the Peddars Way long-distance path, which follows the route of an old Roman road northwards from the end of the Icknield Way and passes another barrow cemetery at Harpley Common (52.8241, 0.6094).

From Thetford head E for 2⅓ miles on A1066 and take R for Rushford, then after Rushford fork L signposted Knettishall and Nature Reserve. Follow 1¾ miles, then L at crossroads to the main car park on L. From here follow signs to woodland trail S over the road, go through the wooden gates, follow the path for 400 metres, and the barrow is just the other side of a small pine-and-birch wood.

52.3853, 0.8708, TL954802, IP22 2TG

5 KINGS FOREST BOWL BARROW WEST STOW

Hidden in this plantation forest, a short walk from the reconstructed West Stow Anglo-Saxon village, is a clearing containing a bowl barrow. The barrow stands to a height of 1.2 metres, but its position on a small hill gives it the appearance of being a lot taller. It is around 32 metres in diameter and there was once a ditch 3 metres wide surrounding it. A monument of such size would have been a considerable effort to construct

in its day, with simple hand tools, and was most likely the product of a large community effort. Along the walk up a long, sandy track to the tumulus, the woods are teeming with life; tiny nuthatches dart along the tree trunks, and the rat-a-tat-tat of the ever-elusive woodpecker echoes through the woods. Although the plantation is transected by only a few long paths, it is very easy to get lost, and a good map or phone mapping is highly recommended.

Head SE from Icklingham village on the A1101 and 1 mile after church take the L turn toward West Stow, and park in the car park L after 180 metres. Walk E along the road for 350 metres and turn L along the Icknield Way bridleway/footpath by house. Follow this track for a little over a mile and look for a path R; there is one marked on the map, but I could not find the end of it on my visit early in 2018. I headed R here through some birch trees and followed the deer fence to join a path SW to the tumulus. Bus routes 16 and 16A Newmarket–Bury St Edmunds and 355 Bury St Edmunds–Mildenhall to Icklingham West Stow turning stop; no Sunday service.

52.3244, 0.6486, TL806729, IP28 6HF

6 STONEA CAMP WIMBLINGTON

In AD 47, a fierce battle took place between the famous Icini and highly trained Roman troops led by Marcus Ostorius, the son of Britain's second governor Publius Ostorius Scapula; Stonea Camp in Cambridgeshire has been suggested as the site of this battle. One of the finds here was the skull of a child of no more than four or five, brutally cleaved in two by a blade like a broadsword, putting paid to any belief that the Romans were benevolent invaders. The barbaric attack on this camp must have acted as a shock warning to the tribes, and may have dissuaded locals from a full rebellion at that time, although the Iceni remained an independent tribe until Boudicca's uprising in AD 61. Despite its bloody end, the use of hillforts such as Stonea as defensive structures has been the subject of debate. Many have little or no evidence of settlement, and some do not make sense as defensive structures; at only 2 metres above sea level, this is the lowest 'hill' fort in Britain, and would then have stood on the southern point of a fenland island. It may be that they were in fact a continuation of enclosed ritualistic spaces like the causewayed camps and henges of the Neolithic. So although battles may have taken place in a handful of them, perhaps they were more places of tribal gathering than ancient castles.

From the A141 in Wimblington head E on the B1093 for 1½ miles. Turn L signposted to Stonea Camp down a very bumpy single-track lane to car park at end. Bus 56 from Wisbech to Boots Bridge stop and walk W to track, 1½ miles in all, or train to Manea and walk 3¾ miles.

52.5165, 0.1323, TL447930, PE15 0PE 🚶

7 FLAG FEN
PETERBOROUGH

In 1982 a team of archaeologists led by Francis Pryor found the remains of a wooden causeway stretching around ⅓ mile across the boggy fens near Peterborough. It would have once linked two areas of dry land, at Northey and Fengate, across the flooded Flag Fen Basin to a central artificial island with a large rectangular building. The walkway was constructed in stages around 1350–950BC. It used a staggering 60,000 timbers driven into the ground like giant cocktail sticks and supporting over 250,000 horizontal pieces of wood. The posts were consecrated with deposits of human and dog bone along with the tusks of boar. Around the central island and the causeway, an astonishing number of artefacts were found, all dating from 1200BC to 200BC. These included swords that had never been sharpened, jewellery, the earliest example of a wheel found in Britain and polished stones brought here from some distance away. All the items were deliberately damaged before being placed in the water. We cannot know for certain why people made these offerings; some suggest they were trying to appease the gods, as the climate became considerably wetter and the landscape more flooded, or were they offerings for the dead? Many have made the link between these watery votive offerings and the story of Excalibur being returned to the Lady of the Lake. Perhaps our practice of throwing coins into wishing wells is also a distant cultural memory borrowed from these ancient times.

From the crossroads at the car dealer on Fengate/Edgerley Drain Road around the E edge of Peterborough, follow Storey's Bar Road E, signposted to Flag Fen. Turn R at T-junction at end, follow bend R and take signed R dead-end road to the site. Train to Peterborough and walk for about 3 miles via the Nene Way riverside path.

52.5745, -0.1897, TL227989, PE6 7QJ 🚌🏕️🏛️

8 SEAHENGE
HOLME–NEXT–THE–SEA

Four thousand years ago the coast at Holme-next-the-Sea was not an expansive, windswept sandy beach as it is today but a tidal salt marsh, more like the area around Thornham, a couple of miles to the east. Amid these tidal marshes at least 50 members of the Early Bronze Age community living here built a circular wooden structure. It consisted of 55 timber posts surrounding the upturned roots of a large oak tree, which had been worked on by bronze axes. Archaeologist Francis Pryor describes it as a timber mortuary structure, and has postulated the body of someone very important would have been placed on the central upturned tree roots for seagulls, buzzards and other local carrion species to dismember down to the bone. In parts of Tibet, Bhutan, China and Northern India, bodies are still laid out for carrion birds like this in 'sky burials'. It has been postulated that such rituals allowed the dead safe passage to the afterlife, as the birds literally tore off the living part of the bodies leaving just the bones. The posts were moved to King's Lynn museum for preservation, so there is little to see on the beach, but you are free to walk along the often deserted sand and allow your mind to wander back to how this area would have looked in 2049BC when the timber was felled and the circle built.

From the A149 just W of Holme-next-the-Sea follow Beach Road N to the car park, R near beach and follow the path to the beach. The monument was found within this small stretch of coastline. About ½ mile E along the sand you may discern the last traces of a second lesser circle from the same date, which was left in situ (52.9777, 0.5484). Bus 36 Coastliner from King's Lynn to Holme-next-the-Sea Beach Road stop.

52.9680, 0.5213, PE36 6LQ 🚌

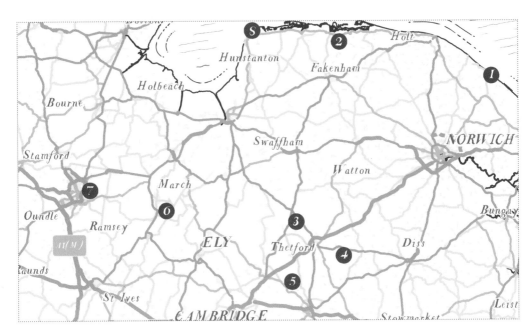

CHAPTER 13
CENTRAL ENGLAND

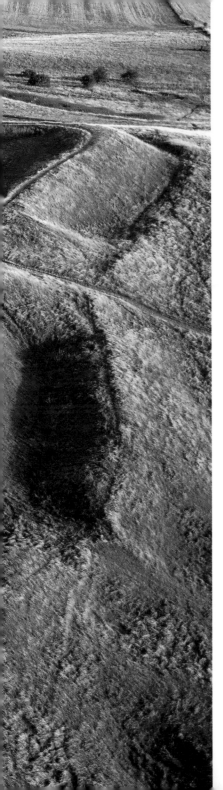

*D*uring the Neolithic, a walk across many parts of England would have meant navigating through dense woodland or boggy ground. So rather than getting stuck in the mud or lost in the wood, people went upwards, navigating across the free-draining, treeless, high chalk ridgeway. Trails, paths and drovers' roads would have criss-crossed this chalk acting as a series of transport arteries running through the centre of the country. The Romans took advantage of these ancient routes, building their own roads and paths along them.

Much of this trackway network, 363 miles of it, still exists as four distinct long-distance paths, from Hunstanton in the east to Lyme Regis on the south coast. Known as the Greater Ridgeway Trail, they are the Wessex Ridgeway, the Icknield Way, the Peddars Way National Trail and of course the Ridgeway National Trail. The last of these runs from the Ivinghoe Beacon in the Chilterns along chalk ridges, through ancient woodland and past the great downs, to Overton Hill near Avebury. The Ridgeway runs seamlessly into the Icknield Way, and both paths pass by many ancient sites. It has been speculated that this was a path of pilgrimage to Avebury, much as the Pilgrims Way to Canterbury was in the Middle Ages. There are several long and round barrows along the route dating from the Late Neolithic and early to mid-Bronze Age. We have the Five Knolls near Dunstable, Bacombe Hill (51.7558, -0.7535) and of course the famous Cotswold Severn-type barrow, Wayland's Smithy. At Whiteleaf there is one of the few Neolithic round barrows in the South of England, along with two Bronze Age barrows (51.7296, -0.8114), all lying above a great chalk cross carved into the hillside, thought to have been cut by monks in the 15th century. Some believe the cross was created to cover up a large chalk phallus that could have dated to a time before Roman occupation, because the area was known as Wayland's Stock, and stock was an old slang for penis – but it also meant a marker post where the heads of executed criminals might be displayed.

The Ridgeway would have had many uses throughout its history, and during the tumultuous Iron Age the strategic nature of this high ridge came into its own and several hillforts were constructed along it. The most notable is of course the great Uffington Castle, with its nearby chalk horse, and Sharpenhoe Clappers has a dramatic setting, but there were others. Near Hitchen is Ravensburgh Castle (51.9531, -0.4022, seek permission from Hexton Manor Estate before visiting due to shoots), Castle Hill or Sinodun Camp is on one of the Wittenham Clumps (51.6278, -1.1787), Cholesbury Camp has a medieval church within it (51.7565, -0.6528), and of course there is the fort on Ivinghoe Beacon (51.8413, -0.6079).

I

1 *WAYLAND'S SMITHY*
UFFINGTON

Nestled in a secluded grove of beech trees just off the Ridgeway long-distance path is the huge mound of Wayland's Smithy, edged by vast sarsen stones. Legend has it that if a horse and a single groat (a silver coin worth fourpence) were left outside the barrow overnight, by morning the mythical blacksmith Wayland would have shod the horse and taken the payment. The tomb was built in two phases, with the earlier lying hidden within the later tomb. This would have been a small wooden and stone chamber where the bones of 14 individuals including a child (likely with their flesh removed) were laid to rest. This was covered in earth and chalk held in place with a kerb of stones, and remained in use for some 15 years, less than a single generation, around 3590–3550 BC. The later tomb, from 3460–3400BC, measuring 55 metres by 14.5 metres today, engulfed and dwarfed the original and mimicked Cotswold-Severn tombs such as West Kennet (see Cotswolds).

Drive to White Horse Hill car park as for Uffington (see entry). From here walk S on road ⅓ mile and take R onto Ridgeway path for 500 metres, until Wayland's Smithy is signed to the R.

51.5667, -1.5960, SU280854, SN7 7QN

2 *UFFINGTON CASTLE*
UFFINGTON

The deeply cut White Horse at Uffington has been dated by Oxford Archaeological to 1380–550BC, in the Mid- to Late Bronze Age or Early Iron Age, making it easily the oldest chalk figure in the country. There are many interpretations of the horse, including a theory it represents the dragon killed by Saint George and the more widespread suggestion that it represents the Gallo-Roman horse goddess Epona, a goddess of fertility and protector of horses. It could have been a tribal totem drawn on the side of the hillfort to mark a territorial boundary between the Atrebates and the Dobunni tribes; it is uncertain which would have controlled the hillfort. Aside from the horse, the hillfort itself would have been an enormous show of power for the tribe. It measures 220 metres from west to east and 160 metres north to south, and the innermost wall would have been lined with huge sarsen stones like those used to build nearby Wayland's Smithy (see entry).

White Horse Hill is signposted from Uffington village. Follow Shotover S to crossroads, turn R towards Ashbury on B4057 then L at next crossroads and continue to White Horse Hill car park on L after ½ mile. Follow signs to hillfort.

51.5753, -1.5693, SU299863, SN7 7QN

3 FIVE KNOLLS
DUNSTABLE

Standing on top of the Dunstable Downs, the highest point in Bedfordshire, the skies are wide open and the chalk downs seem endless. Here Bronze Age people chose to honour their dead in a group of seven barrows just off the Icknield Way, the eastern arm of the Greater Ridgeway path. Archaeological digs during the 1920s found the northernmost of the barrows contained a Neolithic female skeleton with a flint knife, along with much later Bronze Age cremation urns. This was no doubt a case of Bronze Age people appropriating an earlier religious site for their new belief system. In all, bones from almost 100 people have been found here. In Saxon times, the site was used for an altogether different kind of burial, of 30 bodies with their hands tied behind their backs, and victims of a medieval gallows were also buried here.

In Dunstable follow West Street/B489 W to roundabout with B4541 L and take it, towards The Downs and Whipsnade. Follow for just over 1 mile to car park R. Barrows are ¾ mile N along the Icknield Way. Bus 35 from Dunstable to Whipsnade Road stop (near B489 roundabout) and walk S 300 metres up Dunstable Downs on Icknield Way; no Sunday service.

51.8784, -0.5393, TL006209, LU6 2NT

4 HUNT'S HILL
BRADGATE PARK

During the Palaeolithic some 15,000 years ago a hunting party stopped or perhaps even settled for a short time at Bradgate Park. They intercepted vast herds of deer migrating through Little Matlock Gorge, by the River Lin, and worked the deer skins into clothing, removing the flesh with flint knives. People returned here thousands of years later in the Mesolithic, or Middle Stone Age, and surveys suggest they returned again in the Iron Age, as field systems and several house platforms have been found near Old John Tower. Just outside the park entrance, secluded in a wood near the car park, there is a large megalith surrounded by smaller standing stones and several recumbents. The 1.5-metre stone looks like part of a stone circle, and it has been suggested the recumbent stones might be the remains of a cist, but the site does not appear in any archaeological database. This may mean it is a rare example of a site that has escaped the archaeological community, but author Bob Trubshaw suggests the stones were erected by Boy Scouts in the 20th century.

Bradgate Park is signposted from a roundabout on the A50 by-passing Markgate, via Newtown Linford, where you turn L on Main Street to head NE out of village. Follow to ⅓ mile after Grey Lady Restaurant (LE6 0AH, 01530 243558) and turn R into Bradgate Park. Follow the path SE out of the car park into the woods and head L after 75 metres into the trees for about 75 metres to the stones. Bus 120 from Leicester to Newtown Linford Markfield Lane stop and walk 1¼ miles; no Sunday service.

52.7000, -1.2249, SK524116, LE6 0AL

 5 SHARPENHOE CLAPPERS
BARTON—LE—CLAY

In 1897 a Captain Cuttle wrote in *The Shoreditch Observer* of Sharpenhoe Clappers: 'if you want to see the country, climb a hill', and the views from this Iron Age promontory hillfort are a rare treat in a part of the country more associated with urban sprawl. The name Sharpenhoe is said to mean 'sharp spur of land' and clappers from the Latin word 'claperius' referring to the medieval rabbit warren that once covered the site. The countless rabbits once living here have disturbed many of the possible Iron Age traces that could have been discovered. The fort may have been one of a line of defended sites across the Chiltern Hills. Early Romano-British pottery has been found, and postholes suggest the presence of an earlier palisade or huge timber wall, with an enormous four-metre-wide ceremonial entrance. An enchanting copse of beech trees now let in soft, dappled light throughout the summer and in the autumn as the leaves fall, it is a beguiling place to explore.

In Sharpenhoe village turn S on the Sharpenhoe Road and follow ¾ mile to the National Trust car park on the L. Car park can get busy in the summer. Train to Harlington and walk 2 miles.

51.9604, -0.4493, TL066302, MK45 4SH

6 LAMBOURN SEVEN
BARROWS LAMBOURN

There are in fact between 20 and 30 bowl, saucer and disc barrows to be seen in this Bronze Age cemetery. It is thought that at least ten more once stood here, but have been lost to the plough. When they were first constructed, around 2200BC, they would have been covered in chalk and must have been a phenomenal sight to those who lived here. Even today, without the gleaming white coating, you get a real sense of awe walking amongst the mounds of this Bronze Age graveyard. To the north-west of the barrows, just off a path towards the gallops, are the fallen sarsen stones of a destroyed long barrow, where a crouched burial from the Neolithic was found. Carbon-dating of the finds within put it at 4250BC, making the oldest known interment in the country.

From Lambourn follow Oxford Street/B4001 N. After 1 mile take L fork at Mile End signposted to Seven Barrows. After another mile the road bears R, then take the track R with a sign on the bend L; there is grassed space to pull off L with an information board, and the barrows a short walk ahead. Bus 4 from Newbury to Lambourn.

51.5443, -1.5269, SU329829, RG17 8UH

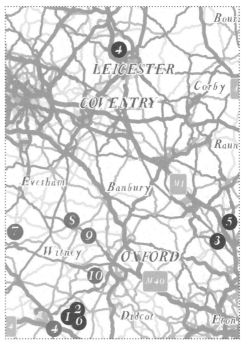

CHAPTER 14

PEAK DISTRICT

It was still painfully early on a spring morning when I visited the Iron Age hillfort of Carl Wark. Visiting wasn't in my original plan, but I decided to squeeze it in following a tip-off from two walkers passing by the chambered tomb of Minning Low. As the mists rose on Hathersage Moor, I caught sight of the two towering outcrops of Higher Tor and Carl Wark. The fort looked ethereal and other-worldly, like a lost city rising up above the desolate moor, and, although the boggy land underfoot squelched over the top of my walking boots as I approached it, I barely noticed the discomfort. I tried to imagine how it must have looked to ancient travellers, all those centuries ago, when the rocky defences were first built. Invading armies and welcomed guests alike must have been in awe of the fort. At once, I understood how constructions such as this, on lonely hilltops, were as much for prestige as for defence. This is by no means the only remarkable hillfort within the National Park; like an ancient way of keeping up with the Joneses, another stands on the peak of Mam Tor. The forts undoubtably had defensive capabilities, and some even showed signs of conflict. Fin Cop, overlooking Monsal Dale (53.2358, -1.7389) shows signs of a violent end, with finds so far of nine bodies, apparently all women and children, thrown unceremoniously into the rampart ditches and buried by the demolished wall. As archaeologists found bodies wherever they dug it is thought there may be hundreds of corpses buried around the site.

Creswell Crags is a limestone gorge 20 or so miles to the east of the Peak District National Park, on the border between Nottinghamshire and Derbyshire. A set of caverns in the crag have been visited by bands of hunters for tens of thousands of years. It has some of the northernmost cave art anywhere in the world and is one of the very few sites where signs of Neanderthals have been found. A decorated bone was also found showing the figure of a man with a horse's head; many of the finds are on show in Sheffield Museum.

Within the rocky crags of the park itself there are numerous caves visited by our Palaeolithic predecessors. They came here seeking shelter during the hunt for large animal prey such as reindeer, red deer, wild horses and bison. At Ravenscliffe Cave in Cressbrook Dale (53.2591, -1.7406) a flint scraper was found amidst a pile of animal bones and, in Elder Bush Cave (53.0912, -1.8551) and Thor's Cave in the Manifold Gorge, flint tools were found with the spoils from a hunting party.

Despite this early history, the Peaks are best known for their Late Neolithic and Early Bronze Age sites. The tiny Doll Tor stone circle is perhaps my favourite in the region, tucked away in a woodland.

1

2

3

4

1 SEVEN STONES OF HORDRON EDGE BAMFORD

It is never clear how names that do not accurately describe a site persist into the modern age. These 'Seven Stones' are ten upright, roughly waist-height stones with another lying recumbent, but the circle may have once contained 26 stones. One of the largest, known as the fairy stone, seems to echo the shape of Win Hill and Loose Hill peaks, to the south-west over Ladybower Reservoir. There are peaks in every direction, and it is possible some of the missing stones also mimicked the shapes of these surrounding hills. I noticed the same phenomenon at stone circles throughout the creation of this book, as have many others. The mind seeks desperately to bring in meaning where there isn't any and it may be nothing more than a trick of the eye, but was there a deliberate effort by the builders of the circles to find stones that matched the shapes in the landscape? It has been suggested the circles were built to harness some power of the hills, or even to worship the gods within them – or the visual effect might have appealed to early people just as it does to us.

Head W on A57 from Hollow Meadows village for a little under 2 miles until you come to a large, separated layby on the L, known as Cutthroat car park. From here, head up embankment and follow path over the fence. The stone circle is on a high plateau beyond a natural rock formation, looking out to the W, 500–600 metres walk in all. Bus routes 273, 274 and 257 from Sheffield to Ashopton Cutthroat Bridge stop, no Sunday service.

53.3781, -1.6779, SK215868, S33 0AX

2 MAM TOR CHAPEL–EN–LE–FRITH

The 'mother hill' or Mam Tor dominates this region now just as it would have done in ancient times. Antiquarian and musician Julian Cope describes it as 'the sacred prehistoric heart of this high peak area'. It is an unpredictable hill, with frequent landslides, and its very name may derive from these natural catastrophic events giving birth to smaller hills from the fallen rock and scree. This was once the site of a hillfort, the largest in the Peak District, with carbon-dated finds from 1180–1130BC. This makes it a very rare Bronze

Age hillfort – however, it would have remained in use during the Iron Age, when the site was reinforced. It is not known whether it was permanently settled but large, possible hut platforms were found here, along with a vast quantity of pottery, some whetstones, a bronze axe and one in polished stone along with items of jewellery. In the south-west corner of the tor there are two round barrows. A 19th-century dig unearthed human bodies, shards of pottery and what may have been a bronze axe.

From Market St/B5470 in Chapel-en-le-Frith take L onto Sheffield Rd signposted for Blackbrook and Edale. After 4¼ miles pull into Mam Nick National Trust car park on L. Follow footpath N to Mam Tor, 20 minutes' moderately strenuous walk. Train to Edale and walk 2 miles S on footpath via Harden Clough to peak.

53.3491, -1.8106, SK127836, S33 8WA

3 FROGGATT EDGE STONE CIRCLE GRINDLEFORD

Also called Stoke Flat West Stone Circle, this is a charming little monument just off a well-used path along Froggatt Edge and Curbar Edge. It is part of a larger prehistoric landscape, together with the moors behind. We know this area was farmed, thanks to the large number of clearance cairns, or piles of rock which have been stacked up to clear fields for agricultural use. This may have been as early as the Neolithic, around 3400BC, although the stone circle itself is more likely to be Early Bronze Age. What is interesting about Froggatt Edge is that these field systems, a place of work, are so close to the stone circle, a ritual monument. It is likely that everyday life was highly ritualised or even somewhat superstitious, and that for early farmers, work, life, death and ritualistic practice were all completely entwined. However, the circles may have been early calendars, set to celestial objects marking key times of the year to sow seed or make the harvest.

From the Chequers Inn (S32 3ZJ, 01433 630231) on the A625 at Froggatt, take the road N for 1¼ miles. Just after the road bends sharply R, on a bend to the L, there is a small car park/layby on the R. Walk back 140 metres to the path starting at the gate L and follow it S on embankment for 5–10mins until the circle appears on the L. Bus 65 from Sheffield to Froggatt.

53.2875, -1.6270, SK249767, S32 3ZJ

4 ARBOR LOW
NEWHAVEN

Positioned on a high moorland plateau, some 375 metres above sea level, on the hills between Bakewell and Matlock, the name Arbor 'Low' is somewhat ironic; in fact it may come from Old English hlaw for mound or barrow. Here the wind gusts over these enormous, recumbent limestone slabs, which lie within a large, round, banked henge. Aubrey Burl advocates the idea that Arbor Low was built in four distinct stages: first, the construction of the central cove, a small, U-shaped group of stones; next, the banks of the henge, built up using nothing but bone and antler tools; much later the clockface-like stones placed within the henge; and finally the barrow built into its banks. An entire burial, a human arm bone, arrowheads, flints, antlers and ox bones, Neolithic and Bronze Age vessels and a stone cist have all been found on the site. Most sources agree that the stones never really stood, although there are those in the archaeological community who dispute this. In 1927 the small Bardic Circle of Imperishable Sacred Land held a Gorsedd (a meeting of modern-day druidic bards) here, the men dressed in green robes, the women in white. A great sword was unsheathed, and the single question 'Is it peace?' was asked, a rather prophetic one, considering this was halfway between the two great wars of the century. Close to the henge there is a Bronze Age barrow called Gib Hill (53.1669, -1.7647), built upon a Neolithic barrow that predated the henge.

Follow A515 from Newhaven N for 2½ miles. Take R then shortly R again, both signed to Arbor Low. Shortly come to a brown sign directing you R to a small car park. Please donate to the honesty box here.

53.1688, -1.7614, SK160635, DE45 1JS

5 NINE STONES CLOSE
WINSTER

Only four stones still stand at this beautifully situated Derbyshire stone circle, often called the Grey Ladies. It is unlikely the name of the site ever represented the number of stones, as many more than nine would have made up this 13-metre stone ring. The name may well come from local folklore instead, and be a corruption of 'noon', the time of day when fairies are said to gather at the stones and dance. Another local legend tells of a giant by the name of Robin Hood (not the famous outlaw) who stood astride the rocky outcrops to the south (53.1573, -1.6659) and urinated into the fields below. Having watched the giant relieve himself, a group of women were turned to stone; they became the Grey Ladies and the rocky outcrop became known as Robin Hood's Stride – although a more suitable name might have been Robin Hood's Urinal. A large monolith, which may have once belonged to the circle, has been built into a nearby farmer's wall. There are faint cup and ring marks on Robin Hood's stride, and a hillfort known as Castle Ring to the north-west (53.1622, -1.6715). The Limestone Way footpath runs adjacent to many of the sites in this area.

From Winster village take the B5057 NW towards Elton, and at crossroads turn R onto B5056 towards Bakewell. After ¾ mile you will come to a pull-in on the R (53.1536, -1.6594). Walk back a few metres then take lane opposite and turn R immediately on it onto Limestone Way footpath. Follow this past Robin Hood's Stride to circle 300 metres due N; OS map or phone mapping is useful. Bus 172 from Matlock to Winster, or to Youlgreave and longer walk S on Limestone Way.

53.1605, -1.6644, SK225626, DE4 2LZ

6 DOLL TOR STONE CIRCLE
BIRCHOVER

Hidden amongst the trees of a small copse is a magical little stone circle, perhaps my favourite of all in the Peak District. It consists of just six stones, with a diameter of 6 metres, and an adjacent cairn. Digs by father and son team J.P. and J.C. Heathcote in the 1930s found a number of cremation urns containing men, women and children, along with burnt flint blades. Two blue faience beads thought to date from 1400BC also turned up with separate cremations, giving us a rare glimpse of one the colours of the Bronze Age. On your way to the circle you will pass the Andle Stone, a 5-metre-long boulder covered in cup and ring marks (53.1635, -1.6420), and in a clearing north-east of Doll Tor is a millstone gritstone circle called Nine Ladies (53.1680, -1.6289). The site is well known, as plans to quarry in the area put the circle under threat. There are more stone circles hidden on the moors, but as the stones are so small and often hidden in bracken and heather, it will take a keen eye and plenty of time to find them!

From Stanton in Peak head S signed Birchover at top of hill, and pull in on R after ¾ mile at 53.1628, -1.6398. Walk W to the Andle Stone, from here the circle is 200 metres to the SW in the woods. Can also be approached from the S through Birchover from visiting Nine Stones Close (see entry). Nine Ladies is best visited from the road E out of Stanton in Peak to Stanton Lees: pull off R at 53.1739, -1.6326 and follow the path SE.

53.1617, -1.6454, SK238628, DE4 2LR

7 MINNING LOW CAIRN
BALLIDON

Mining Low Hill wears its ring of trees like a giant natural crown that can be seen for miles around – it is visible from Arbor Low (see entry). Once up the hill, the trees offer shade for this often forgotten 36-by-44-metre Neolithic chambered tomb, the largest

in Derbyshire. Excavations did find the tomb had passageways with drystone walls leading into at least four burial chambers, and may have been reused during the Romano-British period. The capstones are still in place on two of the cists here, but sadly both grave goods and stones have been robbed from the site over the centuries. The plundering of the cairns, which may have been done by the Romans, has meant there is little known about Minning Low. It is a short diversion off the Midshires Way/High Peak Trail, which runs along the old Roman road from Buxton.

Take A5012 E from Newhaven for 2⅓ miles heading through the hamlet of Pikehall, turn R to Parwich and follow ¾ mile to Minning Low car park on R after a sharp R bend. Join the Midshires Way/High Peak Trail in the SE corner of the car park and walk just over ¾ mile, past the abandoned farming machinery where there is a permissive path up the hill to the cairn.

53.1124, -1.6887, SK209573, DE4 2PN

8 THOR'S CAVE
WETTON

The cathedral-like yawn of Thor's Cave 80 metres above the River Manifold has towered over the Dovedale landscape for many millennia. Carved out of the soft limestone rock by fast-flowing waters of a distant time, there have been signs of Thor's Cave and the adjacent Fissure Cavern being visited since the Late Palaeolithic. It is likely these earliest wanderers were hunting parties, stopping for the night out of reach of roaming predatory animals below. A Neolithic polished basalt axe has also been found here with a crouched burial, suggesting this may have been a site of ritual worship. The presence of a Bronze Age hearth, along with beads and flints, may also suggest semi-permanent settlers in the caves. Finds now on display in Derby and Sheffield Museum also show there were Iron Age and Roman visitors. An alternative name for the cavern is Hob Hurst's House, after a benign supernatural being said to live there. Tourists have been coming here since the Victorian era when the caves had their own station, served by the Leek and Manifold Light Railway (now the Manifold Way walking and cycling path). Adventurous children will simply love getting themselves dirty on the steep, sometimes muddy, climb up to the cave.

Follow minor lanes to Wetton and park in car park at SW corner of village. Take the path over the stile N and turn L onto Leek Road NW out of Wetton. Just after a gated track you will see a footpath sign and stile in the wall. Follow this path in W towards the Manifold Way and Valley, but after 500 metres, in trees, branch off L for the caves.

53.0916, -1.8545, SK098549, DE6 2AF

the footpath along the contour for 200 metres, and as it bends R take less defined footpath to Carl Wark. Bus routes 271 or 272 from Sheffield to Fox House at Hathersage Road stop, at the car park.

53.3293, -1.6106, SK260814, S11 7TY

9 CARL WARK
HATHERSAGE

This rocky outcrop or promontory on Hathersage Moor has the advantage of rocky gritstone cliffs on three of its sides, with a rampart topped with stones, built to protect the vulnerable fourth side. This defensive wall on the western rampart is remarkably intact and quite unique in this part of the country. Although the wall is considered to date to the Iron Age, making this is a possible Late Iron Age hillfort, it may be of Roman construction. Regardless of when it was built, it has baffled those studying it as to why it is here at all. There is after all Higger Tor just to the north, looming 64 metres higher than Carl Wark. Several footpaths crisscross the moors here, in an area very suited to travelling by foot.

Follow the A6187 SE from Hathersage for just over 2 miles. The road zigzags for a while before coming to a sharp R on a bridge; about 200 metres after this pull into car park on L. Take

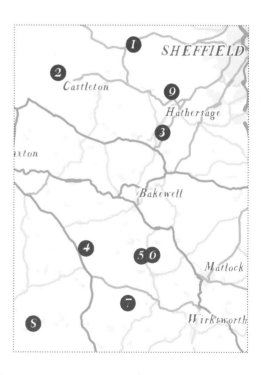

CHAPTER 15

WELSH BORDERS

During the Iron Age, it is thought the Welsh Borders were mostly under the rule of two tribes: the Cornovii and the Dobunni. The Cornovii would have dominated the land to the north in Shropshire, along with parts of all the surrounding counties. Little is known about the tribe but it has been postulated that their name means 'people of the horn', and they were said to worship a horned god known as Cernunnos, who was part man, part stag. The Dobunni have been described as a tribe of farmers and craftsmen, living largely in the southern borders. However, their territory may have spread further to include parts of Somerset, the Cotswolds and Wiltshire. All across this region, the influence of these tribes is written into the landscape; the Welsh Borders have some of the greatest concentrations of hillforts in the country. Some of the largest and best known include the magnificent Old Oswestry, British Camp and Wrekin Hillfort (52.6693, -2.5514). However, there are many lesser-known forts, almost too numerous to mention. These include the tucked away Burrow Hill, Titterstone Clee Hill with its wide reaching views (52.3975, -2.6025), Burry Ditches (52.4470, -2.9916) and Bach Camp (52.2383, -2.6650).

Findings at King Arthur's Cave in the Wye Valley show that settlement in this area, also called the Marches, had its roots much further back in prehistory than these Iron Age remains. People butchered animals in the cave, and it is likely that isolated hunter-gather communities existed all over the region. Although traces of these communities have long since been lost in the mists of time, the remains of later, Neolithic and Early Bronze Age culture are far more evident. The tomb we now known as Arthur's Stone stands, as it has for 5,000 years, overlooking the Herefordshire hills. We still don't know for certain why these early farmers built it or erected standing stones such as the Harold Stones, the Four Stones and the Devil's Ring and Finger. We can only ponder why these enigmatic monuments were put in place and feel humbled by the fact that there are still mysteries in this world.

I KING ARTHUR'S CAVE
MONMOUTH

The last inhabitant of King Arthur's Cave was a trapper named Slipper Jem, who made animal-skin slippers and sold them to tourists. As Jem was reported not to have washed for the entire 30 years he lived in the cave, it is unlikely he had any regular customers! Jem was one of a much longer line of cave dwellers here; archaeologists W.S. Symonds and Herbert Taylor in the late 19th and early 20th centuries found evidence of much, much earlier visitors to the site. Hidden deep in the back of the cave, they unearthed clues to a wilder past; flints were found alongside the bones of great Irish elk, woolly rhinos, lions and bison dating to a staggering 30,000 years ago. What is also remarkable is that people kept coming here: investigations have found evidence of hearths dating to 12,120 years ago, flints from the Mesolithic and Neolithic and artefacts from the Bronze Age, the Iron Age and Roman occupation (and perhaps beyond). In the woods to the north-west is Little Doward hillfort (51.8408, -2.6710) which in recent years has been cleared of trees. The Wye Valley is famous for activities and the more adventurous can take out a canoe down the river (wyedean.co.uk, 01600 890238) or head deeper underground and explore the many cave systems.

Take the A40 NE from Monmouth, take the L to Doward after about 2 miles, before the Symonds Yat roundabout. Follow signs for Crockers Ash L and then after ⅓ mile Doward R, and after nearly 1 mile park in the gravelled pull-in R on bend (51.8398, -2.6572) shortly before the Doward Park campsite. Follow track into the woods, head past the old quarry then L up to the cave.

51.8373, -2.6593, SO546156, HR9 6DU 🚶🥾🏕🌳🚡

2 HAROLD'S STONES
TRELLECH

Measuring 2.7, 3.7 and 4.6 metres tall apiece, these stones are well worth a stop when passing through the area. Their name derives from a tale in which King Harold used the stones to mark the ground where three rival Saxon chieftains fell, but we now know the stones are far older, dating back to the Late Neolithic or Early Bronze Age. Closer examination of the central stone shows enigmatic carved indentations or cup marks, which may have been rudimentary writing or even a calendar; they are said to face the midwinter sunset. Stories of a mythical giant known as Jack O'Church are rife in this part of the world, and another fable has it that during a stone-throwing contest between Jack and the Devil, the giant cast down the three stones to Trellech (which means town or homstead of the stones) from the top of Ysgyryd Fawr/The Skirrid some 14 miles away, thus getting one over on his satanic rival. Within the church at Trellech is a late-17th-century sundial with a Latin inscription of the fable and carvings of the three stones.

Park in Trellech village and follow the main street/B4293 S; around 150 metres after the bend R you will see the stones in a field to the L. Bus 65 from Monmouth to Trelleck opp primary school stop and walk S through village.

51.7426, -2.7267, SO499051, NP25 4PF 🚶🌳🥾

3 BRITISH CAMP
LITTLE MALVERN

Diarist John Evelyn said the view from this hillfort atop Herefordshire Beacon was 'one of the godliest vistas in England', and three centuries later newspaper travel sections still cite it as one of Britain's best views. It certainly is stunning, and it is not hard to see why Iron Age Britons chose to build here. The tiers of ramparts, successively built up throughout the latter Iron Age, stretch for over ½ mile north to south and enclose an area of 32 acres. At the height of occupation there could have been as many as 120 hut circles on the site, housing a substantial population. According to popular myth, Caractacus, chief of the Catuvellauni tribe, made his last stand here against the Romans, but Caer Caradoc also claims the honour. The writings of Tacitus record that despite losing, when he was sent to Rome as a prize Caractacus so impressed Emperor Claudius with his demeanour and eloquence, arguing that the fierceness of his fight brought greater glory to his vanquishers, that he and his family were spared death and lived in Rome. During the 12th century it is thought a Norman castle was built on the summit, on a smaller earthwork known as the Citadel. An easy walk to the south is a second hillfort owned by the National Trust, known as Midsummer Hill (52.0351, -2.3497).

Follow the A449 S from Little Malvern to the Malvern Hills Hotel and Restaurants (WR13 6DW, 01684 540690). Car park is opposite, follow signs from here to the fort. Train to Colwall Stone, about 2 miles' walk.

52.0581, -2.3516, SO759400, WR13 6DW 🚶🌳🥾

4 OLD OSWESTRY
OSWESTRY

Standing on a plateau 150 metres high, its multiple ramparts enclosing an area of over 40 acres, this is one of the largest and most impressive hillforts in the area. Arthurian folklore tells us that it was the birthplace of Guinevere. Flint axes and other tools have been found at the site, suggesting that the land was first used in the Neolithic, thousands of years before it became a hillfort. Traces of huts suggest it began life as an open settlement as far back as the Late Bronze Age before being enclosed by the two innermost ramparts around the 6th century BC. The unusual structure of the earthworks reflects its growth as a stronghold throughout the Iron Age, as it was expanded 200 years later with the addition of a third rampart, and then two more even later, before being abandoned during Roman times. Many have speculated on what the hollows and pits within the ramparts would have been used for, and archaeologist Barry Cunliffe suggests some of the larger enclosures would have been used as corrals for cattle. Although Old Oswestry is well visited, mostly by dog walkers, the centre of the fort and the surrounding paths are often deserted.

In Oswestry head N on the B5069 Beatrice Street, and turn L onto Llwyn Road opposite the iron footbridge, just after the traffic lights by the Morrisons supermarket. Follow over a round-about and out of town to a small car park on L after ½ mile and gate to the hillfort on R. Bus 2 from Wrexham or Gobowen station to Oswestry Jasmine Road stop and walk SW on Gobow-en Road, R onto Coppice Drive, L onto Wat's Drive, and R onto Llwyn Road, ¾ mile in all.

52.8712, -3.0512, SJ295310, SY11 1EW

5 MITCHELL'S FOLD
STONE CIRCLE
PRIEST WESTON

This stone circle is magnificently located on a hillside in a remote and breathtaking corner of Shropshire. It is a land rich in legend, with many tales attached to the stone circle itself. One, often told in verse, says that in a time of great famine an enchanted cow with ever-flowing milk was kept here and fed the locals, but a disgruntled local witch tried to sabotage the bewitched bovine by milking it into a sieve. Things did not go well for the crone as she was trapped within the circle, and as one verse version puts it 'The famine passed, but still this tale is in the country told/Of how the witch was starved to death, walled up in Mitchell's Fold.' In other versions she turned to stone and the circle was built around her petrified form; there was a claim that a stone once stood in the circle's centre. Throughout the area there are cairns, standing stones and even a proposed axe factory to the south of nearby Corndon Hill, and this may have been a very important area in the Neolithic and Early Bronze Age. There could have been ceremonial links with two other nearby stone circles; the Hoarstones to the NE at (52.5927, -2.9991) and the Whetstones, which are nothing more than a pile of stones (52.5711, -3.0280), after possibly being blown up in the 1860s. The nearby Miner's Arms (SY15 6DF, 01938 561352) has a welcoming atmosphere and local ales.

From Priest Weston take the lane E past the Miners' Arms (SY15 6DF, 01938 561352). Just over ½ mile after the pub follow a brown sign at a bend L up a track to the car park for the circle; from here walk on 300 metres to the stones. Bus 553 from Shrewsbury to White Grit opp junction stop and walk 1⅓ miles W towards Priest Weston to track.

52.5785, -3.0251, SO304983, SY15 6BY

6 BURROW HILL CAMP
HOPESAY

Birds of prey circle the open fields and deer hide in the bracken-filled ramparts of this long-forgotten hillfort, just off the long-distance path in a sleepy part of Shropshire. It consists of double rings of banks and ditches with an additional bank on the west side. Although much of the undergrowth has been cleared, it feels as if there hasn't been another soul at the site for years. The presence of two springs and a number of hut circles suggests this site may have been one of permanent residence. Nearby Hopesay Farm (opposite the church, SY7 8HA, 01588 660737) offers a chance to stay on an organic small-holding, or you can pop into their tearooms which periodically open throughout the year.

Park by the church in Hopesay village at (52.4442, -2.8994) and follow Shropshire Way NW from end of lane, keeping to path as it crosses field after tree used as a fence post. After ¾ mile enter corner of woods L via stile. Follow path down, then continue up and bear L around N of hill until you come to a gate to the fort. Bus 745 from Ludlow to Aston on Clun Kangaroo Inn stop and walk 1¼ miles N to Hopesay (signed over bridge).

52.4421, -2.9109, SO381830, SY7 8HA ⛹📷📺

7 DISCOED YEW
DISCOED

At least 2,000 years old, the Discoed Yew is arguably one of the oldest living things in the British Isles. Due to its wide girth it has been claimed to be anything up to 5,000 years old, making it a rival to the Fortingall Yew (see Mid-Scotland). What we see above ground is relatively young, most ancient growth having died centuries ago, for the longevity comes from the tree's ability to regenerate from much older roots underground. It is remarkable to think that all the ancient remains in the area could be contemporary with this yew's sapling years, including standing stones to the south at Kinnerton (52.2572, -3.1060) and the Four Stones (see entry). This is a beautiful area to explore: around a mile south-west of the tree, in aptly named Castlering Wood, are the remains of an Iron Age hill fort (52.2656, -3.0764) and another, known as Burfa Camp (52.2425, -3.0485) can be found over 2 miles due south, just off the Offa's Dyke path on Burfa Bank.

Follow the B4356 W of Presteigne and take the L turn towards Gumma Farm and Cascob as the road bends to the R. Continue to Discoed and park at the sign for the church just past the red postbox. Follow path up and to the L to the churchyard. There is another ancient and fascinatingly furrowed yew further along the lane at Cascob church (52.2903, -3.1174). Bus 463 from Kington to Presteigne, 2¾ miles' walk.

52.2761, -3.0617, SO276647, LD8 2NW ⛷

8 FOUR STONES
NEW RADNOR

Unlike the Nine Stones of Altarnun (see Mid-Cornwall) or the Seven Stones of Hordron Edge (see Peak District), the Four Stones site actually has exactly the four stones claimed. This arrangement, known as a four-poster type, is a bit of an oddity in this part of the world, with similar alignments more common in Scotland. The stones – one now recumbent – seem to mirror the outline of the Cambrian peaks around them, and we can only speculate whether or not this was intentional. There is a legend that the stones mark the falling place of four kings who fell in battle, and a more serious suggestion that they are the terminus of a cursus, or ceremonial walkway, similar to that at Stonehenge (see Wiltshire and Wessex). No one seems certain where the other end is; some suggest it could be anything between 1½ and 2¾ miles away. If correct, this would make it one of the longest prehistoric monuments in the country.

From New Radnor follow the A44 E towards Walton for 2 miles then turn L towards Kinnerton. Pass a white-sided stone farm-house and pull in on the L, avoiding obstructing the gates or lane. The stones are in the field opposite the farmhouse. Bus 463 from Kington to Kinnerton Village Hall stop. Walk S 1½ miles.

52.2402, -3.1059, SO245608, LD8 2RA ⛹🚲📺

 ## 9 ARTHUR'S STONE
BREDWARDINE

For centuries, those of an engineering persuasion have boggled over just how ancient people managed to maneouvre giant stones such as the large capstone of this ruined dolmen, estimated to weigh 25–40 tonnes. Thought to have been put in place over five-and-half millennia ago, in 3500BC, the capstone rests on top of nine sturdy uprights. It is the most northerly of all the recorded Cotswold-Severn-type tombs. Legends about the site and how it got its name vary, with some claiming it to be the burial place of Arthur himself, others that Arthur killed a giant here and the hollows were made by the giant's elbows as he fell. Just over a mile to the south east, beyond the bijoux Dorstone hillfort (52.0732, -2.9828), is the Cross Lodge Long Barrow (52.0695, -2.9755), contemporary with Arthur's Stone.

From The Red Lion in Bredwardine (HR3 6BU, 01981 500303) follow the B4352 S past red phone box. After ⅓ mile take R for Dorstone (signed unsuitable for heavy vehicles) and after about ¾ mile R onto Arthur's Stone Lane. Follow to the small English Heritage car park right next to the monument itself. Bus 448 from Hereford to Bredwardine Red Lion stop.

52.0823, -2.9953, SO318431, HR3 6AX

10 DEVIL'S RING &
FINGER NORTON–IN–HALES

This Neolithic or Early Bronze Age monument, once known as the Whirl Stones, is in desperate need of a bit of love. It lies on the edge of a farmer's field, near a tumble-down wall and a copse of gnarled trees. In all likelihood the stones were dragged there to make way for the plough. Despite its abandoned location, it is an enchanting relic. It consists of a grooved standing (or rather leaning) stone 1.8 metres high and a large circular stone 1.5 metres high and 1.9 metres wide. It has been argued that it might be the remains of a tomb, but equally it could have been part of a stone circle or perhaps even a processional walkway. As the stones are no longer in their original position and very little else has been found locally, we may never know their true purpose. They do, however, seem very reminiscent of other holed stones such as Mên-an-Tol (see West Penwith), which was thought to be part of a stone circle. It is a pleasant walk from Market Drayton and worth carrying on to the Hinds Head in Norton in Hales (TF9 4AT, 01630 695555) for a bite to eat.

In Norton in Hales head S on Main Road, take L onto Forge Lane where road bends R, and park by the houses. Follow lane around bend L, take next L and follow to R to farmhouse. Take L through yard (you should see a footpath sign) and follow line of wall up. Once approaching the brow of the hill look through the woods to your L; the farmer tolerates people hopping the wall through the copse as long as no crops are damaged.

52.9366, -2.4369, SJ707377, TF9 4QN

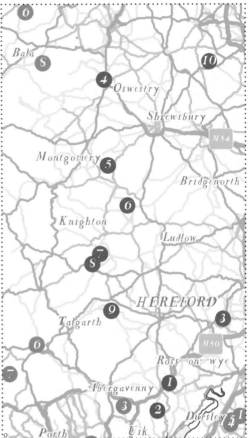

CHAPTER 16

BRECON &
SOUTH–EAST WALES

A young family run excitedly through the muddy banks towards a tidal island. It is late summer, and the children are desperate for the first taste of the wild raspberries that they know grow on its oak- and hazel-covered shores. The adults are equally driven, but on their minds are elderberries, which will later be made into a tart sauce to accompany a leg of wild venison sourced that morning. It is remarkable that this scene is so tangible, yet it happened over 6,000 years ago, in the Mesolithic era, or Middle Stone Age. We know so much about it because the family's footprints, along with clues to the fauna and flora, were preserved under the tidal mud in what is now the Severn Estuary, along the beach at Goldcliff just south of Newport.

Moving up the valleys from the coast and into the Brecon Beacons, the area is dominated by numerous hillforts. To the east of the region is the vast fortress of Y Gaer Fawr on Garn Goch. This wild and windswept hillside feels as though it is at the end of the earth, but in its day, this would have been a thriving hub for the local area and could have been both a strategic stronghold and an important place for trade. To this day, you can still find much of the stone material used for the walls high up on the ramparts of the fort. To the north of the National Park we find the magnificent Pen-y-Crug and down in the valleys to the south is Twmbarlwm. Both of these forts command panoramic views, worthy of the aching legs required to achieve their summits. However, my favourite fort in the region is a far more humble one: the modest little Coed y Bwnydd, just east of the National Park. It is a vastly different place, hidden away in a quiet pocket of woodland. During spring the enclosure in the centre of the fort is awash with wild flowers, and there really is nowhere like it in all of Wales.

1 GOLDCLIFF
NEWPORT

Back in the Mesolithic, the area in and around Goldcliff would have looked quite different. In what is now a tidal estuary stood an island covered in oak trees, surrounded by a dense reed swamp. Footprints of humans, reindeer and wild crane made over 6,000 years ago have been found hidden under the silty mud. Evidence of a series of temporary campsites along these prehistoric shores suggests they must have been prime hunting grounds. It seems inhabitants periodically returned to this area to butcher and cook animals such as deer and wild pig. This stretch of land has a slightly surreal feel to it, like a pocket of rural East Anglia or Kent deposited in the industrial Welsh heartland. The Severn here is at its most changeable, with millions of tonnes of water rushing in to cover the silty mud as the tide comes in. The footprints mostly lie undisturbed under the silt, and it is inadvisable to go paddling in the mud. For many, it is enough to come here knowing that so long ago people much like ourselves looked up at the same sky as we do today.

Follow Goldcliff Road E through Goldcliff and ½ mile after crossing the bridge, as the road bends L to pass a red-brick chapel, take the R turn signposted Seawall. Park at the end beyond the tearoom and follow the steps over the bank to the estuary. Bus 63 from Newport station to Goldcliff Farmers Arms stop.

51.5340, -2.8993, ST377820, NP18 2PH

2 TWMBARLWM HILLFORT
RISCA

Twmbarlwm (sometimes Twyn Barlwm) translates from Welsh as the hump, tump, pimple or even nipple and refers to the shape of the mound in the eastern side of the hillfort. Approaching the fort it does look like a breast rising up from the summit of the hill. It is a medieval motte, set inside the earlier banks, but as is usual with mounds and tumps such as this, folklore tells of a giant's burial accompanied by the obligatory treasure. Many have come in search of this treasure over the last 200 years, but each digging party is reported to have been attacked by bees! As one of the highest hills in the area, it is an effort to climb but on a clear day the views are simply staggering. From this vantage point, it is easy to see why the Silure tribe chose this as one of their defensive locations in their 25-year war

with Rome. There are numerous cycling and walking trails in the area, and it is a popular getaway for those in the surrounding towns.

From Risca & Pontymister station follow Park Road NW to Gelli Avenue, first R over tracks, becoming Elm Drive after crossing canal. Follow 1⅓ miles after canal then turn L onto road signed first for pedestrian and cycle access to Risca Community School and then for Upper Grippath Farm. Follow to end and turn L onto lane (Mountain Road), follow this 1¾ miles NW up hill to car park. Follow path W to summit. Bus 151 from Newport to Risca War Memorial stop; there are more direct paths through Cwmcarn Forest from here if walking or cycling, but they are steep and strenuous and a good OS map or phone mapping is advisable. Train to Risca and Pontymister, or Crosskeys if using alternative routes.

51.6273, -3.0979, ST240926, NP11 6FY

3 COED Y BWNYDD CAMP
BETTWS NEWYDD

Bettws Newydd is a sleepy Welsh village with a slate-roofed, whitewashed pub, a 2,000-year-old yew in the churchyard (51.7479, -2.9251) and the Iron Age hillfort of Coed y Bwnydd just to the north. The hillfort is a thickly wooded Iron Age relic, awash with bluebells and wild flowers during the spring. It has an other-worldly feel then, like a mythical realm quite detached from the lanes below. The inhabitants in their wattle-and-daub roundhouses would have been protected by a stone wall surrounding the fort. It seems it was in use around 400BC, but economic upheaval in the area forced the residents to move out sometime between 300BC and 200BC. The woodland was not always so dense here; even as recently as the early 19th century there would have been wide-reaching views across the Usk Valley and the Monmouthshire landscape. Back in the village churchyard just over ½ mile to the south, the oldest of three ancient yews is contorted like a melting waxwork on one side and has a cavelike yawn large enough to get into around the other, with a new, younger trunk inside. Its exact age is unknown but it is at least 2,000 years old and very possibly older.

Parking is limited in the village, so park at fort and walk back for the yew. Heading N the village take the R after Black Bear Inn (NP15 1JN, 01873 880701), opposite the well. Take first L and after about ⅓ mile you will see a pull-in with a National Trust sign and info board. Hillfort is up a path behind this.

51.756, -2.9201, SO365068, NP15 1JS

4 TINKINSWOOD BURIAL CHAMBER ST NICHOLAS

The first thing that strikes you about Tinkinswood is the huge capstone: a single solid piece of rock over 9 metres long and estimated to weigh over 40 tonnes, it is arguably the largest in Britain. It must have been a monumental effort to move this single slab when the tomb was constructed. The bones of around 45 individuals were found within the tomb, of which 21 were women, 16 men and the rest children. Rather than being laid to rest as single skeletons, they were mixed together. This is a Cotswold-Severn type of tomb, with a characteristic open forecourt at one end of the earth-covered main body. It has been suggested the bones of individuals were left in the forecourt to be stripped of flesh by birds, animals and insects, before being placed within the tomb. According to legend, if you spend the night in the chamber on May eve, St John's Eve, or midwinter eve you will die, go mad or become a poet – perhaps challenges like this are why there are so many bards in Wales?

Take the A48 W from Cardiff to St Nicholas/Sain Nicolas and there turn L signposted Dyffryn, Tinkinswood and St Lythans at the traffic lights. After about ½ mile pull in R (51.4531, -3.3045) and follow signs. Bus X2 from Cardiff to St Nicholas.

51.4513, -3.3081, ST092733, CF5 6ST 🏷🏕🚶

5 ST LYTHANS BURIAL CHAMBER DYFFRYN

Like its close neighbour at Tinkinswood (see entry), this chambered long barrow would once have been covered in earth. It may have also had a forecourt and features similar to Tinkinswood, but these have long since vanished. Very little is known about the tomb other than that it was certainly in use 5,000–6,000 years ago, during the Neolithic. The high placing of the stone makes it possible to take a picture of the setting sun within the dolmen itself. Locally it is also called Gwal-y-Filiast, the kennel of the greyhound bitch, and folklore has it that the capstone spins around three times on Midsummer's Eve before going down to bathe in the River Waycock. Set in accessible pasture (known as the Accursed Field, as it is said no crop will grow there) it makes a pleasant stop on a circular route

taking in Tinkinswood, St Lythans village, the Horse & Jockey pub in Twyn-yr-Odyn (CF5 6BG, 02920 670410), and St Nicholas village.

From St Nicholas/Sain Nicolas on A48 carry on past Tinkinswood and Dyffryn Gardens to T-junction, turn L, and park by the side of the road when you see the Cadw brown sign. Bus X2 from Cardiff to St Nicholas stop.

51.4425, -3.2949, ST100723, CF5 6SW 🏷🏕🚶

6 PEN—Y—CRUG HILLFORT BRECON

The multiple ramparts of this hillfort have been softened by age and appear as ripples in the earth emanating outwards from the central point, but at one time they would not have looked so appealing, especially to an invading army. They would have been protected with stone and wood, providing a formidable defence to this impressive stronghold. It seems this fort would have been somewhat self-sufficient, as stock pens and granaries, along with dwellings in the form of roundhouses, stood behind the defences. At just under 1½ miles from the centre of Brecon town, the fort is very accessible, yet once at the summit you have the sense of being miles from anywhere. If approaching from the town you pass Maen-du well (51.9569, -3.3999), with its 18th-century stone housing; this once supplied the nearby town with water.

From the centre of Brecon take the B4520/Pendre N past the cathedral. Close to the edge of town, just after Pendre Close and postbox on R, take unsigned L into housing estate and then immediately R. Follow this road as it curves L round the top of the estate and park in the car park just past the mini-roundabout, before no entry signs. Follow the signed footpath N to the well then walk up the fainter footpath to the summit; ¾ mile, 20 minutes' strenuous walk. Bus routes to Brecon from most major towns in South Wales.

51.9627, -3.4140, SO029303, LD3 9PN 🏷🏕🌳🚲🚶

7 MAEN LLIA
YSTRADFELLTE

This large, lonely monolith has stood on the desolate moors high in the Brecon Beacons for millennia. As with so many stones in the area, there are stories of Maen Llia coming to life and drinking in the nearby river. For many stones this is a yearly ritual, but this one is far thirstier, as it is said it heads for a drink nightly before the cock crows (at sunset, the pointed shadow creeping toward the river does resemble a tongue). Over 3.5 metres tall and nearly 3 metres wide, but less than a metre thick, the stone resembles a Neolithic hand axe to some eyes. As it marks an important route through the hills, it may be that axe traders first erected Maen Llia to mark their path. Later the Romans used this route through the hills, and there is evidence of a Roman road passing by the monolith, along with a camp in the hills that is now obscured by trees.

In Ystradfellte take the road N past the New Inn (CF44 9JE, 01639 721014). Continue on this road for just under 4 miles. There is a pull-in here on the R (51.8607, -3.5644), the stone is in the field over the stile.

51.8608, -3.5637, SN924191, LD3 8SU

8 CARREG BICA
NEATH

Also called Maen Bredwan or the Hoat Stone, this is a huge Neolithic standing stone in the hills north of Neath. At 4.3 metres it is about as tall as a double-decker bus, and towers above the majority of the megaliths in Wales. Legend has it that the stone rises up every Easter to take a drink in the Neath River, and local traditions also tell of local children racing to the stone every Easter – perhaps to catch it making its way down the hill? We will never really know if these stories keep alive a long-lost religious rite or important ritual attached to the stone. There is a chalk mound just off the track, a few metres from the stone, which is thought to be a burial cairn. Both cairn and stone are in an unashamedly beautiful part of South Wales, worthy of an afternoon spent exploring.

In Neath take A474/Penywern Road N, then L fork signed Bryncoch onto Main Road, and L signed Longford opposite school onto Tyn-Yr-Heol Road. Pass Bryncoch Inn (SA10 7EB, 01639 633472), turn R at roundabout and follow road across the river to a T-junction and turn R. Shortly after take L where road bends R to park at small car park almost immediately on R (51.6841, -3.8275). Walk on up road around bend to R to farm, and then follow forestry track up hill. At the crossroads take the highest track straight in front. Follow as it horseshoes round a rocky outcrop to the top of the hill and the stone should slowly come into view. A map or phone mapping is helpful. Train to Skewen; on foot there is a bridleway up from Drumau Road (51.6652, -3.8437), which is 1½ miles of strenuous walk.

51.6793, -3.8456, SS724994, SA10 7BJ

9 GARN GOCH HILLFORTS
LLANDEILO

High in the hills surrounding the Towy Valley and along remote country lanes stand the twin hillforts of Y Gaer Fach and Y Gaer Fawr. The second of the two is a colossal structure, enclosing an area of nearly 28 acres, and 2,500 years ago would have had walls 10 metres high and 5 metres thick lined with stone slabs; much of the material of the walls still lies around the summit. When the fort was operational, it would have been a meeting place for the surrounding population, and several hundred people lived within the huge stone walls. The panoramic views from the top would have allowed the occupants to keep watch over the valley below, guarding against any invaders. There were eight separate entrances, which may have once been roofed; remains of one with its upright slabs can still be seen on the southern side of the fort. There is a massive stone cairn dating from either the Neolithic or the Bronze Age within the ramparts, which suggests the site was in use long before it was appropriated by Iron Age people.

In Bethlehem village follow the road SW past the village hall/ post office out of village, then at the large 3-storey farm house just after bridge take the L signed unsuitable for heavy vehicles (there is a signed turn in Bethlehem suitable for all vehicles). Follow the lane up to a T-junction and turn R. Take next L to car park just over cattle grid and follow footpath to forts; 20 minutes' strenuous walk to summit. Trains to Llangadog and walk W through Felindre to Bethlehem, 4½ miles.

51.9018, -3.9049, SN690243, SA19 6YY 🚶🏔️♿🚶♿

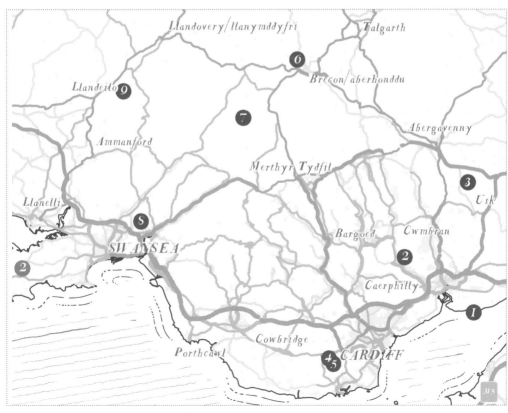

CHAPTER 1:

PEMBROKESHIRE
& MID-WALES

*A*s forecast, the rain started off as a steady drizzle, which my host assured me was good weather for West Wales. We set off with her three children in tow, one of them in a backpack carrier and two under-tens walking. The weather slowly began to worsen, and we found ourselves in a thick fog, unable to see more than a metre ahead of us. Through a mixture of luck, memory and navigational skills, a large, rocky outcrop came into view like a giant iceberg emerging from a sea mist. Here amongst the bog and gorse of the Preseli hills, I found myself looking at one of the suggested quarry sites of the Stonehenge bluestones. The kids went from downhearted and sluggish to positively animated, excitedly exploring the stones for signs of those ancient quarrymen. As I stood there in my failed waterproofs, soaked to the skin, I imagined the effort of moving multiple stones 140 miles away to Wiltshire. Even today, moving the stones would prove a tricky undertaking but almost 5,000 years ago, without any motorised transport, no crane and no metal tools, it must have been a monumentally (if you pardon the pun) daunting task.

The ancient world still echoes through the landscape of Wales, with the roots of its very language anchored firmly in pre-Roman Britain. That pre-literate society left its mark with tombs and standing stones across the hills and valleys. The most iconic of these are the table-like dolmen or cromlechs, tombs consisting of a massive capstone supported by equally giant upright vertical megaliths. These aren't unique to Wales, also turning up in Cornwall and Northern France. Very similar structures, from differing cultures, can also be found as far away as Korea, India, the Middle East and even Africa. However, in West Wales, we find some of the best-preserved of these ancient monuments, such as Carn Llidi near St Davids (51.9034, -5.2938), or Ffyst Samson (51.9730, -5.0489) with its delicately balanced capstone. Such is the profusion of ancient tombs here that in an ordinary residential estate on the outskirts of Newport in Pembrokeshire we find the well-preserved dolmen of Carreg Coetan (52.0185, -4.8282).

I GWAL Y FILIAST OR ARTHUR'S TABLE LLANBOIDY

Sources vary here but the name Gwal y Filiast can translate as the 'greyhound bitch's kennel' or her 'lair', or may be a corruption of the far more sinister 'lair of the wolves'. It is not to be confused with Gwal y Filiast used for St Lythans burial chamber in the Vale of Glamorgan (see Brecon & East Wales). Both sites may have been given the same name because they resemble ancient kennels, or could it have been that wolves once made their dens between these Stone Age slabs? It has been suggested that the dolmen's position tucked away in its beech woodland clearing was chosen because it was where the flow of the Afon Taf, towards which the capstone 'points', turns into rapids. The sites of dolmens were probably already important places, sacred to those who erected the monuments, so this could have been somewhere to honour the dead or a meeting place long before the dolmen was built here. Additional stones scattered around the site suggest that either there was another monument here or the dolmen was a more extensive structure at some point in history.

Heading S from Llanglydwen village take first R. Park in lay-by immediately on R and walk on. Take track R through gate towards Penpontbren, past a house and through woodland, taking L fork past stone gatepost, to dolmen. Bus 221 Carmarthen to Llanglydwen Penybont Inn stop, no Sunday service.

51.8991, -4.6605, SN170256, SA34 0TU

2 ARTHUR'S STONE OR MAEN CETI REYNOLDSTON

The wind can whip this area of coast, gusting across the peninsula and over the 5-mile sandstone ridge of Cefn Bryn. From the top of the ridge, the wide-open sky echoes the expansive moor below, while golden beaches glisten in the sun and the blues and purples of distant hills frame the scene. It is a truly magnificent place to be and one where 4,500 years ago Neolithic builders chose to build the portal dolmen we now call Arthur's Stone. Rather than raising the colossal capstone, some 4 metres long by over 2 metres high and wide, into place, the ancient builders of this site are thought to have dug away the ground surrounding it, inserting the uprights as they removed the earth. People have been coming to see the tomb for centuries; during the 15th

century, Henry VII's troops visited the site on their way to Bosworth Field. By the Victorian era it was recognised as an attraction and became one of the first sites to be protected under the Ancient Monuments Act of 1882.

From Llanrhidian head E on B4271 for 1 mile. As road bends L, turn R to Cefn Bryn/Port Eynon. Follow 1¾ miles to large, makeshift car park on R, and follow path N for 500m. Bus 116 from Swansea to Llanrhidian Turn stop, no Sunday service.

51.5935, -4.1793, SS491905, SA3 1EL

3 PAVILAND CAVE PORT EYNON

Around 33,000 years ago, a man some 25–30 years old was laid to rest at the back of Goat's Hole or Paviland Cave in the Gower Peninsula. As if to prefigure the gravestones of today, his burial was marked with a large mammoth skull. He was adorned with a shell necklace and mammoth bone rings, thought to be bracelets, and his bones were stained with red ochre, a naturally occurring form of iron oxide. It has been speculated whether this was part of a deliberate burial ritual or dye seeping through from red cloth. When he was found in 1823, he was misidentified as a Roman prostitute (due to the jewellery and Creationist dating), and thanks to his red-stained bones, was dubbed The Red Lady of Paviland. Although this man is the earliest known burial in Europe, anatomically speaking, he was little different from you or me. In contrast, the land he lived in would have been wholly unfamiliar to us. With differing sea levels, the area in front of the cave would not have been coastline but a vast plain full of mammoths, rhinos, herds of deer and antelopes. The man was in good health when he died, with a diet of foraged roots and berries along with fish and animal meat. The cave can only be reached at low tide, so it is best to begin your approach as the tide is retreating; a badly timed visit can result in an unplanned overnight stay in the cave.

Approaching Port Eynon on the A4118, in Scurlage turn R onto B4247 towards Rhossili. Remain on road for 1⅓ miles to park on R by the National Trust sign just before Pilton Green (51.5614, -4.2423). Follow the footpath opposite SW to the sea until you reach a rock valley. Climb down this to the shore, then climb up to the cave (not suitable for those with limited mobility). Always check tide times, ideally approach as the tide is going out. Bus 118 from Swansea to Pilton Green stop.

51.5496, -4.2546, SS437858, SA3 1PE

4 KING'S QUOIT DOLMEN
MANORBIER

There is just enough room for two or three people to shelter from a brief summer downpour under the 4.5-metre by 2.7-metre capstone of this burial chamber. Perched on the cliff path, it offers a sweeping view out to sea and down to the sandy beach at Manorbier Bay, and it is likely that it was positioned to be visible from both the land and the sea. Much of the structure is below ground, and it is thought to have been built in the same way as Arthur's Stone (see entry), by removing the surrounding earth rather than raising the capstone. These are known as earth-fast monuments, as part of the structure is held up by an earth support. The beaches along this stretch of coast are some of the most unspoiled in Wales – the coastal caverns of Skrinkle Haven and the spectacular rock arches of Draught Sands further to the east are highly recommended.

Take the road west out of Manorbier for a little under ½ mile, past the large Manorbier car park, until you come to a pull-in on the L (51.6444, -4.8053). Cross the beach and follow the cliff path around to the dolmen, 10 minutes moderate walk. Bus 349 from Tenby to Manorbier House stop.

51.6408, -4.8060, SS059972, SA70 7SZ

5 GOLDEN ROAD QUARRIES & BEDD ARTHUR CRYMYCH

A high trail called the Golden Road runs along the spine of the Mynydd Preseli. When the weather is clear you can see as far as Snowdon and out westward across the sea to Ireland. Many believe that this high ridgeway would have been an important walking route 5,000 years ago, similar to the Ridgeway path running through the Wessex Downs. On such high paths, Neolithic hunters or traders could avoid the woods and undulating terrain below and easily spot bandits or enemies as they approached. A number of rocky outcrops just off the path lay claim to being the quarry sites of the bluestone inner circle at Stonehenge (see Wiltshire & Wessex). The latest research points to Carn Goedog (51.9652, -4.7249), on a path diverting ½ mile north-west off the main path (close to the centre) as the main quarry. Prior to this, the larger outcrop Carn Menyn or Butter Rock (51.9594, -4.7025) was believed to be the source of the stones. Between these two sites is the horseshoe- or oval-shaped ritual site of Bedd Arthur, consisting of 13 upright and two fallen stones. This stone monument is said to echo the earliest stone formation at Stonehenge. It is even possible that the bluestone inner circle there was erected here first and stood for hundreds of years before being moved 140 miles east to its present home in Wiltshire.

The B4329 heads NW through countryside into the hills, until 1½ miles after the crossroads with the B4313, due N of Rosebush there is a car park R (51.9547, -4.8029). The Golden Road starts here and ends on a minor road 1 mile W of Crymych (51.9659, -4.6720); the best way to walk it is to park a car at each end. Navigation equipment is essential to locate the sites, as many of the paths are hard to find.

51.9595, -4.7223, SN134325, SA66 7RB

6 PENTRE IFAN
BRYNBERIAN

Although now called Pentre Ifan, which translates as Ivan's Village, this site once bore the Arthurian name of Arthur's Quoit, like many other sites in Pembrokeshire. Very much the poster child for dolmens or cromlechs in Wales, it is highly popular, and you can expect to take your turn for photographs unless you visit very early in the day. However, this does not take away from the sheer majesty of the structure. Put simply, Pentre Ifan is a Neolithic marvel; the 5-metre-long capstone is poised almost magically on the near pen-point tips of its equally large uprights. In its heyday, it would have been an even more impressive structure, covered in a mound of earth 40 metres long and 17 metres wide, with a large semicircular forecourt. Like other similar tombs, it would have been a communal burial site used by the local community, and the bones of the dead may have been taken out and placed back into the tomb a number of times before the inner chamber was eventually sealed off. Local folklore tells of fairies visiting the site wearing red caps and soldier's clothes.

Signed at the Brynberian turning on B4329, between Rosebush and Crosswell. Follow the road through Brynberian, past the turning L for chapel, and for 1⅓ miles further, around bends, to a large layby on L. Follow footpath at end to the dolmen.

51.9989, -4.7700, SN099370, SA41 3TZ

7 PENDINASLOCHDYN
LLANGRANNOG

The views from this hillfort – also spelled Pendinas Lochtyn – are simply spectacular. Seabirds struggle against the winds that blast in over the Irish Sea, and out in the distance the rain can be seen breaking. Parasol and field mushrooms grow near the summit. The remains of a roundhouse dating to the Romano-British period were found here, but a much earlier Bronze Age post-hole suggests there had been a settlement on this site long before the coming of the Romans, and it overlooks two Iron Age sites. Out to sea is the Ynys Lochtyn promontory fort with its towering rocky cliffs, which must have been impenetrable in its day; the actual 'ynis' or island beyond may also once have been part of it. On private land to the southwest overlooking Llangrannog is another hillfort where a number of house platforms were found; it is not marked on maps, but the banks are visible from below (52.1573, -4.4700, due south of The Ship/Y Llong, SA44 6SL, 01239 654510).

Park in the car park on B4334 on the outskirts of Llangrannog (52.1568, -4.4627) then walk L towards village, L again towards sea, then fork R up hill at white cottage called Pengwern, up the dead end road. Follow this around and at the fork take the R to the top of the hillfort (tarmacked and suitable for pushchairs, although there are stiles) or the L to walk around the base. Bus 552 from Cardigan to Llangrannog stop.

52.1662, -4.4640, SN315548, SA44 6SF

8 BUWCH A'R LLO
PONTERWYD

The twin Buwch a'r Llo stones stand in splendid isolation on the edge of marshland on a long and winding single-track road between Penrhyn-coch and Ponterwyd. Although they are locally known as the Cow and Calf, it takes quite a stretch of the imagination to see anything bovine in these two stones. Archaeology professor Simon Timberlake puts forward an argument that the stones mark the line of a trackway dating to the Bronze Age. The proposed route runs from the west coast along the Afon Clarach through Penrhyn-coch up to the hills around the peak of Plynlimon. Following this on the map, it is possible to pass several Bronze Age sites such as the

Disgwylfa Fach Standing Stone (52.4361, -3.8678) and a nearby stone row, and the Y Garnedd cairns or barrows and well-preserved Hirnant Circle kerbed cairn (52.4392, -3.8355). Some of these would have been contemporary with the stones at Buwch a'r Llo, whilst others, most notably the cairns, were added later. Perhaps what started as a trade route in the Neolithic or Early Bronze Age became a significant path of pilgrimage?

On the A44 head E from Goginan to Ponterwyd. Turn L just before the village, after the garage. Continue 1¼ miles and take L fork signed Penrhyn-coch. After 1½ miles, find stones on roadside.

52.4336, -3.8798, SN723834, SY23 3JY

9 GORS FAWR
MYNACHLOG—DDU

In the shadow of the Preselis with their famous bluestone quarries along the Golden Road (see entry) lies the stone circle of Gors Fawr or 'the great marsh'. Expansive in size, yet lowly in stature, it is an oddity in this part of the country as the stones are graded with the tallest standing on the south side, in the direction of the sun. Aubrey Burl comments that this bears a similarity to the Fernworthy Stone Circle (see Dartmoor), but doubts that a shared culture existed between the two areas. To my mind, the discovery of a Preseli-made mace head at Sidmouth on the Devon coast, a little over a day's walk from Fernworthy, points towards a trade route, possibly partly by sea, running between South Wales and Devon. There is a pair of megaliths by the circle, one of which is called the dream stone, and I was told by a local man that when you sit against this stone, your dreams come true. However, my dreams were never given a chance as his wife hogged the stone the entire length of my visit!

In Crymych follow A478 S past leisure centre, turning R at Haulfan holiday cottage towards Mynachlog-ddu. Continue for 4¼ miles, and 1 mile beyond Mynachlog-ddu park in pull-in on R by gate. Follow path W to the stone circle. Bus 642 from Clarbeston Road station to Mynachlog-ddu stop, Fridays only.

51.9315, -4.7146, SN134293, SA66 7SE

10 CARREG SAMSON
ABERCASTLE

Legend has it that Welsh-born Saint Samson of Dol, one of the seven founder saints of Brittany, placed the giant capstone of Carreg Sampson atop its uprights with nothing more than his little finger. Throughout history the engineering skills of prehistoric people have been set aside in favour of stories such as this, in which saints, giants, the Devil or even aliens created these ancient monuments. There is no doubt that moving these great slabs of stone would have been a tremendous effort, and it goes to show how cohesive and sophisticated the society that managed it must have been. Crop marks found just 500 metres to the south by aerial reconnaissance in 2013 show that the dolmen would have stood on the edge of farmland, just as it does today. An earlier excavation of the site in 1968 uncovered evidence of four more stones besides the present six uprights. One of these would have supported the chamber stones and the others suggest there may have been a passage leading out to the north-west. Carreg Sampson makes an excellent diversion off this section of the Wales Coast Path.

Park in the seafront car park at Abercastle and follow the coast path around the headland until you are directed uphill. Bus 404 from Fishguard to Abercastle Mill stop.

51.9583, -5.1329, SM848335, SA62 5AN

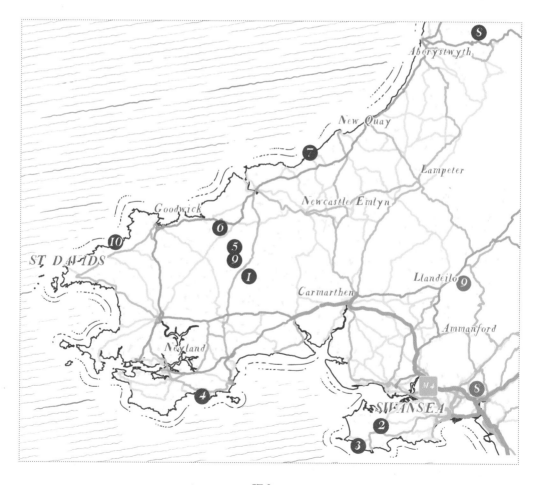

CHAPTER 18

NORTH WALES & ANGLESEY

*T*he mountainous region of North Wales is a place where beauty and industry have been entwined since prehistory. As far back as 1800BC people were mining for malachite, the raw material to smelt into copper, beneath the rocky limestone headland now known as Great Orme. They had nothing more than bone and stone tools to chip away at the rock, lighting their way using tallow candles. It is staggering to think they chiselled out 5 miles of tunnels through the bare rock with such limited tools. Now a popular tourist attraction, the mine lay hidden underground until 1987, when its discovery shifted back the first date of metal mining in Britain by 2,000 years.

Down the coast is the unspoilt Llyn Peninsula. This was the site of an even earlier industry during the Neolithic, 3650–3050BC, when stone axes were carved on the slopes of Mynydd Rhiw for use in the local area. To the east of the mine, close to the hamlet of Treheli, there is a burial chamber that may have been a place of worship for those who carved the axes (52.8275, -4.6171). Further south Mynydd y Graig (52.8149, -4.6308) is one of many Iron Age hillforts on the peninsula; others include Garn Bentyrch (52.9501, -4.3464), Carn Fadrun (52.8866, -4.5578) and Tre'r Ceiri, all further inland to the north-east.

Axes from the extinct volcano at Graiglwyd (54.2597.-3.9210) were so prized they were distributed across the country from Yorkshire to Wiltshire. The active quarry makes this a difficult place to visit but there are countless other sites of interest in the area including the Druid's Circle (53.2258, -3.9157). Another area thick with ancient remains can be reached from the car park (53.2258, -3.9177) to the south of towering Foel Lwyd, and west of whitewashed Rowen YHA (LL32 8YW, 0345 3719038).

Islands have been holy places since pre-Christian times. The Isle of Mona, or Anglesey as it is now known, is famous for being the last refuge of the druids. Around the year AD 57, in an effort to control the unruly tribes of the west, the general Suetonius Paulinus sent troops on horseback across the Menai Strait in flat-bottomed boats. There he led a massacre, with men, women and children indiscriminately cut down by the Roman sword, and sacred oak groves, temples and altars destroyed in an act we would today describe as ethnic cleansing. To get an idea of how these 'unruly tribes' lived you can visit a reproduction of an Iron Age roundhouse at Llynnon Mill (53.3374, -4.4931) or the remains of the Din Lligwy settlement close to the Lligwy Burial Chamber. Elsewhere on the island the double monoliths Penrhosfeilw (53.2957, -4.6618) and the Llanfechell Triangle (53.3966, -4.4620) are well worth exploring.

I LLIGWY BURIAL CHAMBER
MOELFRE

The capstone of Lligwy Burial Chamber is thought to be one of the largest in Britain. Estimated to weigh 25 tonnes, it is a slab of pavement stone 5.9 metres long, 5.2 metres wide and just over 1 metre thick. This colossal stone lies over eight uprights in an astonishing example of Late Neolithic engineering – it is also sometimes called King Arthur's Quoit, with the usual legendary origins. It would have served the local community, and contained the bones of up to 30 men, women and children along with animal bones, mussel shells and both Neolithic and Bronze Age pottery. The capstone may not have always been so prominently on show, but covered in earth like Bryn Celli Ddu (see entry); weathering of its surface, however, causes some to question this. A short walk from the chamber, hidden amongst a grove of trees, is the Din Lligwy settlement. Here are the remains of two Iron Age roundhouses, along with farm buildings dating to the Romano-British era. Findings suggest that metal was worked here.

At the Paradwys Chapel roundabout of the A5052/A5108, SW from Moelfre take road NW signed Traeth Lligwy / Din Lligwy. Follow ½ mile ignoring gateways on bends – a kissing gate and noticeboard for the dolmen will appear on L, but drive on 300 metres for more parking by gate to Lligwy Chapel and walk back. Bus 62 from Menai Bridge to Llanallgo Capel Paradwys stop.

53.3499, -4.2526, SH501860, LL72 8NH

2 BRYN CELLI DDU
LLANFAIR PWLLGWYNGYLL

Reminiscent of a hobbit hole, the Bryn Celli Ddu chambered tomb is perhaps the most recognisable of all the archaeological remains that can be found on Anglesey. The name is said to mean 'the hill in the dark grove'. The tomb was built into an existing henge monument dating back to 3000BC, the Late Neolithic, which had a stone circle within its banks and may have replaced an earlier wooden circle. It has been suggested that the builders of the tomb wilfully destroyed the stone circle as they appropriated the site, in a conflict between their new belief system and the existing one. Inside the tomb is a stone pillar the size of a fully grown person, which resembles a petrified tree trunk but is in fact blueschist, a stone formed under immense pressure. Similar free-standing pillars are found in Brittany, and it has been interpreted as a guardian or protector of the tomb.

Take the A4080 Brynsiencyn Road SW from Llanfair Pwllgwyngyll and after 2 miles turn R. Car park is on L after just over ½ mile. Cross road and walk back a short way to follow footpath signs up and to L. Train to Llanfairpwll station, 2¾ miles' walk.

53.2077, -4.2361, SH507701, LL61 6EQ

4 CAPEL GARMON
CAPEL GARMON

During the spring the meadowland surrounding the Capel Garmon burial chamber, high above the river Conwy, fills with newborn bleating lambs. In full view of Snowdon and its surrounding hills, this is a very rare example of a Cotswold-Severn burial chamber in North Wales. As the name might suggest, these tombs are mainly found to the south in the area around the Severn River and throughout the Cotswolds. There is a chance that they were more common in the region and this is the last remaining example, but it is more likely that those who constructed this tomb came from the south or sought their inspiration there. The tomb has a forecourt and a false entrance, where pieces of quartz and Beaker pottery were found. Only one of the capstones remains, but this is enough to give a sense of atmosphere and fun for any children exploring the tomb. Although it was built towards the end of the Neolithic, Beaker pottery found here suggests the site was still in use long after its construction. During the 19th century the farmer of the land used the tomb as a stable for his horses.

From the White Horse Inn (LL26 0RW) in Capel Garmon, head S uphill to the second footpath sign on R (53.0784, -3.7657). Follow this about ⅓ mile to the burial chamber. Bus 68B from Llanrwst to Capel Garmon St Garmon's Church stop, Tuesdays and Fridays only.

53.0729, -3.7658, SH818543, LL26 0RR 🚶🏃

3 TRE'R CEIRI
LLANAELHAEARN

Few prehistoric sites are as tangible or complete as Tre'r Ceiri. You can still clearly see the footings of the 150 stone huts, which were densely packed inside a perimeter wall 3.5 metres high and up to 4.5 metres thick. The circles date to the earlier Iron Age, while the D-shaped and rectangular remains are later Roman constructions; thought to have been built around 200BC in the territory of the Ordovices tribe, it remained occupied for 500–600 years, until the late Roman period around the 4th century AD. Many of the gateways are also still clearly visible, including the parallel walls of the large south-western entrance. Another entrance marks the route to a spring and it is likely that the 400 or so inhabitants of the fort used this water for themselves and their animals. All over the site, there are stones with a concave dip, resembling the saddle querns used during the Neolithic, but evidence suggests the town was a communal summer centre for stock farmers who used the pastures below, rather than arable farmers with a need to grind corn.

Follow the A499 past Trefor S to Llanalhaiarn roundabout and take the B4417 SW. After 1 mile park at long layby R (52.9707, -4.4155). Walk on 20 metres to footpath by wall R, follow directions on message board to summit; 20 minutes' very strenuous walk. Bus 12 from Pwllheli to Llanaelhaearn Rivals Inn stop.

52.9745, -4.4240, SH373446, LL54 5BB 🏃🏃🚶

5 BRYN CADER FANER
EISINGRUG

A stone crown sits atop a remote Welsh hill in an area with very few signs of habitation. Far below, a distant steam train chugs through the valley but up here there is only the sound of the wind blowing through the stones. A local guide poetically translates the name of the site as 'the fortress of waves on the hill' but it is also interpreted as 'the hill of the throne with the flag'. Neither Victorian treasure hunters nor target practice by the British Army prior to the Second World War even dented the majesty of this isolated Bronze Age cairn. The stones would have once stood upright, but have slipped outwards giving the monument its iconic crown shape. There may originally have been as many as twice the number of uprights. Today the centre of the cairn is little more than a mass of stones, but an Inventory of the Ancient Monuments of Wales from the 1920s describes the remains of an 8ft by 5ft central chamber with a 2ft-high stone 'resembling the gables of the house'.

From Ynys head E on A496, then just after crossing river turn R onto B4573 towards Harlech. First L signed unsuitable for HGVs, to Eisingrug. Follow L round pond in village then R up signed dead end. Remain on this road until you can go no further, by Tynybwlch farm gates, and park. Follow the road to the R for just under a mile E. taking fork S where it turns N, then turn L on the Taith Ardudwy way. Keep to this path for another mile NW until you read a rocky outcrop, after this, the monument should be visible. It is a good 2-mile walk often through boggy ground. Train to Tygwyn; 1¾ miles walk to farm gates.

52.8982, -4.0113, SH648353, LL47 6YB

6 BRENIG 51
CERRIGYDRUDION

Some 4,000 years ago, a community living in the valleys below the Denbigh Moors solemnly made their way uphill to a place sacred to them. There they placed the bodies of an adult and a child close to the centre of a circular platform of level stones, 22–23 metres in diameter, with an open centre and edged by 26 small upright stones, below a towering totem pole. The bodies were cremated, placed in a pot and buried with a bone-handled dagger. This platform cairn was reconstructed in the 1970s and remains one of the most unusual Bronze Age sites in Britain. There is an archaeological trail clearly marked on noticeboards that leads you around the eastern side of the man-made Llyn Brenig Reservoir and takes in sites from the Middle Ages along with several Bronze Age burial cairns, including Brenig 51. Hen harriers are often seen flying over the still waters of the reservoir, and the nearby Clocaenog Forest is one of the few places in Wales to spot the elusive red squirrel.

From Cerrigydrudion village on the A5, follow the B4501 N for 6⅓ miles and then turn R to stay on B4501 for a little under 2 miles more. At a road narrowing sign, turn R and follow ¾ mile to the car park R at fork. Archaeological trail is signed, with markers to the site, but it does help to have a map and compass or phone mapping.

53.0967, -3.5101, SH989565, LL16 5RN

7 BACHWEN BURIAL CHAMBER CLYNNOG FAWR

Looking out over the Irish Sea from the middle of a meadow, close to the historic village of Clynnog Fawr, sits the table-like cromlech or dolmen known as the Bachwen Burial Chamber. Behind it rises the distinctive peak of Gyrn Goch, flanked by the towering bulk of Gyrn Ddu and Bwlch Mawr. The chamber is unusual in that over 100 cup marks cover the surface of the enormous capstone, giving it the texture of a giant crispbread. Traces of a possible mound imply the capstone would have been covered in soil, so these markings raise questions. Had the stone been used for a different purpose prior to the construction of the tomb? Were the markings ceremonial, made when the dead were interred within the tomb? Or were they made long after the tomb had fallen out of use, by people quite different from those who built the monument? Whatever the reason behind the markings, they are rare examples of their kind in this part of the country. During the 1870s the owner of the land nearly destroyed the monument because he was fed up with visitors crossing his fields.

Leave the A499 to drive into Clynnog Fawr and park by the church. Walk back S to the main road and cross at bollards to the driveway towards the holiday cottages. Follow, turning L towards the coast, then L again along path, and after about 350 metres you will see the dolmen on your L. Bus 12 from Pwllheli to Clynnog Smithy stop.

53.0189, -4.3752, SH407494, LL54 5NH

8 MOEL TY–UCHAF
LLANDRILLO

In his book *Standing with Stones*, photographer and writer Rupert Soskin says this cairn circle 'is one of those sites which is very hard to leave'. The name translates as the 'highest house on the bare hill' or the 'high bare hill', an altogether fitting name for almost perfectly placed stones, high on the Berwyn Hills. The 41 stones are rather small, no more than metre high at most, with some as little as 20cm. Gaps in the circle are likely to be from stone robbing, though there may have been an entrance on the south-west side, and it is thought there was a central cist but this has unfortunately also gone. An outlying stone around 15 metres to the north-east may be associated. After a steep but rewarding climb from the village below, the circle will only come into view when you are almost upon it. It is the best-preserved example of several monuments on and around the summit: down the hill from the circle is a cairn made almost entirely from white quartz, and there are four cists and another cairn in the area.

From the B4401 in Llandrillo park in the car park just E of the river. Walk away from bridge and turn R after war memorial. Keep on the track, staying broadly NE and uphill through four gates and over two fords until you reach the crossways with a copse of conifers ahead. Turn R here and the cairn circle is on the L near the top of the hill. Bus T3 Barmouth – Wrexham to Llandrillo Dudley Arms stop.

52.9236, -3.4054, SJ056371, LL21 0SP

CHAPTER 19

YORKSHIRE

Giggleswick Scar

*O*n a crisp autumn day in 3000BC a man dressed in winter sheepskins came to the end of an arduous week-long walk and stood in awe, simply staring at one of three vast henge circles, coated in white gypsum to reflect the sun. Or perhaps it was night, with a clear sky perfectly framed above by the great banks of the henge – under moonlight, it must have looked as if the stars had come down to earth. Perhaps it was the midwinter sunset, and the atmosphere was pregnant with anticipation as a crowd walked through a timber avenue into the most southerly of the henges, a murmur growing as the light faded, before the congregation joyfully erupted in unison as a row of three stars came into view overhead – the circles they stood in reflected in the sky.

We cannot say exactly what took place 5,000 years ago in the great mile-long earthwork of Thornborough Henges, but we do know it must have been magnificent. This has been called the Stonehenge of the north, and not without good reason. It seems that Yorkshire, once the biggest single county in the country, has always liked to do things on a grand scale. The Rudston Monolith is likely the largest standing stone in Britain, and towers nearly 2 metres taller than the biggest stone in Scotland, Clach an Trushal on Lewis.

Although undoubtedly ancient, Thornborough Henges isn't the oldest evidence of human ritual activity in Yorkshire. More than 20 antler headdresses dating to the Mesolithic over 10,000 years ago were found on the banks of the River Hertford at Star Carr, due south from Seamer (54.2144, -0.4252). It has been argued that these may have been used for hunting, but television presenter and archaeologist Neil Oliver points out that they would have weighed down the hunter and suggests they must have been part of a ceremonial costume. Along with the famous antler headwear, the site yielded 180 barbed bone points, evidence of a wide range of hunted animals and the bones of the earliest domestic dog found in Britain.

Heading even further back into Yorkshire's past, to a time when large mammals outnumbered humans, hunter-gatherers would have roamed the hills and dales in search of food. A band of these hunters came to rest in Kinsey Cave, high in Giggleswick Scar (54.0865, -2.3013) at the end of the last ice age over 11,000 years ago. They left behind flakes of flint and the point of a reindeer antler, which may have been used as part of a weapon. The caves of Yorkshire continued to be visited into the Neolithic, when some of Britain's first farmers placed a body in Kinsey Cave and a man's skull in nearby Sewell's Cave (54.0946, -2.3306). Dating to around 3900BC, these were some of the first burials in Yorkshire, and marked a new era where people started to subsist on cereal crops rather than wild game and foraged plants.

1 RUDSTON MONOLITH
RUDSTON

Standing in a village churchyard is a colossal tapered megalith, over 8 metres in height and about 1 metre by 1.75 metres on the sides. It is the largest standing stone in the country and estimated to weigh 26–40 tonnes; it is hard to know because excavations suggest it may go down as far as it rises up. Considering the size and weight, it is remarkable to think it was carried here from Cayton Bay, some 10 miles to the north, near Scarborough. The stone would not have stood alone in the landscape: there are two long barrows in the area and the stone marks the convergent point of three cursus monuments, large dug-out ceremonial walkways, that were found following an aerial survey of the region. Rudston Beacon, a nearby hill, may also have been sacred to those who erected the monolith, and the two may have been somehow ceremonially linked. Further barrows can be found on top of the hill and in the surrounding landscape. Local legend tells us the Devil hurled the Rudston Monolith at the church but was such a poor shot that he missed it completely. Given that the church dates to around AD 1100 and the monolith dates to around 2500BC in the Neolithic or Bronze Age, it seems the Devil missed by at least 3,600 years!

From the A164 around Bridlington take the B1253 W signposted for Rudston and the crematorium, and follow for 4½ miles. Turn L into Rudston; the monolith is signposted. Parking is tricky on School Lane, where the churchyard is, so aim to park on streets to the S. Bus 124 from Bridlington to Rudston, Wednesdays and Thursdays only.

54.0938, -0.3225, TA098677, YO25 4UY

2 THE DEVIL'S ARROWS
BOROUGHBRIDGE

The Devil's Arrows is the modern name for three large, Late Neolithic or Early Bronze Age monoliths forming a row 174m long. The tallest stone, at a height of nearly 7 metres, is the most southerly, with the following two 6.7 metres and 5.5 metres high. With so few stones in the row we cannot tell if it was intended that they descend in height, as with the Down Tor stone row (see Dartmoor) or the Gors Fawr stone circle (see Pembroke). There may have once been as many as

seven stones in the row; we know one was dragged off to make a bridge sometime in the 17th century. They were quarried at Knaresborough over 6 miles away, and would have formed part of a broader Thornborough-Hutton Moor ritual complex. It is likely they were placed on the site of a ford crossing the river. The Devil is said to have fired the 'arrows' from Howe Hill in an attempt to destroy Aldborough, but missed – he has a reputation as a poor shot in Yorkshire, it seems. Two of the stones are in the open field and the third lies across the road to the south within its own garden. To get a sense of the scale of the stones, just lean against one of them and look up!

Leave the A1(M) at junction 48, to join A168 heading N parallel with motorway. At the roundabout take the third exit into Boroughbridge, then first L to park at small pull-in R. Bus 21 from Knaresborough to Boroughbridge opp high school stop and walk N on Horsefair to turn L into Roecliffe Lane to stones; no Sunday service.

54.0932, -1.4037, SE390665, YO51 9LR

3 THORNBOROUGH HENGES
WEST TANFIELD

A much-forgotten and sadly neglected gem of the Yorkshire countryside, Thornborough consists of three huge, 240-metre diameter henge circles, spaced about 1,000 paces apart from centre to centre; the three are not quite in a straight line, but mirror the stars of Orion's Belt in their setting. It is one small part of a larger ritual landscape that included six henges, a cursus and as many as 28 barrows. Two of the three henges are left open to the elements, and the third, the best preserved and most atmospheric, lies hidden in a dense patch of woodland. To experience the henge circles it is best to walk into the very middle of one on a clear night and lie down. The world beyond the banks is cut off, and all you can see is the dome of the night sky. This may have been the intention of those who built this monument around 5,000 years ago: a way of creating an enclosed space for ceremony, much like later cathedrals. Archaeological evidence shows the presence of a timber walkway leading to the southern circle, which would have only enhanced the sensory experience. The banks of the central henge appear to have been coated in gypsum, which would have glowed in the moonlight. Henges such as these were in use between 3000BC and 2000BC, but as little has been found within them, at present we know little about them. Thornborough Henge recently passed back into the ownership of Yorkshire Council.

In West Tanfield turn E off the A6108 past playing field and village store on L to a mini-roundabout on the edge of the village, and turn L for Nosterfield. After ½ mile park in the

Nosterfield Nature Reserve car park on L. For the north circle walk 300 metres further along road to crossroads, turn L and continue for 300 metres; the henge is through a gap in the wall near the end of the trees on the R. For the other henges turn R at the crossroads on track/green land path, L when this meets the road, and walk for 300 metres to centre henge on L and broad field leading to south henge on R.

54.2101, -1.5639, SE285794, DL8 2QZ

4 AGRA MOOR STONES
MASHAM

Agra Moor is a wild place of heather, rock, bog and dark, winding, stony streams in the beautiful, hidden Vale of Costerdale. Despite being rich in archaeological remains, Agra Moor is seldom found on any tourist trail – or indeed in archaeological records! Lost amid the undergrowth on the western side of aptly named Brown Beck is a 1.4-metre-high monolith sometimes called the Brown Beck Standing Stone (54.2375, -1.7944). The presence of more stones sinking into the moorland peat has led many to believe this may have once been a stone circle or burial cairn. In the West Agra Plantation woods to the south-east of the stone are a number of fascinating stone carvings, which date from the Late Neolithic and into the Bronze Age. One is a cup mark surrounded by a series of concentric rings that are bisected by two narrow parallel lines on one side (54.2313 -1.7829). This labyrinth design occurs again and again throughout the ancient world, from ancient Egypt through Spain and Italy to Scandinavia and India. As the rock carvings are on private land, a certain amount of discretion should be exercised.

From Masham follow Fearby Road 3⅓ miles through Fearby and Healey, then take fork R for Colsterdale. After a further 1¼ miles park in Gollinglith Foot car park L. Follow Six Dales Trail opposite N for 580 metres, past farm, and take path (dotted road/track on OS maps) through trees to the W. Remain on this path as it runs L and along the edge of the wood. Before you reach Slipstone Crags look for the rock art on L of path. The standing stone is in the moors to the N and can only be reached by returning to the car park, heading W on road to footpath N (54.2280, -1.7819), following it up Slipstone Crags, and crossing L over valley once ground levels out.

54.2306, -1.7831, SE141817, HG4 4NL

5 TWELVE APOSTLES
ILKLEY

Just off the Dales Way Link foot-and-cycle path, 381 metres up on Ilkley Moor, the Twelve Apostles Circle is one of many prehistoric remains on the moor. For once the numbering is correct, and this 16-metre diameter circle is indeed made up of a dozen stones of local millstone grit. However, it is thought originally there would have been as many as 20; the small mound at the centre of the circle may also be the remains of a cist or burial. On older maps it was simply referred to as 'circle of stones' and has gone by the names of the Druid's Chair, the Druidical Dial and Druidical Circle. Although it can be a boggy walk to the stones, and the depressions around them often become pools, it is worth the 20–30-minute trek across the moors to see them. The Grubstones, a double-ringed stone circle sometimes referred to as an enclosure, stands 800 metres to the south-east of the Twelve Apostles, off the Millennium Way footpath on Burley Moor (53.8984, -1.7938). Across the north and western edges of Ilkley Moor there are around 40 carved stones, including the Idol Stone (53.9094, -1.7995) and the Swastika Stone, named long before the Nazi era (53.9187, -1.8559), west from the White Wells car park on the Millennium Way.

In Ilkley follow Wells Road S from the B6382 at the station to White Wells car park at the end. Walk S on the track until you reach White Wells Spa Cottage. Join the Dales Way Link Path here, heading SE then S for 1⅓ miles to the stone circle. Train to Ilkley station, 2 miles' walk in all.

53.9016, -1.8094, SE126450, LS29 9JS

6 MIDDLETON MOOR
ROCK ART LANGBAR

Rock art in Britain is generally thought to date from Late Neolithic into the Bronze Age around 3,500 to 6,000 years ago but some believe they may be later, Iron Age markings. Like so much of prehistory, it remains an enigma – no one quite knows who made the marks or why. We do know they were often made in places with wide-reaching views, such as on rocky outcrops or high, exposed areas. They fit into several categories, but the most common are cup and ring marks, so

named because they are cup-like indentations often surrounded by rings. Where pick marks can still be seen, they indicate pointed and chisel-like tools possibly of metal, bone or antler were used. On Middleton these marks are dotted all over the moor, and it is worth spending some time exploring all the rocks. There are some excellent examples clustered near the path between Badgers Gate and Delves Ridge, just south of Dryas Dike (53.9574, -1.8349).

Follow A59 E from Bolton Bridge and turn R for Beamsley just after crossing river. At Beamsley take L towards Langbar. Remain on the road 2¾ miles, through Langbar, until it curves hard to the R and you come to a car park L just after a cattle grid. Walk back to the bend and take the footpath on the R. After 820 metres this will join a path heading N; remain on this path for another 800 metres to the first concentration of stones.

53.9593, -1.8373, SE107514, LS29 0ET

7 VICTORIA CAVE
SETTLE

Yorkshire was far warmer 130,000 years ago than it is today, and supported a thriving population of large mammals. Hippos, rhinos and elephants all thrived in these fertile planes before coming to rest in Victoria Cave, perhaps dragged there by spotted hyenas making it their lair. The first people didn't come to the region until thousands of years later, following the retreat of the last ice age. It appears hunters used the caves sometime around 12,500BC, leaving a decorated rod made of reindeer antler as evidence. About the same time, a scavenging wild animal dragged in the head of a horse that had been butchered by humans, to finish its meal undisturbed. As time moved on, so did the sophistication of the people who lived in the area around Langcliffe Scar. In 1870 a double-barbed harpoon head was found in the caves, which was dated to around 10,900BC. Considering the vast timescale of this cave, the pottery and coins dating to the Romano-British period found here feel like they were left almost yesterday. An Iron Age burial was also found at nearby Jubilee Cave (54.0854, -2.2496).

Head N from Settle on B6478, after ½ mile take R to Langcliffe village and park in car park at far end of Main Street opposite church. Follow the road NE for 700 metres and join the Pennine Bridleway where road bends L. After 800 metres go through the gate then turn R along the wall on path to cave (for Jubilee Cave go straight on after gate). Train to Settle, 1⅓ miles walk to Langcliffe, or Giggleswick 2 miles.

54.0810, -2.2487, SD838650, BD24 9RD 🚶🅿️⛺️

8 YOCKENTHWAITE
CIRCLE YOCKENTHWAITE

This is a small but perfectly formed stone circle, on the banks of the River Wharfe in the Langstrothdale Valley, deep in the Yorkshire Dales. In the Late Neolithic the river would have been an important route through an area that would have been difficult to navigate through on foot. The stones are quite tiny, around 40cm in height; there are larger stones nearby, but it is not clear that these are part of the monument. A slight impression in the centre has led some to believe this may not be a stone circle but a burial cairn with a missing stone cist. The stones lie just off the long-distance path called A Pennine Journey, which follows the route taken by Alfred Wainwright in the 1930s. The name of the moor and stone circle may sound familiar, as it was used for an intellectually challenged troll in the 1990s children's puppet series *Roger and the Rottentrolls*.

Follow the B6160 N up Wharfedale Valley to Buckden. Here fork L signposted Hubberholme, remain on road 3 miles to tiny Yockenthwaite hamlet. Park in the pull-in L when you see the bridge. Cross bridge and take Dales Way L ⅓ mile to stone circle.

54.2099, -2.1552, SD899793, BD23 5JH 🚶🅿️⛺️

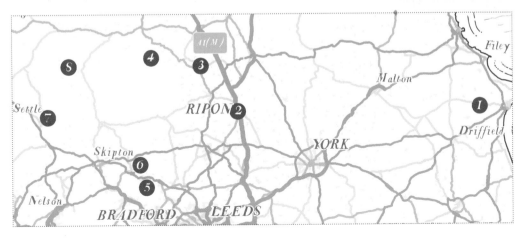

CHAPTER 20
LAKE DISTRICT

I *had* seen Castlerigg in pictures many times and always meant to visit. It looked beautiful and remote from my home in the south, but little prepared me for quite how stunning this stone circle really is. Early in the morning, long before the crowds arrived, the air was fresh and still, and, although it was during a very warm spell of weather the heat of the day hadn't yet hit. A man who had arrived even earlier with his two husky dogs said with eyes full of wonder, 'I can't get over it – this is such an amazing place'. Few would dispute his words: it is a perfect site, like a grand open-air cathedral on a plateau surrounded by vast mountains. The other stone circles of the Lake District have their own, no less impressive charm. There is the remote, hard-to-get-to Sunkenkirk, described by antiquarian Aubrey Burl as 'the loveliest of all the circles in North West Europe'. To the east of Ullswater the prehistoric remains on windswept Moor Divock punctuate a fine day of walking, with the Cockpit Stone Circle being the perfect point for a sandwich and a rest for the legs. To the south of the region you'll find the Birkrigg Druid's Circle with views out to seemingly endless sandbanks – once more highlighting how important the landscape was in the construction of these ancient monuments.

As you approach the summit of Pike of Stickle you can understand how sacred a place this could have been to the people of the Late Stone Age. Climbing the Langdales from the east, you reach a plateau of land between the peaks of Harrison Stickle, Pike of Stickle and Loft Crag. Up here, it feels as if you have reached some mythical home of the gods; Cumbria's answer to Mount Olympus. It is a place very much removed from the everyday world: birds fly below you, the clouds can drop to shroud the area in fine mist and on a clear day it is just as awe-inspiring as it must have been 5,500 years ago. Up here, near to England's highest mountain, Neolithic man carved beautiful stone axes from the green-flecked local rock. When polished, these axes were things of beauty, highly sought-after items, as much a status symbol as the latest smartphone or Swiss watch. Around a thousand years before the Egyptians began building their pyramids, these axes were traded throughout Britain and even across the seas to Ireland and France.

1 CASTLERIGG STONE CIRCLE KESWICK

With a backdrop of Cumbrian peaks, including Helvellyn and High Seat, Castlerigg is arguably the most recognisable prehistoric construction in Northern England. Dating from the Neolithic era sometime around 3000–3200BC, it may also be the earliest stone circle in Europe. Three stone axes were found here, and its position marks a clear route along the Borrowdale Valley from the Langdale axe factories in the south (see entry), which you can still walk on the modern Cumbria Way footpath. It is very likely that this was an important meeting point for Neolithic axe traders on their way to the coast. The circle has a strange quirk: if you stand in its centre looking out at the stones, you can match each with a corresponding peak or outcrop behind. It is impossible to say if this is a coincidence or a genuine attempt to line up the hills with the stones of the circle. Perhaps this was an early form or mapping, or a ceremonial representation of the surrounding landscape? To avoid the crowds, visit early in the morning; at this time of day the air is fresh and the site can be enjoyed at its best.

Take the Penrith Road/A591 E from Keswick. Bare L at Woodside B&B, following signs to Castlerigg along the A591. Take 1st R to follow road for ¾ mile until you see layby parking on L. Circle is on R. Bus 555 Lancaster–Keswick to Castlerigg Castle Lane stop and walk N on Castle Lane, 10 minutes.

54.6028, -3.0984, NY291236, CA12 4RN

2 MAYBURGH HENGE EAMONT BRIDGE

Around 4,500 years ago, the banks of a vast henge began to take shape at Mayburgh. Locals gathered stones from the nearby river and piled them up to 6.5 metres high to form a large ring over 100 metres in diameter. It must have been a huge undertaking, as it is thought over 20,000 tonnes of stone were used. Although we see construction as a commercial or personal venture today, it is likely that the building of the henge was as an important communal, even ceremonial task. Four megaliths up to 3 metres high were placed in the centre, with two pairs to mark the entrances. Of these, only one remains, slightly off-

centre and dominating views of the hills behind. The eastern entrance faces nearby King Arthur's Round Table, so named as the king is said to have enjoyed a jousting tournament here (54.6482, -2.7404); together with the now-destroyed Little Round Table 200 metres further south, there may have been a triad of rings as at Thornborough Henges (see Yorkshire). It is a good place to stretch your legs on a long journey up the motorway. A pleasant walk can be plotted to Brougham Castle (54.6540, -2.7191) and the adjacent Roman fort bank via Eamont Bridge. The Narrowbar Café in Penrith (CA11 7SR, 01768 891417) provides vegetarian and vegan choices and is well worth a stop.

Leave M5 at junction 40 to take A66 E for Scotch Corner and Brough. At next roundabout take fourth exit for A6 to Shap. Cross bridge then turn R at mini-roundabout and cross onto B5320 for Mayburgh Henge, past King Arthur's Round Table (no parking here). Take first R signed dead-end and pull into parking bay on L at bend. Follow the road on to signed gate. Bus 508 Penrith–Kendal to Eamont Bridge The Beehive stop.

54.6487, -2.7466, NY519284, CA10 2BX

3 FOUR STONES HILL HAWESWATER

The more megalithic sites you visit, the more you find that the number of stones in the name has no relationship to the number actually there! Four Stones Hill is a prime example, with its pair of megaliths overlooking the long expanse of Haweswater. Although the reservoir is the product of the Haweswater Dam, the views from the stones would have always been dramatic. They could have been marker posts, showing a route through this part of the Lake District or the edge of a territory. However, the number of burial cairns in the area argues against these theories, nodding more towards this being an area associated with funeral rituals. Perhaps the dead were brought through the stones to mark their transition from this life to the next?

In Burnbanks at the E end of Haweswater Reservoir park near red phone box (54.5378, -2.7618). Follow the lane to R of phone box up to the northern path around the reservoir 1½ miles, turning R away from the water after crossing The Forces waterfalls (54.5316, -2.7953). After ¼ mile cross a bridge to R and ascend track for ⅓ mile.

54.5393, -2.7889, NY489164, CA10 2RW

4 THE COCKPIT STONE CIRCLE MOOR DIVOCK

On a high moorland plateau amid the hills, the stones of the Cockpit Circle have been exposed for millennia to the winds blasting across this desolate Cumbrian landscape. It is a contradictory place, both barren and full of life, bleak and beautiful. It is uncertain if this was a true stone circle or a ring cairn, but given its age it is likely its use changed across time. The stones lie off a well-used path frequented by walkers and mountain bikers who continue on to nearby Ullswater. Walking along this path, the number of monuments suggests it was also a well-trodden route some 3,000 years ago during the Bronze Age. There are several piles of stones gathered up from farmland when this area was first worked thousands of years ago, known as clearance cairns. When you descend, the nearby village of Askham has two heated outdoor pools for all ages to enjoy.

From Askham village take Helton Road S, and as you enter Helton after 1 mile take the R lane uphill. When this splits take the R fork, signed dead-end, for about 1 mile and park by side of the road L opposite track (54.5857, -2.7796). Walk NW on track/path for a little under a mile then turn L and follow path for ⅓ mile.

54.5926, -2.8021, NY482222, CA10 2QA

5 LANGDALE AXE FACTORY GREAT LANGDALE

Nearly a third of all the highly prized stone axes we have from the Neolithic in Britain were made of Langdale hornstone, or greenstone, found near the summits of Pike of Stickle and Harrison Stickle. This is not only a difficult place to get to but also a dangerous place to be. The axes were distributed throughout Britain and Ireland, with rare examples discovered as far away as continental Europe. With such a wide distribution of axes, some showing no sign of actual use, it is thought that their purposes must have been ceremonial as well as practical. Many were retrieved from peat bogs, discarded thousands of years ago in a ceremony long forgotten. Archaeologist and broadcaster Neil Oliver believes that the site of the Langdale axe factory, high up in the mountains of the Lake District, may have been as important as the axes themselves. Perhaps the hardship of getting there, the beauty of the mountains, the danger of the slopes all added to the value of the axes. Such was the industry on this site that rejected axes can still be found to this day on the scree slope, east of the summit of Pike of Stickle. The slope is not for the faint-hearted or the inexperienced, as the loose scree is perilous. For those willing and able to brave this treacherous place, a man-made cave can be found around 50–100 metres down the scree slope. It is possible this was a Neolithic construction, built for the axe carvers to retreat into when the weather turned on the mountainside.

Follow the B5343 from Skelwith Bridge towards Great Langdale. About 2½ miles beyond Elterwater pull into the National Trust New Dungeon Ghyll car park. The path begins to the L of the toilets at the back of the car park; keep to the L fork as path splits and follow up to summit (take a map and navigation aids). Scree slope is roughly 100 metres to the E of the summit of Pike of Stickle. Scree can be unpredictable and dangerous, only attempt if you are competent to do so. Bus 516 from Kendal to Dungeon Ghyll.

54.4563, -3.1199, NY274073, LA22 9JU

6 SUNKENKIRK STONE CIRCLE SWINSIDE

Part of the charm of this circle is its relative inaccessibility. It lies in an unpopulated part of Cumbria at the end of

long, winding farmer's track and can only be reached on foot or by bicycle. It may well be the best-preserved stone circle in Northern England, with 55 of its original 60 or so porphyritic slate pillars still standing. The midwinter sunrise is said to shine between the two entrance or portal stones. It seems that the site was home to some very early landscaping, as digs in the early 20th century suggest the ground was levelled before the circle was built. The name Sunkenkirk has arisen from an old story that when a church was being built on the site the Devil came and pushed it underground at night, making the stone circle.

From Millom take the A5093 N for just over 2 miles through The Green and turn R onto the A595 towards Broughton. After ½ mile, at Broadgate turn L and park at the small layby L after another ½ mile, before the road forks at Cragg Hall (54.2738, -3.2589). Take the L fork on foot and walk for just under a mile (20 minutes, moderate). The stone circle is on private land but next to the footpath.

54.2825, -3.2737, SD171881, LA18 5LD 🚶🚴⛰️

7 BIRKRIGG DRUID'S CIRCLE BARDSEA

The Druid's Circle consists of two concentric circles and is the only one of its kind in Cumbria. The inner circle, which pokes its head above the bracken in the warmer months, comprises 12 small limestone pillars and is the most complete of the two. Archaeological evidence suggests the central area would have been paved or cobbled, and below this cobbled surface five cremations have been discovered. It is likely the outer ring, much of which can lie all but completely hidden in the bracken, was a retaining kerb for a platform rather than a second stone circle. The area continued to be important throughout the Bronze and Iron Ages, with the remains of cairns and settlements found further up Birkrigg Common. The circle is in an unusual part of Cumbria: rather than mountains and lakes dominating here, the surreal expanse of Ulverston Sands and Morecambe Bay stretch out seemingly to infinity. On a windy day the clouds above whizz by and the sun casts its dancing light across the stones. A picturesque village of whitewashed houses and a towering church spire sit below the circle to the north-east, completing this contradictory landscape.

From Ulverston follow A5087 S along coast, passing car park for Ulverston Sands and R turns into Bardsea, to take R uphill just after entering trees. Follow ½ mile and park in pull-in on the R (54.1554, -3.0861). Take path through bracken R for 200 metres to circle. Bus 11 Barrow-in-Furness–Coniston to Bardsea Olde Mill stop, no Sunday service.

54.1566, -3.0850, SD292739, LA12 9RE 🚶🚴⛰️🚉

8 LONG MEG & HER DAUGHTERS LITTLE SALKED

With a backdrop of the rolling Cumbrian hills, this is the sixth-largest stone circle in Britain. The usual legends apply: Meg and her offspring received the traditional disproportionate punishment of being turned to stone for the heinous act of dancing on the Sabbath, and if you are able to count the same number of stones twice the curse will be lifted, and Meg and her daughters will go free. 'Meg' is the large, 3.4-metre megalith of local red sandstone standing outside the circle, in line with the midwinter sunset from the circle centre. It doesn't take much imagination to see her

cup-and-ring-marked 'eye' on the flat side, and the downturned mouth and nose on the adjacent, rougher side. She looks a little world-weary, which is perhaps not too surprising as she is 3,500-year-old mother of 59 stone children! Her daughters are mostly of a whitish-grey glacial erratic stone called rhyolite. A smaller stone circle called Little Meg, most likely a Bronze Age kerbed cairn, can be reached by following the path to the NE of the large circle before heading E along the edge of a field (54.7305, -2.6585). To the north is the Glassonby Stone Circle or ring cairn (54.7472, -2.6652). Little Salkeld Watermill nearby has delicious snacks and lunches (CA10 1NN, 01768 881523).

At Langwathby turn off A686 to take Salkeld Road N through Little Salkeld, following the road as it bends R, signposted Long Meg Druids Circle. Continue for ½ mile then turn L at cross-roads and follow road R to the circle – it passes through it, but there is a pull-in on R at the edge. Bus routes 137 (Thursdays) and 139 (Tuesdays) from Penrith to Little Salkeld stop. Lang-wathby station 3 miles, buses also stop here.

54.7281, -2.6673, NY571372, CA10 1NW

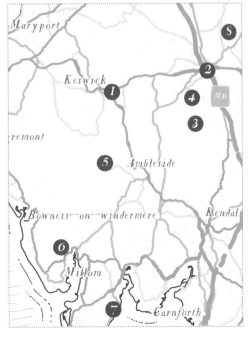

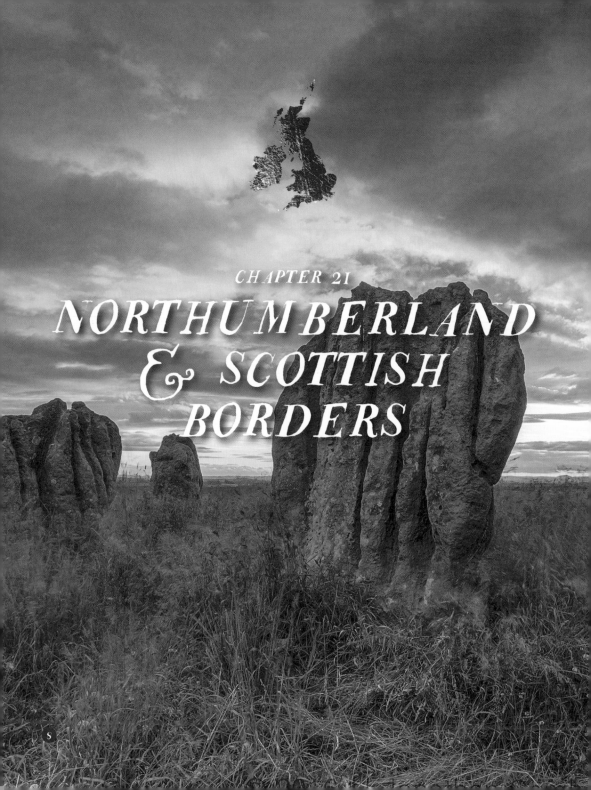

CHAPTER 21

NORTHUMBERLAND & SCOTTISH BORDERS

*T*his region not only boasts a disproportionately generous share of Neolithic and Bronze Age rock art – it also has some of the most beautifully located examples of this ancient enigma anywhere in Britain. There are currently estimated to be around 7,000 carvings across the British Isles, and 1,000 of them are found in Northumberland alone (compared with just 75 in Wales). Most of the rest are in Northern England and Scotland, with 750 also occurring in the Republic of Ireland. One theory suggests that the iconic cup and ring marks may have spread from a culture across the Irish Sea, and there are indeed similar examples at the great 5,000-year-old tomb of Newgrange in County Meath. However, it could also be that both were influenced by a culture from the Iberian Peninsula, where early examples of the markings can also be found. They have been interpreted in countless ways throughout history; in the 19th century people left milk out in the indentations for fairies to drink, hoping for good luck in return. They also believed that rainwater collected in the marks could heal all kinds of problems, from improving a woman's fertility to banishing eye ailments. These folk remedies have no relationship with the marks' original purpose, but with no written record, a whole range of theories have been put forward. It has been postulated that they could map settlements, mark tribal boundaries, represent rebirth, act as astronomical charts, commemorate the dead or even catch the blood of sacrifices. They are commonly found in places with uninterrupted views, often looking over rivers, leading some to believe they marked hunting ground or routes, or sources of water. The resemblance of the concentric circles to the ripples of a stone dropped into water encourages this aquatic association, and much of the rock art in North America is linked with a source of water. Lordenshaw, below Dove Crag in the Simonside Hills, has some of the most extensive examples of the markings, sharing its pre-eminence with the profusion at Roughting Linn (55.6241, -2.0271), close to a magical secluded waterfall. There are more scattered on Doddington Moor nearby.

1

2

3

3

1 TRESTLE CAIRN & FIVE STONES *JEDBURGH*

Numerous remains lie either side of the Dere Street Roman road in this remote part of the Scottish Borders. The positioning of the road so close to so many ancient remains is probably no coincidence, as it is thought to follow the route of a much more ancient track. When it was first used during the Neolithic, the route would have been a functional one, perhaps for trade or hunting, but it may have later taken on a spiritual aspect when the cairns and stone circle were in use. It could be seen as a path for the rites of the dead, similar to those found in Dartmoor. We will never know if the Romans chose this route for its convenience or as a show of power to keep the locals subdued. There are spectacular views of the mountains here, and if you stop for a moment you will hear the songs of countless birds ringing across the barren landscape.

From Jedburgh head S on A68, then 1¾ miles after Camptown take L towards Howman and Hindhope. Follow for 1¾ miles, continuing straight at the crossroads onto the smallest of the four roads. Park in the pull in R with information board for Penny-muir Roman camp before cattle grid (55.4219, -2.3890). Join the Dere Street path L to the NNW over stile just after cattle grid. Follow path for approx 1¼ miles, Trestle Cairn will be on the L through two gates. Continue for another ½ mile for Five Stones (or Stanes) circle on R (55.4450, -2.3925).

55.4383, -2.3938, NT751161, TD8 6NH

2 WODEN LAW HILLFORT *JEDBURGH*

It has been suggested that Woden Law was the stronghold of the Votadini tribe, whose territory stretched across north-east England and south-east Scotland. To the west of Woden Law, beyond the snaking silver line of Kale Water below, the land was occupied by the Selgovae tribe, and the fort may have been built as a show of power just as much as a defensive structure. Some suggest the Roman road was built here to separate the tribes from each other. Although they were not fully assimilated into the empire, the Votadini seemed to profit from the Roman occupation as a 'buffer' on the northern border, and by the 2nd century AD the fort was used by the Romans,

who built the complex of siegework banks here. The border forts of Yeavering Bell (55.5573, -2.1156) and Eildon Hill North (55.5867, -2.7083) and the more northern Traprain Law (55.9634, -2.6734) may also have been Votadini sites.

Follow directions for Trestle Cairn (see entry) to crossroads by Pennymuir Roman Camp but continue straight on over cattle grid. Follow road as it bends R, then at T-junction turn R signed Hindhope. After about a mile, on a bend with a road off R, park on verge to L. Walk on over cattle grid to take Dere Street L up and then where it branches head R up to the fort on the summit.

55.4062, -2.3684, NT768125, TD8 6NL

3 HETHPOOL STONE CIRCLE *WOOLER*

Below the great rocky outcrops of the Newton Tors, at the head of the College Valley in the northern Cheviots, the Hethpool Stone Circle stands – and lies – hidden in a lush green meadow. This is a much-ruined but very rare example of a Late Neolithic stone circle, once part of a double stone circle, both of a similar size. The southern one measures 61 by 42.7 metres, and the northern one, now largely buried, measured 60 by 45 metres. The landscape is full of archaeological remains, and towering far above the stones just to the south is the defended Iron Age settlement of Great Hetha. It is a very strenuous but highly rewarding climb of some 200 metres from the circle to the summit, where traces of Iron Age structures can still be found. A short walk down to the right is the neighbouring fort of Little Hetha, thought to date from the same era. Three further hillforts can be found to the NE; West Hill Camp (55.5590, -2.1458), St Gregory's Hill (55.5609, -2.1347) and the largest hillfort in Northumberland, Yeavering Bell (55.5573, -2.1156), where over 130 circular house foundations and platforms have been found inside the hillfort built around its two peaks.

From Wooler take the A697 NW to Akeld, turn L onto the B6351 signposted Kirknewton and Yetholm. Follow 3½ miles to Westnewton, here take L, then L again, following signs for Het-hpool, and follow the road for 1¾ miles to the car park L shortly after village, just past conifer plantations on both sides and over cattle grid (55.5458, -2.1698). Walk S on road to stones and continue past the trees to the footpath on R for Great Hetha.

55.5438, -2.1721, NT892278, NE71 6TW

4 THE GOATSTONES
STONEHAUGH

On a high ridge between the great rocky outcrop of Ravensheugh Crags and the Kielder Forest plantation, the Goatstones are a rare example of a four-poster stone circle on English soil. The name 'circle' is a little misleading here, as the four stones make up a 4m square – hence the name four-poster. In keeping with the 22 other examples of four-posters in England, it is on high ground, commanding views over this remote, beautiful part of the country. It is thought that there may have once been a burial cairn in the centre, possibly present before the stones. This four-poster is unique in that it is the only monument of its kind to bear cup marks on one of the four stones. Aubrey Burl suggests that its name could be a corruption of gyet stanes, meaning wayside stones, as it was near a known droveway. Today it is a short diversion off the Pennine Way, and only a short drive or an afternoon's walk from Hadrian's Wall.

Heading N on B6320 from crossing the North Tyne at Choller-ford, after 3¾ miles at Nunwick pass the L turn to Simonburn and St Mungo Church and take immediate next L towards Stonehaugh. Towards the far end of Ravensheugh Crag after 3 miles you will see a pull-in on the L, next to a footpath sign. Park here and follow the track up towards the crag. The stones are 450 metres away to the W of the crag.

55.0666, -2.2686, NY829747, NE48 3EJ

5 LORDENSHAW ROCK ART
ROTHBURY

The rock art at Lordenshaw, close to the Simonside Hills, can only help to bolster the theory that the markings chiefly occur on high ground with uninterrupted views – here mostly to the north-west from the slope below Lordenshaw hillfort. Apart from the beautifully placed cup and ring marks on the most prominent stone, seek out the Horseshoe Rock, named for the curved groove enclosing several cups (55.2870, -1.9212). The latest thinking is the carvings may be as early as the Neolithic or Early Bronze Age, meaning they could predate the hillfort by 2,500 years, or more! The hillfort itself is a large, sprawling earthwork, probably created in several phases. Inside the ramparts are several hut circles of varying sizes, at least three large and four smaller. The cairns to the north of the fort were dug at the same time and the remains of burnt bones and a femur were found. To explore the area fully, set aside a whole morning or afternoon, and for a very rewarding day include a walk around the hills to the south.

Take Station Road SE out of Rothbury, becoming B6342, and continue for 2½ miles then R with a brown sign for Simonside on a bend to L (55.2736, -1.9075). Continue ¾ mile to car park on R. Follow path to hillfort NE, and rock art NNW of that.

55.2864, -1.9192, NZ052991, NE61 4PU

6 BLAWEARIE CAIRN
OLD BEWICK

The grey stones of this Bronze Age cairn, coupled with the equally grey ruins of Blawearie farm behind, stand in stark relief to the brown expanse of Berwick Moor. The cairn is a steep climb from the right-angled terraces of Old Bewick, through often boggy terrain. The loose, rocky central cairn and equally rocky outer wall are surrounded by a kerb of stones 11.6 metres across, some of which are falling outwards. An excavation in the 19th century by Canon Greenwell uncovered four stone-lined graves containing grave goods including a jet and shale necklace made up of 102 beads. A dig in the 1980s by archaeologist and author Stan Beckensall, aided by local children, found an amber necklace and the remains of several burials including that of an adult and child. He also uncovered an area of burnt soil beneath

the cairn. This led him to believe a large oak tree was burnt on the site prior to the monument being erected. Towering above, dominating the northern skyline, are the double banks of a sprawling Iron Age hillfort. The outer bank protected a small collection of round houses on the western side, with the eastern serving as a corral for cattle. Strewn across the rocks to the east of the fort are several cup and ring marks, which may predate the fort by some 1,000 years, if not more. Like so many other examples of their kind, they are placed in a location with far-reaching views of the valley below.

From A697 S of Wooler take B6346 for Eglingham/Alnwick, then at crossroads after 2 miles take L towards Chatton to park at Old Bewick and follow the track up between the farm and the terrace of houses. Remain on this track/path heading NE for a mile, to a rough path branching L 100 metres to the cairn. For the hillfort, walk on towards the ruined farmhouse then take path R across the moor S and SW. Bus 470 Wooler–Alnwick Leisure Centre to Old Bewick Schoolhouse stop, no Sunday service.

55.4945, -1.8724, NU081223, NE66 4DZ

7 BUTTONY CUP & RING
DODDINGTON MOOR

Searching for the Buttony cup and ring marks, hidden deep amongst a grove of trees, is a bit like looking for a hidden treasure. There are six carved panels altogether in these woods to the south-east of Doddington Moor.

The most intriguing are a series of concentric circles radiating out, as if a pebble had been dropped in water, bisected by a long groove running out from the centre. Many are lichen-covered, giving them a greenish hue, and it has been speculated that some of the designs may once have been coloured with pigments. To the NE of the rocks is Buttony Wood Camp (55.5744, -1.9720), which may have served as a fort or an animal enclosure during the Iron Age. Across the moor there are several other examples of rock art and Iron Age settlements including the impressive Ringses Hillfort (55.5890, -1.9803) a mile to the north and the three hillforts around the summit of Dod Law (55.5784, -1.9899 and 55.5790, -1.9917 at the very top, and 55.5791, -1.9947 slightly below). There are more carved rocks, the best of them located between the two Dod Law forts just north of the cottage called Shepherd House (55.5790, -1.9922). Finally, at the centre of the moor are the remains of a small stone circle (55.5791, -1.9808). It is worth pointing out that the footpaths on a paper map bear little or no resemblance to those now running across the moor; a GPS device or phone mapping may come in handy here.

Best explored from the village of Doddington. Take the B6525 N from Wooler to Doddington and park in the village. Follow signs from the Wooler Golf Club NE and then back S over moor to Dod Law. The Buttony cup and ring marks are in the large plantation of trees ¾ mile SE from the summit of Dod Law.

55.5726, -1.9745, NU017309, NE71 6AL

8 DUDDO FIVE STONES
DUDDO

Not to be confused with the Five Stones near Jedburgh (see entry) Duddo Five Stones is an exquisitely located Bronze Age relic, standing on a large knoll close to the Scottish border. The stones command breathtaking views over the Cheviots and the Lammermuir Hills north of the meandering River Till, and overlook the Tweed to the west. The deep grooves running down from the tops are a result of 4,000 years of weathering on the soft sandstone. Until 1903 it was known as Duddo Four Stones (and still is on OS maps), with a fifth lying flat on the ground nearby, but that year the Duddo Estate was let out to new tenants who felt the need to improve the monument by re-erecting the last stone. It is often said this was not an act of considerate restoration, merely an attempt to 'improve the skyline'. The new tenant did not manage to fully re-create the 10-metre diameter circle, as two more stones originally stood in the gap on the western side.

Duddo is on the B6354 from Berwick-upon-Tweed to the A697. Look for the Stone Circle brown sign turning off the through road and park on the verge where directed. The stones are a 20-minute moderate walk away signposted across fields on a permissive path. Bus 267 from Berwick-upon-Tweed to Duddo Tower Cottage stop.

55.6868, -2.1120, NT930437, TD15 2PT

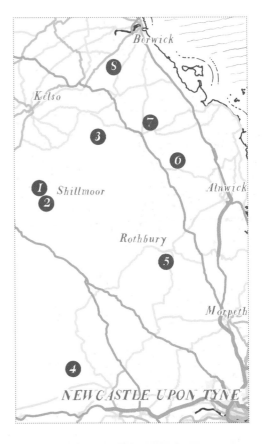

CHAPTER 22

DUMFRIES &
GALLOWAY

*D*umfries and Galloway can be undeservedly over-looked, as tourists often rush past it to get to Loch Lomond and the Highlands in one direction, or the Lakes in the other. Great swathes of its gently rolling countryside are remote and sparsely populated, yet it remains well connected to the outside world. It is home to the twin tombs of Cairn Holy, one of which is probably the most recognisable Neolithic structure in Western Scotland. Overlooking Wigtown Bay, with the Isle of Man on the distant horizon, it is also one of the most beautifully located. In the west of the region, on the slopes of the Water of Luce valley north of Glenluce, are a handful of Neolithic cairns collectively known as Mid Gleniron (54.9107, -4.8298). The two chambered cairns have the most to offer, with Mid Gleniron I still retaining one of its three capstones and all three chambers. Mid Gleniron II was originally two Early Neolithic circular chambered cairns, later joined up to make one long cairn. All over this region are reminders of the Neolithic. In the area east of Stranraer are the twin stones of Laggangarn, which could have been part of a larger stone circle. The number of cairns nearby suggests that this now-remote part of the country once held some significance to those who lived in the wider region.

Unlike the far north of Scotland, this area saw Roman inroads. The small number of their military installations around the defended settlement of Barsalloch Fort (54.7386, -4.5683), thought to have been a stronghold of the Novantae, shows that the Romans did not feel the need to subdue the tribe. Instead, to begin with at least, it is likely that they struck deals with them. Barsalloch shows evidence of Mesolithic activity, with a hearth and microflints found at the site. To the north-west of here are two more perfectly situated hillforts, likely to have been used by the tribe: Knock Hill (54.8655, -4.7206) close to Glenluce, and the Tor of Craigoch (54.9371, -5.1095) north of Stranraer.

To the east of the region, the Damnonii and the Selgovae shared a border, and would have built hillforts overlooking their territory as a show of power to the neighbouring tribe. We do not precisely know these tribal boundaries; it is likely that Arbory Hill fort stood between the two tribes, but we have no way of knowing which of them had control of it.

1 ARBORY HILL FORT
ABINGTON

On top of Arbory Hill are the well-preserved concentric banks of a multivallate fort, with extensive views over Clydesdale, commanding a position over the narrow Clyde Valley. Today the west-coast railway line and the M74 both take advantage of this opening in the hills, but it would have also been an important through route for the Romans, with the remains of their road still visible as a scar in the landscape. It is even probable that they in turn built over an existing Iron Age trackway or trade route. The fort was constructed in two phases, with the wide outer rampart built first, and the inner ramparts added later. On the eastern side, the lower rampart diverges outwards to create a large enclosed space where cattle may have been kept. The fort may have supported a small population, as remains of a timber-framed house and a rectangular stone foundation have been found within the inner circle. For a bird's-eye view of Arbory fort, continue up the neighbouring Tewsgill Hill.

From A702 heading S through Abington, turn L onto Station Road over Clyde River and railway line. Turn L at T-junction to large pull-in on L after ¼ mile. Follow track from gate opposite along stream/burn until it runs out, then cross the water and head upwards. A strenuous 30–45 minutes.

55.4965, -3.6719, NS944238, ML12 6RW 🚶🏔⛩

2 GIRDLESTANES & LOUPIN' STANES
ESKDALEMUIR

In an area of low, rolling hill and green pastures, nestled between the White Esk River and the road are the Girdlestanes and Loupin' Stanes, the remains of two stone circles some 500 metres apart. The western side of the Girdlestanes, the more southerly of the two (55.2539, -3.1757), has succumbed to the ever-changing path of this tributary of the Esk and washed away downstream, leaving just 26 of a possible 40–45 stones. Dating from 2500–2100 BC, the Girdlestanes have similarities to the stone circles of the Lake District and are thought to be aligned with Samhain, or Halloween. The Loupin' Stanes or Leaping Stones are so named because 'it is said that lads, and even a lass, were in the habit of jumping from the top of one to the other' of the widely spaced flat-topped pillars, according to one sceptical 1897 account. Like many sites, they are believed to have astrological significance, showing an alignment with the midsummer sunset. The two circles are undoubtedly connected, and there are indications of a possible ruined stone row between them. Further upstream in this tranquil, isolated valley is the Samye Ling monastery, the largest Buddhist monastery in Western Europe. The stone circles are one element of the Eskdale Prehistoric Trail, a route for motorists and cyclists prepared to do some walking. The trail, marked by brown signs, includes several Iron Age and Romano-British sites within the Castle O'er Forest. Over Rig (55.2298, -3.1875) is the most unusual of these, a uniquely formed earthwork within a natural amphitheatre, dating from the 1st century AD now cut in half by the river.

From Langholm follow the B709 NW for almost 12 miles, passing Bentpath, towards Eskdalemuir. You will see the back of an information board and a pull-in R, a stile and fingerboard L. Park, cross the road and follow the path 300 metres or so to the Loupin' Stones. Bus 124 Langholm to Eskdalemuir Clerkhill stop, no Sunday service.

55.2582, -3.1705, NY257966, DG13 0QQ 🚶🚴⛩

1

3 CASTLE HAVEN DUN
BORGUE

Prior to 1905, the remains at Castle Haven were nothing more than a pile of rubble. With the zeal and enthusiasm of many Victorian and Edwardian antiquarians, James Brown, the Laird of Knockbrex and owner of the land, had the galleried dun expertly restored. The results of his work have become swamped with ivy, but this only serves to enhance the romance of this coastal ruin. It is D-shaped and as such classed as a semi-broch, as opposed to a circular broch. It would have been a formidable home for an Iron Age family, measuring over 18 by 10.5 metres, with walls 4.5 metres thick. An unusual feature of the dun is that passage to the upper levels is by a series of stone slabs protruding from the inner wall, rather than the typical enclosed staircase. It is a great site to explore, with stairs, lintels and narrow passageways all lovingly restored. To get the best view of the semi-broch, leave through the narrow door in the south wall to the rocky shore, where the local cows enrich their diet with seaweed; from the land side, the building is almost completely hidden from view by weeds and ivy.

From Borgue on B727 head W past the churchyard towards Carrick for 2 miles. Park by the side of the road after Roberton Farm driveway and farm track R, and before bend to R and castle ruin further on (around 54.8109, -4.1865). Dun is at the cliff-top in field to L, above Castle Haven Bay; an OS map or phone mapping will come in handy. Bus S1 from Kirkcudbright to Borgue Roberton Farm stop.

54.8096, -4.1900, NX595481, DG6 4UB

4 CAIRN HOLY
KIRKDALE

Cairn Holy is the name given to two well-preserved, Neolithic chambered cairns of the Clyde or Clyde-Carlingford type, superbly placed overlooking Wigtown Bay, with the hills of the Isle of Man visible on the distant horizon. The first cairn is the most iconic and recognisable, its horn-shaped forecourt made up of eight towering megaliths: the two tallest either side of a chamber, flanked by three shorter stones each. A dig at Cairn Holy I in the late 1940s uncovered evidence of several fires in the forecourt, suggesting some sort of ritual activity such as funeral rites or cremation. The

most fascinating of the finds here were the fragments of a jadeite axe head (a real status symbol of the Neolithic) in the outer chamber. Jadeite is a brittle substance that shatters easily, and each axe head represents at least a thousand hours of painstaking work. It was also quarried far from here, in the Italian Alps, so its presence suggests that there must have been a series of indirect trade routes linking this remote corner of Scotland with the Italian Alps some 6,000 years ago. Cairn Holy II is a 150-metre walk away and, although clearly signposted, it is often missed (54.8590, -4.3101).

Head W from Gatehouse of Fleet on A75 past Cardoness and Auchenlarie Holiday Park to Kirkdale. Take R signposted Cairn Holy ½ mile; Cairn Holy II is further along track to the N. Bus 500 Dumfries–Stranraer to Carsluith Cairn Holy stop, 15 minutes' walk.

54.8578, -4.3106, NX517538, DG8 7EA

5 TWELVE APOSTLES
HOLYWOOD

The largest stone circle on the Scottish mainland, the Twelve Apostles is a sprawling 88-metre-wide oval-shaped stone circle. A great number of Langdale stone axes (see Cumbria) were found here, and some say it is the most northernly of the Cumbrian group of stone circles. There are now only 11 stones, with local legend attributing the loss to Judas Iscariot. However, since it was lost sometime between 1789 and 1837, the culprit is more likely to be a local builder; there were originally 19 stones, but the rest had vanished centuries before. A mile or so to the east another stone circle, or 'Druidical temple', thought to have measured 285 by 35 metres, was also broken up for building material some time before 1837. Both circles, along with a north and south cursus – a proposed Neolithic walkway similar to that at Stonehenge (see Wiltshire and Wessex) – were probably part of a group of sites known as the Holywood cursus complex.

From Dumfries head N on the A76 signed Kilmarnock, L after 2 miles on B729 towards Dunscore. Pass first L (unsigned, on bend) and park in pull-in immediately after it. Stone circle is in the field SE of the corner. Bus routes 213 or 246 from Dumfries to Holywood village stop, or train to Dumfries and walk 3 miles.

55.0978, -3.6517, NX947794, DG2 0HZ

3

5

6 LAGGANGARN STANDING STONES
STRANRAER

There are several ancient monuments to the east of Stranraer, on and around the Southern Upland Way between Castle Kennedy and Bargrennan. The most remote of these, at least 3 miles from the nearest road, are the Laggangarn stones. These are the two lonely survivors of a group of 14 stones, half of which survived right up until 1873. Due to a series of crosses cut across their surface, it was once believed this was the site of an early Christian settlement dating to the 8th century. However, no evidence was found to back up this claim, and it is now believed they are the remains of a large stone circle. Hidden in the heather 5 miles along the Way to the south, a few hundred metres off the path, is a stone tomb marked on OS maps as the Caves of Kilhern (54.9417, -4.8141). Like White Cairn (see entry), this cairn is a round, Bargrennan-type chambered tomb. Although it is in a robbed and ruined state, one of the four inner chambers still has the capstone in place, and it is well worth hunting out. Between the two sites, in the shadow of the turning turbines, is the Neolithic chambered long cairn of Cairn na Gath (54.9691, -4.7938) or 'cairn of the wildcat', close to the remains of a number of hut circles.

From the E end of Glenluce, off the A75, take minor road 5 miles N to New Luce. At the start of the village before the church, turn R and follow to Balmurrie Farm, 2½ miles (limited space to pull off). Follow the Southern Upland Way from here N for 3½ miles. Path can be boggy, a map and GPS are essential for navigation.

55.0076, -4.7813, NX222716, DG8 0NB

7 WHITE CAIRN CHAMBERED TOMB
CANNICH

Beautifully sited in a serene clearing in the forest at Glentrool, on the western edge of the Galloway Forest Park, is the White Cairn chambered tomb. It is a superb example of a passage grave, set in a round cairn only found in southwest Scotland and now known as the Bargrennan type after this example; Cairnderry chambered cairn, just along the road (55.0853, -4.6401), is another. A dig at White Cairn in the late 1940s found the remains of fires, an area of paving, cremated bones and fragments of Neolithic pottery. A later dig in 2004–2005, led by Vicki Cummings and Chris Fowler, revealed a quartz scraper inside. They also found a stone axe head, a bone belt attachment and an urn containing the cremated remains of a teenager and a Bronze Age urn with a man's cremated bones. The tomb is large enough and complete enough to explore the inner chamber, and it is a great place to bring children, despite the reasonably long walk. The path to the tomb is marked by white-banded posts, but it is still very easy to get lost in the woods, so bringing a map and compass or phone mapping is advisable.

From Newton Stewart take A714 NW for 8 miles, then at Bargrennan take R to Glentrool village. Take the second turning into the village, past the school L, and find somewhere to park. As this road bends round to the L look for a path up into the forest and a post with a white band around the top. Follow these markers to the clearing with the cairn, 700 metres' moderate walk.

55.0722, -4.5820, NX352783, DG8 6SY

CHAPTER 23
MID-SCOTLAND

In the summer of AD 84, in the shadow of the Grampian Mountains at the beating heart of Caledonia, the historic Battle of Mons Graupius took place between the invading Roman Empire and the tribes north of the border. Twenty thousand Romans led by Agricola faced 30,000 native troops from disparate, previously warring clans, united under the leadership of Calgacus, the first Scot to be named in history books. Although they no doubt intimidated the Roman army, and were described by Tacitus as fierce warriors with long limbs and red hair, the native side was defeated. We only have biased Roman accounts to go on, but they claim 10,000 Britons were killed and the remainder retreated to the surrounding hills. Although there were only 360 casualties among the highly trained invading Roman army, this was to be a Pyrrhic victory for them. Prior to the Roman invasion, there would have been small-scale conflict between the tribes, with minor border conflicts and cattle rustling; it is possible the battle served to unite these clans within Scotland, turning them into the 'troublesome Picts' north of the wall. Along the central belt the tribes built brochs to protect themselves, such as Tappoch Broch (56.0434, -3.8744), Coldoch Broch (56.1576, -4.1010) and Leckie Broch (56.1198, -4.1054). On the lochs they used water as a defence and built island homes, like the Isle of Spar on Loch Tay (56.5817, -3.9991). And of course they had great hillforts such as Castlelaw near Edinburgh and Tom a' Chaisteil (57.3386, -3.6696) near Grantown-on-Spey.

The other-worldly practices of those who preceded these Iron Age tribes are as alien to us as they are compelling. We cannot know if there was a universal belief system, as with our churches and cathedrals but we can group together similar monuments. The Clava Cairns at Balnuaran give their name to a distinctive group of cairns close to Inverness, which include nearby Corrimony, Druidtemple (57.4492, -4.1928), Allanfearn (57.5004, -4.1439) and Cullernie (57.5014, -4.1293), along with Moyness (57.5608, -3.7521) and Easter Clune (57.5425, -3.7517) near Nairn. They are unusual kerbed, circular cairns inside a ring of standing stones, part cairn and part stone circle. Some, such as Corrimony, had a passageway in from the angle of the midwinter sunset in the south-west to a central domed chamber large enough to stand up in. Few bones have been found within them, so it is debatable if these were family tombs. Instead it has been postulated that cairns are in fact temples and the burials were sacrifices or honoured elite of the tribe and the monuments function more like the great pyramids of Egypt. In that case, these would have been places of ancestor worship, perhaps of ritual and celebration, rather than simply cemeteries.

1

2

3

3

I FOWLIS WESTER STONES
FOWLIS WESTER

Farming has taken place in this area for millennia under the gaze of these ancient stones, with their panoramic views over a large pastoral plain and moorland. There are two circles, each paired with a great monolith – one of which is still standing, the other lying flat on the floor. In 1939 the eastern circle was excavated, and finds indicated that it rested on a clay floor, with scatters of quartz, charcoal and burnt bone fragments found near the centre, mostly in scoops under thin stone slabs. Similar fragments lay under one of the standing stones, and there was evidence of cremation fires within the stones of the western circle, as well as a bedding of tiny white pebbles.

There is nowhere to park at the stones; park in car park by the village hall N of the church in Fowlis Wester village. Take the road NE, after ⅓ mile follow bend L to continue N. After just under ⅓ mile go through gate on L, opposite the woodland to the R. Follow track W, keeping ruined shelter in sight; you will soon see a great monolith near to the stone circle. Bus 46 from Crieff to Fowlis Wester at postbox stop, Tuesdays, Wednesdays and Fridays.

56.4041, -3.7452, NN923249, PH7 3NL

2 SMA' GLEN CAIRN & GIANT'S GRAVE CRIEFF

The stones in this area have confusing names: as well as the Sma' Glen 'valley' cairn tucked away in a woodland by the cool waters of the River Almond, there is one atop the peak (56.4507, -3.8029). The valley cairn and the monolith (56.4456,-3.7781) have also shared the name Giant's Grave over the centuries. It is far enough from the main road for a secluded picnic and is a great spot for kids to explore or – if they can brave the cold – paddle in the stream. Before the road was built and the wood was planted, both the stone and the cairn would have stood in open land with the backdrop of the mountain. There is another great boulder, Ossian's Stone, a little further up the valley (56.4544, -3.7940), which was moved when General Wade built his military road through the area. This disturbed ancient remains, which the Highlander soldiers promptly reburied – possibly at this more southerly monolith. The cairn is prehistoric but it has never been excavated, so it is hard to pinpoint it to an exact date.

Travel NE from Crieff on the A85, join the A822 and continue N. Just after the turn for the B8063 look for gravelled parking area R and walk through woods; if this is blocked, there is a layby R at the other end of the woods (56.4492, -3.7874).

56.4476, -3.7807, NN904295, PH1 3SH

3 LYNCHAT OR RAITT'S CAVE KINGUSSIE

This 'cave' is a souterrain – an underground, tunnel-like structure similar to the fogous of Cornwall. Like those underground structures, its purpose is uncertain; both are widely considered to be either ceremonial or for food storage. It was built using material robbed from a nearby stone circle, which predated the souterrain by 2,000 years. The Iron Age people here may not have had any cultural ties to the stone circle, which could have been just as much of a mystery to them as it is to us today. A local legend tells that a 'freebooter' named Cummings and his eleven sons dug the souterrain in one night and built a cottage on top to hide it, in which two women of the family lived. When cattle started going missing from the neighbouring Macpherson tribe, a disguised local collapsed outside the cottage, claiming to be a traveller suffering from 'gravel' or kidney stones, so the old women brought him in. He either noticed they were baking more bannocks than they could eat, or discovered a hole in the floor through which he saw the missing cattle, and ran from the cottage to fetch reinforcements, who wrought on-the-spot vengeance on the family. But to this day the spy's descendants are said to suffer from kidney stones.

Join the A9 E of Kingussie, heading E, and follow 1½ miles. After layby 116 (blue sign) pull off L in smaller layby with gate at end (57.0937, -4.0025). Park and follow the track N and then W, as if back to Kingussie. You will soon come to an information board and a sign to the souterrain. Train to Kingussie, 1½ miles' walk.

57.0921, -4.0205, NH776019, PH21 1LT

4 KINNELL PARK STONE CIRCLE KILLIN

This stone circle stands in a tranquil farm meadow a stone's throw from the Falls of Dochart, close to where the Lochay and Dochart rivers join forces and flow into the great Loch Tay. It is one of the most enchanting small stone circles in all of Scotland. There are six large slabs of stone (six-stone rings are common in Central Scotland) ranging from 1.4 to 2 metres high, forming a small 10-metre-wide circle. The northernmost stone bears three cup marks, which may be contemporary with the circle or made some time after it was erected. Although the circle is undoubtedly ancient, it is questionable whether it always looked as it did today. Some believe that the former owner of Kinnell House may have 'improved' it, in keeping with the fashion of the late 18th and early 19th centuries for antiquities within the grounds of stately homes. There were 18 crannogs, homes built on artificial islands, on Loch Tay, and to the north-east of the loch is the Scottish Crannog Centre (PH15 2HY, 01887 830583) with an authentic recreation of one of these Iron Age homes.

Park in the free car park off Main Street in Killin and cross the bridge to the Falls of Dochart. Follow the lane to the NE, away from the town, along the banks of the River Dochart toward Kinnell Farm Cottages. The circle is in the field to the R before the farm buildings. It is on private land, so respect busy farming times and do not take dogs into the fields.

56.4658, -4.3112, NN577328, FK21 8SR

5 FORTINGALL CIRCLES & YEW FORTINGALL

In a field just to the east of Fortingall village there are three groups of three standing stones, two of which are the remains of a four-poster and the third a recumbent stone circle (rare outside of Aberdeenshire; see chapter for more). They were excavated by Aubrey Burl and University of Leicester in 1970, and Burl suggests that the odd formation of the stones may be a result of a mixing of beliefs. Perhaps the stones were altered or added to in antiquity, just as old Christian churches are today being used as places of worship by different faiths. The finding of Late Bronze Age cremated bones supports this theory, as these may well have been buried there long after the stones were erected. The other main object of interest in the area is the ancient yew tree in the village churchyard (56.5981, -4.0510). The tree is much diminished in size due to souvenir hunters removing parts of it in the 18th century and children lighting fires within it; markers show the original girth, but sadly it has had to be walled off to protect it, and is now viewed through railings. Although there is no way to accurately date yew trees, it is at least 2,000 and perhaps as much as 5,000 years old – it is amazing to think that it could have germinated around the time the stones were put into place. There is also a cup-marked stone in the churchyard. The Fortingall Hotel (PH15 2NQ, 01887 830367) next to the yew is worth a stop-off for a light lunch or a malt whisky.

The yew is well signposted in the churchyard in Fortingall. For the stones, head E along road away from village for 300 metres, they are in field to R. Bus 91 Aberfeldy Circular to Fortingall opp hotel stop, weekdays only.

56.5978, -4.0453, NN741470, PH15 2NQ

6 CASTLELAW HILLFORT EASTER HOWGATE

The Castlelaw Hill Fort (not to be confused with the vitrified hillfort by the same name in Forgandenny) is a stone's throw from the city of Edinburgh, on the north-eastern end of the Pentland Hills looking down to the Glencorse Reservoir. During the middle of the 1st millennium BC, the fort would have a large wooden gateway guarding the entrance, of the kind later built

for timber colonial forts in the Wild West of America. There would have been a wooden lookout tower on a raised platform over two large gates big enough to allow cattle to pass through, a wooden ladder giving access to the platform, and a chamber for the guards either side. Later in the fort's history, two more earth ramparts were built, and it is thought the earth house or souterrain was constructed after the Roman occupation. The Votadini who constructed this fort also commanded that on the extinct volcano of Arthur's Seat in Edinburgh (55.9430, -3.1599). Despite its obvious strategic value, there is no evidence of the fort ever acting as a defensive structure.

From Edinburgh head S on the A702, continuing for 3 miles after crossing over the A720 through Hillend and past Easter Howgate Farm to R turn signposted Castlelaw Hill Fort and Ranges. Follow the single-track lane to the car park L opposite information board; 10 minutes moderate-to-strenuous walk to summit. Bus 101 from Edinburgh to Easter Howgate Farm stop, 1-mile walk to car park.

55.8618, -3.2334, NT229638, EH26 0PB

7 CORRIMONY TOMB
GLEN URQUHART

An impressive feat of ancient engineering, the Corrimony chambered tomb shows just how complex and sophisticated the people living here were over 4,000 years ago. If we consider what any one single part of the construction must have entailed – the gathering of hundreds of tumbled stones from the river to make the cairn, or the placing of the capstone on the once-domed centre – we can see this monument must have represented thousands of hours of communal effort. A dig by Professor Stuart Piggott in the 1950s uncovered the outline of a single crouched burial here, thought to be a female. Whoever she was, she must have been held in very high esteem by the tribe for them to commit so much time to the construction of the tomb. Perhaps she was a tribal leader, or a pre-Christian equivalent of a saint, and the tomb became a site of worship? Her anonymity only adds to the tragedy that we know so little of these people. There are several hut circles close to the tomb, which is in beautiful countryside a short drive from Drumnadrochit and Loch Ness, with the Corrimony waterfall only a mile to the south-west.

From Bearnock on A831 head W towards Cannich for approx 1½ miles. Turn L signed to Corrimony Cairn. Park in the Historic Scotland car park on L after ¾ mile and walk 60 metres to the tomb. Bus 17 from Inverness to Corrimony Road End stop.

57.3344, -4.6879, NH383302, IV63 6TW 🐾⛺🗻

8 CLAVA CAIRNS
CULLODEN

The Bronze Age burial cairns of Balnuaran of Clava are more commonly known by their abridged name the Clava Cairns. These are three tombs close to the battlefield of Culloden (but some 4,000 years older), and part of a seven-cairn cemetery south of the River Nairn. They were the first of the Clava Cairns type of ring cairn to be discovered, and gave their name to a larger group of between 45 and 50 tombs in the area around Inverness. Two of the three cairns – the North East and South West – are passage graves. These had long, low, narrow passageways, leading into a central 3-metre-high, dome-shaped chamber, all now open to the elements. There are cup and ring marks on stones around the chamber entrances. The passageways on two of the tombs are apparently aligned with the setting midwinter sun on the south-west horizon, suggesting they mark the winter solstice. The return of the sun at this time of year would have been of the utmost importance for these early farmers, and it is no surprise many of their monuments are aligned this way. The third of the three cairns, the central cairn, lacks a passageway to the central chamber. The use of colour in the Clava Cairns has regularly been discussed: there are red stones facing the sunset, black at the back of the chambers, and grey or white stones in the mounds facing the sunrise.

From Inverness take B9006 E past Westhill. After Culloden Battlefield Clava Cairns are signed R at crossroads with Culloden Moor Inn (IV2 5ED, 01463 790022). Remain on road over smaller crossroads, then as it bears L then R over river, and take next R to car park. Bus 5 from Inverness to Culloden Moor stop near crossroads, 20 minutes' walk.

57.4735, -4.0732, NH757444, IV2 5EJ 🐾⛺🚶🎿

CHAPTER 24

ABERDEENSHIRE

About 10,000 years ago, hunter-gatherers north-west of Stonehaven in Aberdeenshire built a unique monument: a 50-metre-long arc of 12 pits that mimicked the waxing and waning of the moon. Calibrated by the midwinter solstice, this ancient construction in Warren Field (57.0612, -2.4307) appears to be the world's earliest-known calendar. To us, calendars are a way of keeping track of events we create or control, for appointments or holidays, but to these people, so reliant on the land and seasonal change, tracking the passage of days would mean the difference between life and death. Being able to mark time had tremendous social implications, allowing early humans to anticipate the movement of migratory herds or runs of fish in the nearby River Dee. Knowing when large, natural resources such as this would be available, they could meet in larger groups for the first time.

We can never know for how long a cultural memory of this monument was orally handed down; perhaps subsequent generations made copies of the calendar, using wooden posts that have vanished from the archaeological record. What we do know is that 6,000 years after this early Mesolithic timepiece was developed, communities in this region had begun to build more permanent lunar calendars in the form of recumbent stone circles. Of the world's 200 recumbent stone circles, 99 come just from this part of North-Eastern Scotland, with the rest far off in South-Western Ireland. They consist of rings of stone in which two large uprights flank a large flat or recumbent, stone. It is thought the two 'flankers' would frame the cycles of the moon as it passed over hills on the distant horizon. Richard Bradley of University of Reading suggests that in some cases, the stones would have been symbolic markers, as the view may have been blocked by cairns or other stones. Just a few miles from the Warren Field site is the 22.5-metre diameter Esslie the Greater, part of the beautifully located Banchory triad of monuments. With 99 recumbent circles in Aberdeenshire it is impossible to feature them all. However, to the north of Banchory, in a line west of Aberdeen, there are the wonderfully remote Sunhoney, Cullerlie and Tamnagorm (57.1588, -2.5785), and about 4 miles north of Sunhoney, to the west of the Castle Fraser Garden and Estate, is Balgorkar (57.2026, -2.4733). Other examples worth visiting are Balquhain (57.3066, -2.4414) and the famous Loanhead of Daviot to the north-west of Inverurie (57.3495, -2.4209), where the cremated remains of over 30 people, including young children, were found in an adjacent Bronze Age enclosure. Further afield are Stonehead (57.3470, -2.6646) and Upper Ord (57.3302, -2.8611) to the west, and Aikey Brae (57.5137, -2.0704) to the north-east, west of Peterhead.

1

2

3

1 ESSLIE & NINE STANES CIRCLES BANCHORY

The three stone circles of Banchory stand in a sparsely populated corner of Aberdeenshire, south of the River Dee. There are more complete examples of their kind, and ones which are far better cared for, but it is unlikely you will come across another soul here, so it can feel as if you are the very first to discover this trio of ancient monuments. Two of the circles overlook each other, and the third also would have once, but is now hidden in a woodland. There is no doubt that the three are somehow linked as part of a ritual landscape, but we can only speculate what happened during any ceremonies. The most northerly of the three circles, thought to be a ring cairn within a stone circle, is Esslie the Lesser. This is now covered in bracken and it is hard to make out its features clearly. To the south-west, in a field close to Knock Wood, is Esslie the Greater, a 22.5-metre stone circle enclosing a 17.7-metre ring cairn. This is in much better shape than its near neighbour up the hill, and it is said to be aligned on the midsummer sunrise. Finally, hidden within a forest plantation, is the Nine Stanes Circle. This is by far the most atmospheric of the three, partly because of its forest location. The stones make a good focus for a day's walk from Banchory, and if you come at the right time of year the salmon may be leaping by the Bridge of Feugh, south of the town.

From Banchory head S on Dee Street/B974 over the Dee, then L over bridge at Falls of Feugh. Take immediate R after bridge then turn L after 1½ miles, opposite driveway to Blackness Farm. Follow to T-junction and turn R, then L at the next T-junction. Within ½ mile, just after road bears L, a forest track heads N (57.0104, -2.4581). Pull in here; Nine Stanes is R of this track. The other two circles are ½ mile NW (57.0146, -2.4674) and ⅓ mile N (57.0197, -2.4001).

57.0113, -2.4574, NO717916, AB31 6LB

2 CULLERLIE STONE CIRCLE WESTHILL

The eight megaliths that make up the outer stone circle at Cullerlie were first erected in the Late Neolithic or Early Bronze Age. It was constructed on a ridge of well-drained gravel in the middle of swampland, and the lower parts of the circle have been eroded by the

acidic peat. Then around 1800–1200BC, in what must have been an important ceremony, twigs were piled up and a huge fire was lit inside the stones. The fires have been interpreted as a consecration of the land, because after this ritualistic burning small cairns were built inside the circle, containing human bones, pottery and flints. Archaeologist Richard Bradley has suggested that bonfires were a way of bringing the stones to life, animating them with the flickering light and shadows. Today, the stone circle lies behind a farm, approached by walking between two rows of conifer trees. Save for the caw of a distant crow, the circle is a quiet, peaceful place. The remains of two other circles are nearby: three remaining stones of Gask Stone Circle 1½ miles to the north-east (57.1479, -2.3291) and the much-ruined stone circle of Wester Echt 3¾ miles to the north-west (57.1651, -2.4343). Also to the west is the picturesque Sunhoney (see entry).

Take the B9119 W from Westhill and take the first L past the Garlogie Inn (AB32 6RX, 01224 743212), signposted Bachory. Circle is signed at first L, follow until you see the pull-in to the L with wall and conifers and signs. Walk through trees to the stone circle behind the farm.

57.1288, -2.3565, NJ85042, AB32 6UX

3 SUNHONEY CIRCLE ECHT

Concealed within a circle of trees on an Aberdeenshire hillside, Sunhoney is a wonderfully atmospheric 4,000-year-old, recumbent stone circle. The recumbent has 31 cupmarks and is grey granite, whilst the stones of the circle are red granite and gneiss. Recumbent stone circles have been interpreted in several differing ways. In 1935, a young Glaswegian archaeologist by the name of John Gentles put forward an idea that Sunhoney predicted solar and lunar eclipses. The modern consensus, however, holds these circles to be far broader lunar calendars, used by the local farming community to chart the seasons. In 1865 Sunhoney was excavated by gentleman antiquarian Charles Elphinstone-Dalrymple, who found eight deposits of cremated bone in the centre and fire-marked stones. It is thought that in around 1500BC, centuries after Sunhoney was erected and when the belief system may have been vastly different, the site was reused for cremation burials. It continued to be held in some reverence by the local population, and to this day local pagans gather at the site at key dates such as solstices and equinoxes. Although a little more off the beaten track than many of the recumbent stone circles in the region, Sunhoney is well worth the effort of visiting.

Head W from Echt on B9119 for a little under 1½ miles to a large farm with track heading off the road L and R. Park where you can here (be careful with the verges on the bridge) and head N for 250 metres along the track; turn L at top of track to copse. Bus X17 from Aberdeen to Echt parish church stop.

57.1412, -2.4710, NJ715056, AB32 7AL

4 TOMNAVERIE STONE CIRCLE TARLAND

Dating to the Late Neolithic or Early Bronze Age, Tomnaverie means 'hill of worship'. It is an excellent example of a recumbent stone circle, the dark basalt of the recumbent stone contrasting with the circle stones of pale red granite. These monuments can be seen as observatories, built to follow the path of a celestial object across the sky. In the case of Tomnaverie, the mountain of Lochnagar is perfectly framed between the two uprights and above the large recumbent stone. This allows an observer in the middle of the circle to track the movement of the moon over a summit at key points of the year, just like East Aquhorthies (see entry) and the famous Loanhead Circle (57.3495, -2.4209). This would have been of utmost importance to hunters and farmers. During the early 1900s, a quarry was opened dangerously near to the site and the circle was almost lost. In the Aboyne Castle grounds, some 4 miles to the south, is the curious Image Wood stone circle (57.0799 -2.7869). An unarguably enigmatic site, due to its odd shape many have debated if this is a true Late Neolithic or Early Bronze Age monument or a folly dating to the late 18th or early 19th century.

Follow Bridge Street/B9119 S out of Tarland, take first L onto B9094 toward Aboyne. Look for the signed car park R just after ½ mile and follow path to circle.

57.1193, -2.8496, NJ486034, AB34 4YR

5 EAST AQUHORTHIES STONE CIRCLE INVERURIE

Farmland still covers the slopes surrounding this stone circle, just as it would have in the 3rd millennium BC, or Early Bronze Age, when the stone circle was erected. It is likely this circle served the local community who worked the surrounding fields. Indeed, the name Aquhorthies is often translated as 'field of prayer'; it is sometimes called East, sometimes Easter. The stones on the east of the circle are whitish-pink and, in the west, dark grey, with the recumbent made of red granite with flecks of white quartz. The large recumbent stone looks similar to a Christian altar at first sight, and you can see why Victorian antiquarians often described these as 'druidical altars'. This highlights how easy it can be to superimpose our belief system onto one so far removed from modern religious practices. Rather than an altar, it has been suggested that this circle acted as a calendar and the setting of the moon can be tracked between the two uprights, recording the progress of the seasons so vital to a farming community. The stone circle is in sight of Millstone Hill to the west, which has a cairn near a rock carved with Ogham writing and a cross (57.2772, -2.5064), and Mither Tap Hillfort to the north-west (57.2906, -2.5283). Mither Tap (which means 'mother of the top') has traces of hut circles and could date to 1000BC, but the earliest charcoal remains date from AD 340 at the earliest.

Follow brown sign for 'Aquorthies Stone Circle' NW from Black-hall roundabout on the A96 at Inverurie (the northernmost of the three roundabouts bypassing the town). Follow just under 2 miles to car park on L and follow path S to stone circle. Bus 421 from Inverurie, to Burnhervie Birken Cottage stop and walk N to Aquhorthies Farm (57.2702, -2.4683) turn R to walk NW on track/path then R again at T-junction to car park, 2/3miles walk, or train to Inverurie, 3 miles' walk.

57.2770, -2.4456, NJ732208, AB51 5JL

6 COLMEALLIE STONE CIRCLE EDZELL

Colmeallie is a sweet little stone circle, looking more like a garden ornament than an ancient monument. Set in a valley, not far from the river and flanked by mountains, it couldn't be in a more beautiful spot. Sadly, like so many other stone circles, it was plundered

some time before the 1850s for building materials. Before this date, it is likely to have been a much larger monument, comprising two concentric rings. The inner circle may have been a recumbent stone circle, but as the large recumbent stone is now damaged, this is somewhat hard to make out. The circle is on private land but the owner doesn't mind the odd respectful visit. He let me know, with a twinkle in his eye, that some visitors provide payment by 'doing a Billy Connolly' – in other words, dancing around the stones naked!

From Edzell head N on High Street/B966 for 1½ miles. Cross the river, taking L towards Glen Esk and follow for 5 miles until a bridge over a brook and a lane off to R; there is a bench in the field by river L. Park here and follow the lane to the stone circle.

56.8923, -2.7146, NO565781, DD9 7YW

7 FINZEAN CAIRN
BANCHORY

The cairn at Finzean is hidden away in mixed plantation and native woodland, up a muddy track off a minor road on the edge of the Highlands. At 3.5 metres high and 33 metres long, it appears to be a Neolithic trapezoidal long cairn, and was probably once even larger. Craters in the pile of stones resemble caved in or robbed tombs elsewhere in Britain, and this could be a chambered cairn used to bury the dead. Unchambered cairns also exist, and it has been suggested that these, often placed in prominent positions such as the tops of hills, may have been built to mark territories or meeting points. In various cultures, both modern and ancient, trees have been used in much the same way. The 'smaller cairns and tumuli' noted near it in the 19th century have since been identified as clearance cairns, stones piled up to clear the land for farming. The cairn makes part of an excellent walk or run that includes Tom's Cairn hill to the east. There are also great mountain bike trails in the local area in the Blackhall Forest beyond Tom's Cairn.

Take the B976 E from Aboyne, and 1½ miles past the Butter-worth Gallery and Ballogie Nursery you'll see the war memorial by a layby R. Pull in to the larger layby L with the Dardannus Standing Stone (held together with iron staples after it was broken in the 19th century) and cross the road to follow the path into the woods on the S, bearing L as it branches to the cairn.

57.0333, -2.6740, NO591937, AB34 5EA

8 SCULPTORS CAVE
COVESEA

On the rocky shores of the Moray Firth, a mile-long trek across shingle beaches and slippery rocks, is one of Britain's most grisly Bronze Age sites to modern eyes. In an area now visited more by fulmars and sea otters than people, stands a huge cave that once served as a temple to dead children. Around 3,000 years ago, people would make the pilgrimage here and in what seems a macabre act to us today, put their offspring to rest by displaying their heads or skulls in the entrance to the caves, possibly on sticks. Can we presume that they felt this ritual could prevent more young members of the family coming to a sticky end? Were these children honoured, or sacrificed? Other skulls, showing signs of decapitation, date from the Iron Age, in the 4th century AD, and there are several Pictish symbols carved into the rock at the entrance, which is how the cave got its name. At the back of the cave there were deposits of Bronze Age metalwork apparently left as offerings, Roman pottery and coins, signs of fires and possibly of structures: the cavern is large, bring a proper torch! Other caves along this stretch are also being explored by archaeologists and yielding bones; this may have been an entire coastal necropolis. During high tides, the cave becomes inaccessible, so it is advisable to begin your walk as it is falling, 2½ hours before low tide. Although the walk is arduous at times, this is a particularly unspoilt section of the coast and the bays are often sunny and sheltered from the wind.

From Lossiemouth head W on the B9040 past the Moray Golf Club and 1 mile past the caravan site. Park in layby on R just past the crossroads (57.7166, -3.3629). Check tide times before you begin the walk from here. Follow track to the coast, continue straight as it bends L, and make your way down to the shoreline. Head W over the rocks and beaches, passing a set of steps carved into the rock (follow these up on the return leg). After 1 mile look for the double entrances of the cave in a squarish opening; one entrance may be boarded up.

57.7186, -3.3866, NJ174707, IV30 5QS

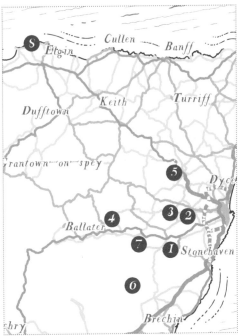

CHAPTER 25

WEST SCOTLAND & ARRAN

With its towering mountains, deep, still lochs and empty, white-sand beaches, the West of Scotland is one of Britain's best-kept secrets. During the Bronze Age 4,200 years ago a now fertile glen would have been one of the most significant trading posts in all of Britain and Ireland. Boats loaded with tin from Cornwall and copper from Northern Ireland were funnelled between the Mull of Kintyre and Jura to Kilmartin Glen. They stopped here before trade continued north across the Great Glen, the rift from Fort William to Inverness that separates Lowland and Highland Scotland. Archaeologist and author Neil Oliver describes the area as a prehistoric customs post, where local inhabitants took advantage of the trade route to take their cut as the goods moved north to the bronze-working region of North-East Scotland. The newly discovered bronze, an alloy of tin and copper, would have made those living in the Kilmartin Glen very rich indeed, and one legacy of this wealth can still be seen thousands of years later, with over 150 prehistoric monuments discovered within a 6-mile radius of the village of Kilmartin. One of the most impressive groupings of ancient sites is the 3-mile linear cairn cemetery south-west of the village, which includes the three Nether Largie cairns. Away from the crowds, the Ri Cruin Cairn (56.1170, -5.4997) has a number of carvings including an axe head of Irish design, which experts often link to a Bronze Age axe-worshipping cult. Rock art is not unusual in this area, with two more examples only 600 metres away on a rocky outcrop at Baluachraig (56.1160, -5.4902) and on the Ballymeanoch Stone Rows (56.1110, -5.4862). Further south there is, of course, the extensive cup and ring marking at Achnabreck, and at Kilmichael Glassary (56.0861, -5.4444 with parking opposite) a fenced rocky outcrop shows a number of keyhole-shaped carvings unique in the area. Just off the west coast is the Isle of Arran, often described as Scotland in miniature. In the south-west of the island are the famous stone circles of Machrie Moor which stand alongside hut circles, standing stones, cairns and cists, thought to be family tombs dating from the 3rd millennium BC. Aubrey Burl believes that Machrie Moor and the whole south-west of the island may have been a centre of cultish worship similar to the Kilmartin area.

To the west of the island, in a clearing in the South End Forest, there are two Neolithic chambered tombs known as the Giant's Graves (55.4764, -5.0973). These are just two of the 20 or so chambered cairns on the island. To the north of here in another woodland clearing is Meallach's Grave of Monamore, while Torrylin (55.4407, -5.2343) is a short walk from the road near the village of Lagg on the south coast.

1

2

3

4

1 GREADAL FHINN CAIRN
ARDNAMURCHAN

On the remote Ardnamurchan peninsula, Greadal Fhinn Cairn is arguably the most westerly Neolithic monument in Britain. It stands unloved and forgotten on marginal land amidst the gentle hills, at the back of Kilchoan village and overlooking Kilchoan Bay. Like Barpa Langais on North Uist (57.5706, -7.2915) and Rubh' an Dunain on Skye (57.1638, -6.3132) it is a Hebridean chambered tomb, a type of passage grave characteristic of the Hebrides, Skye and Far West Scotland. The capstone has slipped from its original position, and much of the stone is missing, but enough of the tomb remains to make this a worthwhile diversion.

Park in Kilchoan on B8007 and walk W towards Ormsaigbeg. Take a R just after stream through gate towards Grianan Croft. Turn L around the buildings, giving them as wide a berth as possible and make your way up through the fields; you should see the cairn on the hillside. Although there are rights of access in Scotland, the owner of the land is said to be a little tricky.

56.6991, -6.12354, NM476639, PH36 4LQ

2 RUBHA AN DÙIN BHÀIN
SANNA

Just around the headland from the beautiful beaches of Sanna Bay, you will find Rubha an Dùin Bhàin or Burnbank fort, a promontory hillfort from the Iron Age, jutting out of the rocky cliffs. The fort would have made use of its natural position on cliffs towering above the rocky shores to defend against raiders from the western seaboard; on a clear day, you can see the islands of Muck, Eigg and Skye. Some of the stones that went to build the inland wall are still visible as a line of rock. There is a small white-sand bay with crystal waters just behind the fort; were this anywhere else in the world it would be a private beach tied to a luxury hotel.

From Kilchoan follow B8007 N then R for Sanna and follow just over 4 miles to the car park R. From here follow track across the bridge to towards the north shore and around the headland to the E the best you can. It can get very boggy so bring walking sticks and welly boots. The fort is on a rocky promontory due N of the car park, and is marked by a modern cairn (pile of stones).

56.7551, -6.1759, NM448704, PH36 4LW

3 DALINEUN CHAMBERED CAIRN KILMORE

South-east of Oban a narrow road, often used by walkers and cyclists seeking a slower pace, winds its way down to the calm, sheltered waters of Loch Nell, with its lichen-covered trees and distant calls of springtime cuckoos. The Dalineun cairn overlooks the water from just off this winding road. It is a Clyde-type chambered cairn, which consisted of one or more inner chambers and may have served as a family tomb over a long period of time. It began life in the Neolithic and seems to have stayed in use right up until the middle of the Bronze Age; during this later phase a large stone cist, which is still visible, was inserted behind the main chamber. The large number of cairns and chambered cairns in this region point towards this being an area of huge ritual significance, perhaps even comparable to Kilmartin. The sites are all in varying degrees of completeness but nonetheless worthy of your time. A crannog – a man-made island that would have once housed an Iron Age dwelling – now home to a large tree, can be seen from the cairn; another lies to the north-east end of the loch.

Turn off the A816 at Kilmore and head along the river for 1 mile to Loch Nell, following signs for Glen Lonan. At the loch pull into a passing space at 56.3843, -5.4333 just past fishing permit sign next to a bench. Enter the field via the gate in front, you should see the capstone of the cairn on a rise ahead.

56.3849, -5.4358, NM879267, PA34 4XU

4 KINTRAW
KILMARTIN

Kintraw is a magical site with a 4-metre-high monolith dominating a number of nearby cairns. There are clues that there may have been a platform above the cairn to the north-east. This could have acted as an observatory for the midwinter solstice, aligned with the standing stone and a wooden post that once stood in the centre of the cairn. However, the stone fell during a storm in 1978 and it is widely held that it has not been returned to its original position. It is thought this cairn was covered in white quartz when it was first constructed during the Early Bronze Age. Elsewhere in the country white quartz is associated with lunar worship, and it is likely that the moon held some significance to those who built the

KILMARTIN CAIRN CEMETERY

Within the centre of Kilmartin glen and visible from the museum is a linear cemetery of burial cairns, the earliest of which dates to 3000BC, some 5,000 years ago. Such a linear layout is more common in the Stonehenge region (see Wiltshire & Wessex), and this is the only example in Scotland. The differing ages of the cairns here show a tradition and continuity of belief lasting a thousand years. Further down into the glen is Dunchraigaig Cairn (56.1146, -5.4871), a large circular Bronze Age burial site that contained cremated remains from eight to ten people, and a good starting point to explore the Ballymeanoch Stones (56.1111 -5.4857) and further sites in the south of the glen.

cairn. From up here the boats on the loch below look like part of a Lowry painting framed by distant Scottish hills.

Follow A816 N from Kilmartin just over 5 miles, when approaching sea pull off at bend with two opposite gateways (56.1872, -5.4971) if safe. Stone and cairn are in field just N.

56.1878, -5.4974, NM830049, PA31 8UW

5 GLEBE & NETHER LARGIE NORTH KILMARTIN

Taking the cairns in order, we begin with the Glebe Cairn, a mound 30 metres in diameter and 3 metres high, which was probably once considerably bigger. A cist, or stone coffin, was found in the cairn containing an inhumation and a tripartite (three-sectioned) pottery food bowl. Also in the cairn was a bowl of Irish design, submerged in gravel with a jet necklace placed on top. A short walk south is Nether Largie North Cairn (56.1295, -5.4918), perhaps the most impressive of all the Kilmartin Cairns. It is possible to enter the inner chamber of this tomb and examine the submerged cist within its ancient walls. The end slab and capstone contain a number of carvings, including those of axe heads. It has been debated whether or not they were originally part of another stone monument, or if these carvings were meant for the eyes of the dead.

In Kilmartin on A816 park in the museum car park. Follow road N to the garage, then L to walk along footpath S to cairns.

56.1338, -5.4890, NR832989, PA31 8RN

6 NETHER LARGIE MID & SOUTH KILMARTIN

The Mid-Cairn is perhaps the best from which to view the alignment of all the burial mounds stretching out in front and behind you along this tranquil glen. It contained two cists, both empty; the large stone slab or capstone that once covered one has been raised, showing what limited space there was for a body. Interestingly, this only allows the inhumation to be placed in the foetal position: could it be the builders believed the exit from this world had to mirror its entrance? It is thought another, lost cairn would have stood between this and the South Cairn (56.1245, -5.4952). This last one is the earliest of all, a Clyde-type chambered round cairn dated to the Neolithic by pottery, flints, and arrowheads found within. It is reminiscent of the Cotswold-Severn chambered tombs far south of here, and young explorers will appreciate its long central chamber. When I made my visit, a family of house martins were in residence! From the South Cairn follow the old tin Ministry of Works signpost to the Temple Wood Stone Circle across the lane (56.1236, -5.4987). A timber circle predated the one of stone here, and for 2,000 years this was a place of ritual and funeral rites, with cremated remains found in cists within. It is thought to be one of the earliest stone circles in Scotland.

Continue further down the footpath from Glebe and Nether Largie North Cairns (see entry) to visit the rest of the cairns and the circle.

56.1280, -5.4925, NR830983, PA31 8RN

7 ACHNABRECK ROCK ART KILMARTIN

A few miles south of the village of Kilmartin, Achnabreck, which means 'rock of the host', is widely accepted as one of the best, if not the largest, examples of prehistoric rock art in Scotland. Consisting of double, triple and horned cup and ring marks, they show up best after rainfall or any dousing of water, and it is sometimes debated whether they were once coloured

6

with pigments. Along with the cup and ring marks, there are ringed stars and most intriguingly, spirals similar to those found in Ireland. This cements the idea of a trade route from the copper mines in Ireland to the North-East of Scotland via Kilmartin Glen. It is a short walk through a Forestry Commission plantation and best explored during the months of May and September, outside the main midgie season. On a wooded hill just to the west of the main car park traces of wall can be found at the Dun na Maraig Iron Age fort (56.0610, -5.4510), best visited before the trees come into leaf.

Head S from Kilmartin village on the A816 for 5½ miles, then turn L at the Historic Scotland brown Achnabreck sign. Follow ½ mile over crossroads to the main car park R, then follow the track at the top of the car park on foot E to the rock carvings, 400 metres' moderate walk.

56.0607, -5.4460, NR855906, PA31 8SG

8 BALLOCHMYLE ROCK ART
MAUCHLINE

In 1986 a works party for the Kingencleugh Estate began to clear away years of undergrowth from a large rock face to the east of the estate. As they cut away the branches, brambles and bracken they gradually revealed one of the most extensive pieces of prehistoric rock art to be found in Britain. The carvings are mostly true cup and ring marks – deep cup indentations surrounded by circular grooves or rings – but there are also star-shaped marks within circles, and abstract shapes thought to

be deer (although these could have been made later). Additional to these marks there are rectangular and square cups, along with a group of linear indentations forming strange shapes and patterns. The carvings were made over a long period of time, with successive marks being made on top of each other. As with so much of prehistory, we do not know why the marks were made. Were they rudimentary writing, waymarkers, star charts – or could they even have been made by travellers to the region, to appease gods of the place before returning back down the River Ayr? The river was held sacred to many pre-Christian cultures, a belief which could have persisted from more ancient times. Today it can be traversed from source to sea along the River Ayr Way long-distance path, and the markings make for a welcome diversion just off the route.

From the centre of Mauchline, head S on Earl Grey St/on the A76 for 1⅓ miles and take a R marked no through road. Park just before the road bends to the L. Follow the footpath into the field and towards the edge of the wood. Here ignore the path heading SW and enter the woods heading due W over the small brook to the rock face and carvings. Bus routes 343, X50 and X76 from Auchinleck station to Catrine opp Cooperative Avenue stop, walk SW on Newton Street/B713 to A76, cross over to lane opposite and follow through gate straight on at bend (the other end of the no through road, it can be walked) to footpath.

55.5006, -4.3595, NS510255, KA5 5JN

9 CAISTEAL GRUGAIG
GLENELG

Standing on a hillside overlooking a confluence of Loch Alsh, Loch Duich and Loch Long, it is not hard to see why a defensive structure was built on this spot. The family or tribe living and farming here would have had ample time to bring in their cattle or protect their family if they spotted invaders sailing down the lochs. Considering it was built in the Iron Age, at least 2,000 years ago, the broch is remarkably intact. A triangular lintel is clearly visible above the doorway, along with a guards' chamber and stairs in the interior. An interesting account of the broch, written by anthropologist and archaeologist Euan W MacKie, suggests that the narrow cavity running within the parallel inner walls may have been used for storing food, as has been suggested with the souterrains and fogous of Scotland and Cornwall respectively. This

granite, and it has been suggested that this reflected a symbolism of bone and flesh or blood. The different stone circles may have been important focal points for different tribes or lineages: archaeologist and writer Aubrey Burl comments that Machrie 4 has an arrangement of 'male' and 'female' portal stones similar to the circles of Western Ireland (and contained an Irish tripartite bowl), whereas Machrie 5 is more similar to those of north-west England. There is a main path to the stones, but a pair of good boots is advisable, especially if you also want to explore the countless cairns and hut circles near to the stones themselves. Overlooking Machrie Bay to the north of Machrie Moor are the stones of Auchagallon (55.5598, -5.3428), a stone circle surrounding a burial cist, often marked on maps as a cairn.

From Blackwaterfoot head N on A481 for 3½ miles to car park on R. Take the path from it over the stile and follow for just over a mile through many twists heading ESE. Ground can be boggy.

55.5409, -5.3138, NR910324, KA27 8DX

idea of food storage arguably makes more sense than the inner walls acting as a refuge or hiding place from attackers. The broch is at the end of ½ mile of coastal path above Loch Alsh, with views out to the magnificent Eilean Donan Castle. The area is rich in wildlife, and sea eagles have been spotted swooping over the nearby loch.

At Shiel Bridge take the turning off the A87 by the red phone box to Ràtagan, Glenelg Brochs and the Glenelg-Kylerhea Ferry, then shortly take a R to follow the coast road 5½ miles past the Ratagan Youth Hostel until it runs out at Totaig. Follow the path uphill for just over ½ mile to the broch. The coastal road is best travelled by bicycle.

57.2664, -5.5392, NG866250, IV40 8HT

10 MACHRIE MOOR
ISLE OF ARRAN

There is very little flat land on the wild, windswept Isle of Arran. To the west of the isle, just south of the winding rapids of Machrie Water, there are six stone circles on the flat boggy expanse of Machrie Moor. James Bryce in 1861 recorded ten monuments here, the first five being stone circles, then two probable cairns, two standing stones, and another circle. Machrie Moor 11, another stone circle, was discovered sometime later. All are thought to have been erected around 2000BC, and at least two would have replaced wooden circles built some 500 years prior to this. The stone circles are a mix of sandstone and

CHAPTER 26

SKYE & THE WESTERN ISLES

*O*ut in the swell of the Atlantic waters, the sparsely populated islands off the north-west coast of Scotland feel distinctly different from anywhere else in the British Isles – so much so that when Stanley Kubrick filmed *2001: A Space Odyssey* in 1968, he chose the barren Hebridean landscape of Harris to stand in for the surface of Jupiter. Sea eagles, puffins, seals and otters all eke out a living where the azure waters lap pure white, sandy shores, and on a calm, warm day the empty beaches are unrivalled anywhere in the country. Even at the height of the season you can find corners of both the Hebrides and Skye where there is not a single soul for miles.

People have been coming to these picturesque islands for millennia; in recent years, Mesolithic shell middens have been found on the island of Oronsay in the Inner Hebrides and in Northton on Harris. However, it was during the Neolithic that farming settlements really began to take hold, and sites such as the iconic Callanish Stone Circle were built. Callanish would have been part of a much larger ritual landscape, and for the intrepid stone-hunter it is worth donning your wellies and waterproofs and hunting out the other rows, circles and monoliths in this region. Callanish 2 and 3 are perhaps the easiest to find as they are signposted from the road, but there are at least 16 other stone monuments in and around the area. The sites in this region were in use for over 1,500 years, but probably not all at the same time. On a hilltop near the village of Breasclete there is a chambered cairn (58.2196, -6.7514) and travelling further up the SW of Lewis we find Clach an Trushal or Truiseal (58.3934, -6.4929), Scotland's tallest standing stone at over 5.8 metres. Rather sadly local folklore suggests this was once part of a much larger stone circle that rivalled Callanish, but by 1914 all but this giant had been broken up and used in local building projects.

Over the Sea of the Hebrides, in a remote corner of Skye, substantial remains of a Neolithic chambered tomb and a large Iron Age wall stand remarkably intact on the uninhabited Rubh' an Dunain peninsula (57.1638, -6.3132). This is not the only Iron Age relic on these islands to the West of Scotland; Skye has over 50 brochs, including the Dun Beag, a well-preserved and accessible broch to the north of Struanmore (57.3603, -6.4257), and Dun Mor a little further to the NE. Over on Harris and Lewis there are more Iron Age remains such as Dun an Sticir (57.6815, -7.2077) and the rebuilt Iron Age house with its living museum at Bosta in the west of Lewis (58.2553, -6.8817).

1 CALLANISH/CALANAIS STANDING STONES *LEWIS*

These are perhaps the most iconic of all the standing stones on the Hebrides, erected in 2900–2600BC, before Stonehenge (see Wiltshire & Wessex). They consist of a stone circle with cruciform double stone rows and an almost central monolith towering 4.75 metres high. Callanish went through several forms before it ended up as it is today: a central cairn, or stone coffin-like structure was added in the centre about 1,000 years after it was built and some 500 years after that, later in the Bronze Age, was possibly used as a dwelling. The site gradually became covered in peat sometime after 800BC. Unlike the Stonehenge bluestones brought in from Wales, the Callanish stone, Lewisian gneiss, was sourced from the local area. The stones are a popular tourist attraction and it can get busy, especially around peak times, so it is worth visiting early in the morning or late in the evening, when the visitor centre is closed but the site is still open.

Visitor centre with car park is well signposted off the A858 at the W coast, to the S of Callanish village. Standing stones are a short walk N on path, and can also be entered from Callanish. Bus W2 from Stornoway to Callanish at Stones Visitor Centre stop, no Sunday service.

58.1984, -6.7462, NB212331, HS2 9DY

2 CEANN HULAVIG *CALLANISH, LEWIS*

This hilltop stone circle, sometimes known as Callanish IV, is not signposted, nor does it have its own car park or visitor centre. Lying just off the B8011 it is visible from the road but easily missed. It would have once had 13 stones, leading to theories that it was linked with a lunar calendar, but now has just five large stones measuring 2–2.75 metres. The stones have a thick coat of lichen, and can look almost hairy in some lights. It is one of many sites that make up the wider ritual landscape around the Callanish Stones. Like most of the monuments on Lewis these are Lewisian gneiss, a strange rock with swirling patterns and an ancient, other-worldly appearance. Indeed, this stone is some of the oldest on the surface of the earth, about the same age as the rocks on the moon.

Head S from Callanish on the A858 for approx 1½ miles, then turn R onto the B8011 signed Timsgeaidh. After 1 mile look up to the R you should see the stone circle; look for a small gravel pull-in L and a boardwalk to a gate R. Pull in on gravel or wherever you can best (road is two lanes and straight) and walk through the gate, over the moors to the stones. Bus W2 from Stornoway to Garynahine at bus shelter stop and walk W a short way to turning, no Sunday service.

58.1753, -6.7134, NB230304, HS2 9DS

3 DUN CARLOWAY BROCH *LEWIS*

With parts of the wall towering a massive 9 metres high, Dun Carloway broch is one of the tallest and most complete Iron Age structures in the British Isles, thought to date to around 200BC. An inner staircase links a series of galleries within the broch, and for children the dark interior is a fun site to explore. It stands in a field grazed by wild-looking (and acting) horned Hebridean sheep on a hillside overlooking a crofting village. From this vantage point you can see the coastal gusts rippling the waters of the inland Loch an Duin, and on a clear day there are far-reaching views out over the surrounding sea lochs and hills. The purpose of these brochs has been debated for some time, and many now believe they were defensive structures to enclose a family and their animals during troubled times.

From Breasclete in the NW head N on the A858 and take the third L signed Dun Carloway after 4⅓ miles. Park at the visitor centre shortly on R (free) and follow the path to the site. Bus W2 from Stornoway to Carloway Bridge stop and walk 1¼ miles S to turning, no Sunday service.

58.2696 -6.7939, NB189412, HS2 9AZ

4 DUN BORRANISH *LEWIS*

Flanked by dunes and distant hills, this flat expanse of sand is one of the not-to-be-missed sights on the Hebrides. At the top of the beach a meandering, peat-rich burn wends its way around the ruined remains of Dun Borranish or Borranais, also known as Dun Ciuthach or 'fort of the Giant Ciuthach'. Legend says that the Fenian warriors Fionn and Oscar despatched him, and the marks of his buttocks and shoulders were left on a nearby rock. This Iron Age relic is thought to have been a D-shaped broch or fortified tower; it is generally thought that these were strongholds of a wealthy elite who could afford to build such protected environments. Roughly carved pottery found at the site was donated to the National Museum of Antiquities of Scotland. On the lane leading down to the beach is a giant statue commemorating the 12th-century chess pieces carved from walrus ivory that were found in the dunes here. People are permitted to camp on the dunes around the beach – Tràigh Uige on OS maps but Traigh Eadar or Ardroil on signs – for a very small fee. It is somewhat open to the elements, so ideally find a sheltered position.

Head to the most westerly point of the B8011 and follow on around the coast to the S signed Breanais (Brenish). Pass the turning for Timsgearraidh and the community shop, then after 2 miles take R signposted to car park and Traigh Eadar/Ardroil Beach. From the car park follow the beach N and look out for the bridge over the far side of the bay. Cross the bridge and follow the headland around; cross the stepping stones to the remains of the broch. Bus W4 PML from Stornoway to Ardroil Beach Road end stop, no Sunday service.

58.1890, -7.0211, NB050332, HS2 9EU 🔲👣📷

5 STEINACLEIT
LEWIS

In the 1920s crofters cutting peat in the north of Lewis stopped when one of their cutting tools clanged and shook as it hit a stone. The crofters could not have known at the time that the stone their tools met with was laid there by humans as much as 5,000 years ago. At first it was thought they had found a stone circle, or a cairn, but it has since been suggested that the stones belong to a Neolithic farmstead with a house and a yard. If this theory is correct, it is one of the only examples of such a structure in the region. Steinacleit has never been properly excavated, but pottery, flint and bones were found there in the 1930s; the artefacts were subsequently lost without a trace, only adding to the enigmatic qualities of the site.

From Barvas on the north-west coast head N on the A857 towards Butt of Lewis for 4 miles. At Shader take R with brown Steinacleit sign just after church to wide layby L on bend with 'Park here for Steinacleit' sign. Follow signs through the gate to stones. Bus W1 from Stornoway to Lower Shader opp Steinacleit Road End stop, no Sunday service.

58.3973, -6.4579, NB396539, HS2 0RL 👣

6 BORVEMORE
HARRIS

The lonely single stone at Borvemor stands on the headland overlooking the island Taransay and two long, often deserted, sandy Hebridean beaches. The stone, also known as Scarista, Sgarasta or Clach Stèinigidh, was not always so solitary but probably once stood as part of a stone circle; at least two other stones lie nearby, but their original positions cannot be discerned. It is also unlikely the circle was in isolation, instead making up one small part of a larger ceremonial landscape. On the promontory of Àird Niosaboist, just north-east from Borvemor, Macleod's Stone or Clach Mhic Leòid (57.8658, -6.9920) towers over 3 metres in height and overlooks more of the crystal-blue Harris coastline. It can be seen from the beach below and makes for a blustery but worthwhile wander. Between the two lie the remains of a chambered cairn (57.8450, -7.0075).

Following the A859 SW along the coast, shortly after Borve/Na Buirgh and Borvemor Cottages, the road widens and there is an area big enough to pull into on the R. Head through the gate across the road and follow the headland to the stone. Bus W10 from Stornoway to Borve House stop, walk on to gate.

57.8351, -7.0219, NG020939, HS3 3HX 👣📷

7 KILVAXTER SOUTERRAIN
UIG, SKYE

Like fogous in Cornwall, souterrains are long underground passages associated with Iron Age settlements. Their purpose has never been fully understood. It is often said they must have some form of ceremonial or ritual purpose, but this can be archaeological shorthand for 'we haven't got a clue'. Other schools of thought claim they may have been refuges when the village was under attack. However,

given that most are long tunnels only wide enough for a single file of people, the refugees within would have been sitting ducks to any invader. What could be likely is that they were used for storing food such as cheese and butter; this souterrain is associated with the adjacent remains of a roundhouse. The Kilvaxter Souterrian can flood after heavy rain, which is much of the time on Skye, and a pair of wellies or even waders (perhaps even a wetsuit) are a must to explore the tunnel. Light is also very limited so bring along a head torch to explore all 17 metres of this underground marvel.

Travel N from Uig on the A855 about 4¾ miles until you come to Kilvaxter and the small car park R. Souterrain is a short walk from the car park. Bus routes 57A and 57C from Uig to Kilvaxter Village stop.

57.6409, -6.3753, NG389696, IV51 9YR

8 SUARDAL CAIRN
BROADFORD, SKYE

In the wild Strath Suardal Valley, a short walk from the hotels and hostels of Broadford, the turf-covered knoll of Suardal chambered cairn is magnificently set off by the peak of Beinn na Caillich behind. Also known as An Sithean or Aant Sithe, a Highlands name for a fairy hill or mound, folklore says those who cut turf from it will hear terrible screams from their homes. The cairn is 12 metres in diameter and 2 metres high, and its most prominent features are the large upright stones, which would have once been part of the inner chamber. It is hard to get a true sense of what it must have looked like in its day, because many stones once belonging to the tomb are now scattered around the landscape, and both the cairn itself and the stones are much reduced in height. There are two hut circles to the east.

From the W end of Broadford on the A87 take the B8083 S past Broadford Hotel for just under 1½ miles to a layby L and the knoll R. For an easy stroll on a good path, park earlier, after just over ½ mile at pull-in R just after an 'allow overtaking' sign. Cross the road and take the path S, it bends round NW to meet the road again just before the layby opposite the cairn. Bus routes 55 and 612 from Kyle of Lochalsh to Broadford Suardal Houses and walk ½ mile back up road, weekdays only.

57.2272, -5.9326, NG627220, IV49 9AS

9 POBULL FHINN
NORTH UIST

There are several ways to translate (and spell!) this place: it could be the White People or Finn's people or if spelled Pùball Fhinn, Finn's tent, a common reference to the nomadic life of the legendary hero. It is marked on OS maps as Sornach Coir' Fhinn, or Finn's cauldron, a name also given to other sites. The circle is thought to date to around 2000–1000BC in the Middle Bronze Age, far later than many elsewhere in the country, which date to the Early Bronze Age and Late Neolithic. Rather curiously, it appears to have been erected on a man-made terrace on the lower slopes of Beinn Langais, rather than a natural plateau. The circle is located on the banks of Loch Langais, and the waters here are often said to be the most reliable place to see otters on North Uist. This is a stunning and tranquil part of the island, and on the way to the circle you can visit the chambered tomb of Barpa Langais/Langass on the north-west side of Beinn Langais, an impressive cairn thought to be built for an eminent warrior.

Take the A867 SW from Lochmaddy for just under 5½ miles. After the rounded cairn becomes visible on top of the hill L you will see the signed Barpa Langais/Langass Burial Chamber car park on L, just before you reach the Scottish Salmon Company and the turn-off for Langass Lodge Hotel (HS6 5HA, 01876 580285) from where you can also walk to the circle. From Barpa Langais make your way across the top of the hill then due S to stone circle. Bus W18 from Lochmaddy to Langass at Road End stop, no Sunday service.

57.5644, -7.2825, NF842650, HS6 5HA

CHAPTER 27

NORTHERN
HIGHLANDS

*I*n springtime, as the gorse comes into full flower, the Highland hills turn a rich golden yellow. To my mind, this is the best time to be here, heading up the coastal stretch of the A9 and A99. The Buldoo Standing Stone (58.2845, -3.3659) marks the point where these Highland arteries meet at Latheron, and is just one of many well-preserved ancient sites found close to the two. To the north-west, between a meandering burn and a minor road, is the Guidebest Stone Circle (58.2968, -3.3988), but it is in the hinterland of the coast from Lybster to Wick that we find one of the highest proliferations of ancient sites. The strange Hill o' Many Stanes are often called Scotland's answer to Carnac (Brittany) and more rows lie hidden in the heather close to the Cairn of Get. An archaeological trail around the banks of the Loch of Yarrows allows you to walk through thousands of years of prehistory, past chambered tombs and a well-preserved broch.

Brochs are commonly associated with the north and the Western Isles, yet Caithness boasts more per square mile than anywhere else. Resembling small cooling towers, they were the homes of Iron Age chieftains, powerful figures who ruled tribes and controlled land, grain and resources. By 100BC, some may have been so powerful that they could be described as the first aristocrats, living a life of luxury with goods imported from the Roman Empire. Brochs have thick walls and guardrooms, so obviously have a defensive purpose, but could this have been as much a symbolic show of power as a strategic stronghold? Perhaps, like Martello towers constructed during the Napoleonic era, they were built as a response to a real or imagined coastal threat? Many are found overlooking the sea: Nybster, Bruan (58.3382, -3.1787) and Dùn Beath on its estuary on the east coast, Clachtoll (58.1955, -5.3421) and Caisteal Grugaig (57.2664, -5.5392) on the west coast, and Castlehill (58.5992, -3.3892), Heilam (58.5059, -4.6444), the Kyle of Durness (58.5758, -4.7729) and the Kyle of Tongue (58.4414, -4.4819) along the north coast. However, with so many also inland, like the five brochs at Westerdale (58.4479, -3.4952), the Borg (58.4329, -3.8867) and the Yarrows in the east, or Dun Telve and Dun Troddan (57.1946, -5.5867) to the west, it has been suggested these could be places where farmers hid their cattle and families in response to marauding enemy tribes. It seems likely that different brochs were constructed for many different reasons, changing and developing over time.

1 NYBSTER BROCH
AUCKENGILL

Also called Mervyn's Tower, this broch village overlooks the wild Caithness coast from atop a promontory with steep rock cliffs. Rather than an isolated roundhouse, the broch was visibly part of a larger settlement. It has been described as one of the most spectacular Iron Age settlements in the North of Scotland, and is not to be missed if travelling on the A99. Much of the remains surrounding the fort can still be seen, although the raging North Sea has already claimed its share of the buildings. To one side of the broch is a monument to Sir Francis Tress Barry, the first archaeologist to excavate here in 1900. The broch itself is no doubt the main attraction; the walls are over 4 metres thick and the internal diameter is more than 7 metres!

Follow A99 N from Wick for 3 miles to Reiss, and turn R signed John o'Groats to stay on A99 for 6½ miles to the hamlet of Auckengill. At the Auckengill sign, a R turn leads to a car park at the end and path to the broch. A little further along the road on the L is a 19th-century schoolhouse with a picnic bench and parking in front; this is the Caithness Broch Centre, and you can also park here, see associated collections inside and follow signs to the broch. Bus routes 77 and 177 from Wick to Auckengill opp petrol station stop, no Sunday service.

58.5518, -3.0839, ND370631, KW1 4XR

2 YARROWS ARCHAEOLOGICAL TRAIL SOUTH YARROWS

This circular walk of a little over 2 miles spans thousands of years of prehistory. There are chambered cairns and a standing stone dating to the Neolithic, Bronze Age hut circles, an Iron Age hillfort (58.3635, -3.1911) and a broch (58.3744, -3.1844). The northern cairn, a good place to start an anticlockwise circuit, is roofless, with two flagstones standing upright on the moor marking the former entrance. The southern cairn (58.3715, -3.1906) is far more complete, and you can still make out its chambers, along with the covered entrance to the tomb. The broch's now grass-topped walls stand guard over the Loch of Yarrows, a well-preserved Iron Age building, still showing its guard chamber and doorway complete with lintel. Roman pottery and glass were found at the broch, suggesting that an important

person with links to the outside world must have lived here. The route is by no means clear, and a map and compass or a suitable GPS phone mapping will be needed to explore all the sites. The ground can get boggy here so wellies are also essential!

From Wick on A99 head S for 4¾ miles to Thrumster and a crossroads with church and war memorial. Turn R here signposted Yarrows Archaeological Trail, L following sign at next crossroads, and L at loch to car park. Bus routes 81, 81S, 175 and 275 from Wick to Thrumster opp church stop, 2¾ miles' walk, no Sunday service.

58.3740, -3.1900, ND304434, KW1 5SE

3 CAIRN OF GET
WHALIGOE

Close to the 365 steps carved into the cliffs in the 18th century at Whaligoe, a short but boggy walk brings you to this well-preserved Neolithic chambered burial cairn of the Orkney-Cromarty group (named after the region they are mostly found in). The roof of the tomb has long since gone, allowing you to clearly see the inner chambers and the long entrance passage. It also means that unlike other more complete Neolithic tombs, you don't risk scuffing your knees or banging your head as you explore inside here! Around 3000BC, when the tomb was first built, its central chamber would have been more than 3 metres high, large enough to stand up in. Ceremonies may have taken place in the 'horned' forecourt (the walled area at the front of the tomb) and the bones of seven people were found in the antechamber, along with cremations in the main chamber behind. There are stone rows hidden in heather nearby (58.3544, -3.1766 and 58.3516, -3.1765)

From Wick take A99 S to Whaligoe, 7 miles. At Whaligoe, follow brown sign R for 'Cairn of Get ¾'. Follow road to the pull-in R at start of loch (58.3507, -3.1655) and take footpaths to the cairn, ground can get boggy. Bus routes 81, 81S, 175 and 275 from Wick to Whaligoe opp Smithy Cottage stop and walk back to turning, no Sunday service.

58.3531, -3.1750, ND313411, KW2 6AA

4 DÙN BEATH BROCH
DUNBEATH

It is a short, pleasant walk past the ruins of a medieval monastery to Dùn Beath broch, which lies within a clump of trees on a promontory between the Burn of Houstry and Dunbeath Water. A substantial ruin, its wall are 4.3 metres thick around an interior with an 8-metre diameter. The broch was first dug in the 1860s by WS Thomson Sinclair, younger; as the landowner, he fell very much into the category of Victorian gentlemen antiquarians, keen to 'have a go' but leaving no real detailed drawings or lists of finds. However, some of his discoveries were recorded in a letter to the more practised Joseph Anderson who excavated Yarrows (see entry). He discussed details of the guard chamber (which can still be seen) along with finds of deer antlers, butchered bones and the remains of fish such as cod and haddock, shell middens and traces of fire.

Approaching Dunbeath from the S on the A9, turn L immediately after the bridge and follow lower road below houses past the white bus shelter. Take R fork just before stone bridge to follow road round to car park at end. There are noticeboards marking the trail to the broch: follow river N and it is hidden in a clump of trees over a small bridge. Bus 81S from Wick to Dunbeath Layby stop and cross to turning, weekdays only.

58.2547, -3.4410, ND155304, KW6 6EG

5 ACHAVANICH STONES
LOCH STEMSTER

The Achavanich – or Achkinloch – stone setting is an unusual horseshoe-shaped monument with 'sideways' facing stones, somewhat reminiscent of the oval stone circle of Bedd Arthur (see Pembrokeshire). This horseshoe configuration can be seen at Stonehenge and it was built into the early phases of Croft Moraig stone circle in Tayside (56.6018, -3.9602), but nationally it is very scarce. Only 36 of the original 54 stones remain here, the tallest of which stands some 2 metres high. It is large setting, 69 metres long and over 30 metres wide. Visible from the stones to the south-east is a chambered cairn that shares their name, but predates the stone setting by around 1,000 years. With the two sites so close together, and a further cist containing a young woman having been dug out a little to the north (58.3706,

-3.4064) it seems that the area had some important ritual or religious significance during the Neolithic and into the Bronze Age. Close by, over the A9, Greysteil Castle broch (58.3558, -3.4038) protrudes out into Loch Rangag. The two lochs and their associated prehistoric remains make for an enjoyable walk.

At Latheron turn inland on the A9 towards Thurso and Scrabster. Remain on this road for 6 miles then just after parking layby L take a hairpin R turn toward Loch Stemster and turn shortly L to parking by the shore. Walk on S and you will see the stones by the side of the road. From here you can walk to Loch Rangang – or park there and walk to the stones.

58.3566, -3.3895, ND187417, KW5 6DX

6 CAMORE WOOD
DORNOCH

Now a Forestry Commission conifer plantation and a welcome stop-off when travelling on the A9, 2,000–3,000 years ago Camore Wood was a thriving community. Between 25 and 32 roundhouses have been found here, and even if a quarter of these were empty at any given time, it would still have been a substantial settlement. Part of the success of this village was its location, built on a glacial esker or gravel ridge, a geological remnant of the last ice age. The inhabitants would have also been able to take advantage of the Dornoch Firth, and shell middens have been found all over this area. Some of the huts are more visible than others, and there are information boards around the wood close to the remains of some of these dwellings. Elsewhere in the woods lies its main prehistoric attraction, a large Neolithic chambered cairn that resembles some of the Bronze Age burial mounds in the South of England. It is mostly overgrown, but some of the stonework can be seen protruding from the bracken. A large slab of quartz was found within the tomb, which would have been transported here from some distance away. There is a play trail for kids and plenty of picnic benches.

On the A9 heading N, cross over Dornoch Firth Bridge and then take first R to Cuthill. Remain on this road 1½ miles, you will see the Forestry Commission sign L into Camore. Bus routes X98 and X99 from Inverness to Dornoch opp Clydesdale Bank stop, 2 miles' walk along Cuthill Links Road SW.

57.8796, -4.0727, NH771896, IV25 3RW

7 THE GREY CAIRNS OF CAMSTER LYBSTER

Beneath an often grey or misty sky, amidst patches of conifer plantation and vast, barren, windswept moorland, are two unfathomably ancient burial cairns, which stood hidden away for thousands of years. These great isolated mounds of grey stone were built 5,000 years ago and restored to their present glory in the 1970s. The larger of the two, at 70 metres in length, is the aptly named Camster Long. It contains two inner chambers, both of which can be crawled into on hands and knees via a narrow passage behind a sturdy iron gate on the side of the cairn. Inside, light from the modern translucent roof (the original collapsed) allows the explorer to see the ancient drystone walling made up of flat flagstones. It is reminiscent of the tombs on Orkney, and indeed belongs to the Orkney-Cromarty group. In the 1880s a French governess crawled into one of the cairns and refusing to leave the way she came in, became stuck. After what must have felt like an eternity in the dark tomb, a ladder was found, and she left via the hole in the roof! The second tomb, Camster round, is 18 metres in diameter and 3.7 metres high. Its central chamber is also accessed by a narrow passageway; be prepared to be surprised by nesting birds shooting past you as you crawl down this dark tunnel to the inner chamber.

From the crossroads of Lybster head E on A99 for 1 mile, then at Occumster turn L signposted Camster Cairns for 5 miles. You will come to a long layby with signs on the L (58.3790, -3.2642). Park here and follow the boardwalks to the cairns.

58.3800, -3.2669, ND260442, KW3 6BD

8 HILL O' MANY STANES MID CLYTH

As its name implies, this very unusual site on a wild hillside close to the coast of Caithness comprises many small stones, the largest only a metre high. They radiate in a fan shape (it can be hard to make out) from the top of a rocky knoll, as if from a cairn, though there is no sign of one. In 1780, the Reverend Charles Cordiner wrote 'There are twenty rows, and twenty stones in each, so that there are not less than 400 in that one spot'. In 1871, a survey of the site, carried out by Sir Henry Dryden, found this number had dropped to 250 and by 1910 just 192 were still erect. It

is thought there could have been three times the present number here in around 2000–1900BC, when the stones may have been used to mark the maximum moonrise in summer and winter. Local folklore tells us the stones mark a battleground, following a clash of the rival Keith and Gunn clans. The Gunns are said to have come out the victors and marked each fallen warrior, on both sides, with a stone. They now stand amongst gorse and heather, particularly beautiful in early autumn.

From Lybster head E on A99 for 4 miles, then L at brown sign for Hill o' Many Stanes. Small layby R after ⅓ mile. Follow old Ministry of Works sign to stones through gate on L of road.

58.3284, -3.2054, ND295384, KW3 6BA

9 DÙN DORNAIGIL BROCH ALLTNACAILLICH

This isolated, filled-in Iron Age ruin stands on a meander of the Strathmore River, miles down an overgrown single-track road that winds between great exposed rocky outcrops, through thick heather, bracken and patchy tree plantations struggling to grow in the poor Highland soil. The landscape here is wild and barren, but nevertheless utterly beautiful. Dùn Dornaigil has been sculpted by the ravages of time to resemble the soaring summit of Ben Hope, which towers up behind it to the north. On the north-east side of the broch, above the lintelled doorway, the wall still stands to a height of 7m. We do not know who lived here; the alternative name of Dornadilla hints

at a link to the early king Dornadille – unfortunately he was probably fictitious. The 2nd-century Greco-Roman geographer Ptolemy wrote of a Smertae tribe whose territory included much of modern-day Sutherland. He claimed them to be fearsome warriors, and suggested they smeared their enemies with sacrificial blood! However, Ptolemy may have never left Alexandria and is therefore also not the most reliable of sources. To the side of the broch the river has deposited enough stones to form a rocky beach, and on a clear day, this is a perfect stop-off point for a picnic, where you can take in the dramatic scenery. Back in the Iron Age, however, this was likely a fiercely guarded trade route, perhaps the reason for the broch's existence.

From Altnaharra on the A836 head N through over the river and take the L at the crossroads signposted to Hope. Remain on this road for 10¾ miles until you see the broch. It can also be reached from Hope on the A838 to the N, following the road signed Altnaharra on the E side of the loch S for 10 miles.

58.3662, -4.6391, NC457450, IV27 4UJ 🅻🅰🅴🅰

CHAPTER 28

ORKNEY & SHETLAND

*A*s my car was pushed off the ferry onto Mainland Orkney, its dead battery somehow seemed fitting for my arrival; as if the technology it represented had no place on these islands. Orkney is a strange place, starkly beautiful, barren and desolate; life seems to cling to the rocky shores and windswept fields. The treeless landscape lets the eye pass up to the vast sky and out to the wild seas, where seabirds, seals, porpoises and whales can be spotted making a handsome living from the rich waters. Like Shetland to the north, the islands were under Norse rule until the 15th century, and the culture still feels split between Scotland to the south and the lands across the North Sea to the east. You can still hear this in the lilt of the local accent, rising and falling, with words coming to a hard stop more familiar in Scandinavia than the Highlands. Both the Shetlands and Orkney have a wealth of well-visited ancient sites, like the Ring of Brodgar and Maeshowe, not to mention countless brochs, souterrains, tombs and standing stones scattered across farmland, in gardens or even tucked away on industrial estates. Part of this wealth of finds is due to the geology of the area: the islands have an abundance of easily worked flagstones. If you take a walk down to the shoreline close by the Broch of Gurness you will find not only a family of friendly seals but also stones just waiting to be quarried out. They seem almost cut into shape and ready to use, like the squares of a chocolate bar or the Neolithic equivalent of a prefabricated building. Studying the nearby broch, along with settlements like the Knap of Howar on Papa Westray (59.3493, -2.9108) and Skara Brae, you can see the uses these stones were put to.

Current thinking about the islands puts them at the centre of Neolithic activity. It suggests that the Orcadian culture was predominant, and its ideas moved south to influence that of the mainland, rather than the other way around. It may even be that Orkney was more important than sites such as Stonehenge and Avebury far to the south.

1 STANYDALE TEMPLE
WALLS, SHETLAND

On the rough moors of Shetland, almost hidden from view, are the remains of the Stanydale Temple. It is somewhere between an oval and a heel shape, with a concave end, measuring 20 metres by 16 metres with drystone walls 3.5 metres thick. We cannot know for certain if it was a temple, but it is not a cairn, and its sheer size tells us it was certainly an important building in the community. It could have been a meeting hall or the home of an important family, the Neolithic equivalent of a local laird. Large quantities of barley were found here, which could also suggest it was used as a storage barn. The 'temple' stands in close proximity to five houses thought to be contemporary with its construction, and there are several standing stones forming an arc to the south. There are remains of a Neolithic farm known as the Scord of Brouster 2 miles to the north-west off the A971 (60.2479, -1.5409), comprising three houses along with field boundaries, and numerous remains around the two sites, so it is well worth spending some time in this corner of the island.

Take the A971 NE from Walls for 2⅓ miles towards Lerwick over bridge, then R turn towards Skeld and Gruting for 1½ miles. At crossroads take L towards Hulmalees and after ½ mile park in the passing place L at sign (do not fill it up if others are there!). Follow trail across the moor, 1-mile moderate but wet walk. Bus 9 Lerwick–Walls to Skeld Road End stop, 2 miles' to trail start.

60.2354, -1.4865, HU285502, ZE2 9NS

2 BROCH OF MOUSA
SANDWICK, SHETLAND

Of the 500 or more Atlantic roundhouses or brochs found in Scotland and its islands, Mousa is perhaps the most complete and impressive. The 13.3-metre-high tower is in such good condition that it has been described as the best-preserved Iron Age monument in Europe. It is bigger and better conceived than most brochs, and the 12th-century history the Orkneyinga Saga noted it as impregnable. Originally, it would have measured at least 15 metres tall and must have been a formidable sight for any would-be invaders. It owes much of its longevity to its sheer size and its remote position on a now-uninhabited island, far from prospective stone robbers. Brochs are a uniquely Scottish construction, and it is thought they were built to defend families during a turbulent time in the nation's prehistory. All are constructed with an inner and outer wall, almost like a Russian doll; a tower within a tower. This reduces the weight and allows for their great height and for staircases to be built running between the two walls, to a lookout at the top. Being so remote and uninhabited, the island is a haven for birdlife, and seals can be found basking in the sun along the coast.

Mousa is only accessible by boat from the main island. It runs from April to mid-September, Sunday to Friday, from Sandsayre Pier, Sandwick (current timetable at mousa.co.uk).

59.9952, -1.1820, HU457236, ZE2 9HW

3 JARLSHOF
SUMBURGH, SHETLAND

Just like Skara Brae (see entry), the ancient remains at Jarlshof were first revealed by a violent storm. Archaeologists began work on the site in the 1920s and found evidence of around 3,000 years of occupation, the earliest dating to the Neolithic and found on the landward side of the museum. They also found six Late Bronze Age houses with cell-like chambers, at the back facing onto a large courtyard, and the workshop of a bronzesmith with clay moulds for weapons such as swords. Early Iron Age stone roundhouses and souterrains followed, and by the 2nd century BC a 'wheelhouse' with a roof supported on radial walls. Finally, Vikings built farmsteads here in the 9th century, and the large laird's house was built in the 17th century. It is astonishing to think that people first chose to farm at Jarlshof over 4,000 years ago and have been working the land there ever since. On the other side of the stretch of sea known as the West Voe of Sumburgh, a spit of rocky land called the Ness of Burgi juts out into the North Sea. Taking advantage of this near-island promontory, the Iron Age population built a substantial fort, the remains of which can still be seen today (59.8590, -1.3088).

Take the A970 S past Sumburgh Airport, L by Sumburgh Hotel (ZE3 9JN, 01950 460201) signed Jarlshof ¼ mile. Bus 6 from Lerwick to Sumburgh opp Hotel Rd End stop.

59.8693, -1.2906, HU398095, ZE3 9JN

4 QUOYNESS CHAMBERED CAIRN SANDAY, ORKNEY

You have to be very determined to visit Quoyness, a chambered cairn of the Maeshowe type with six small cells inside the walls. It lies in the north-east corner of the Orkney archipelago, on the remote (but beautiful) island of Sanday, at the end of the Els Ness Peninsula, down a track that is better by bike than by car! When you get there, the main chamber can only be accessed by a 9-metre crawl along its entrance passage – a cist found here contained bone fragments of ten adults and four or five children. The precision of the 4-metre-high drystone walling, laid over 5,200 years ago, is staggering; it is hard to imagine modern building lasting half as long as this. Remote as it is, Quoyness is not alone; the remains of Augmund Howe chambered cairn are to the south, a grassy knoll with exposed stonework being claimed by the sea on the coastal side. Spread across the south end of the peninsula are the remains of a Bronze Age cemetery, a little harder to spot than the two main Neolithic cairns.

Regular ferries run from Kirkwall to Loth in SW Sanday (ork-neyferries.co.uk, 01856 872044). From here follow the B9070 NE to T-junction and turn R towards Kettletoft on the B9068, then take L for Lady Village on B9069. Where the road bends L at 1¼ miles, just past a ruined church, take the rough track R with a poorly placed brown sign for the cairn. Follow until you reach a pull-in on the R, then follow the coastal path for ¾ mile to the cairn.

59.2255, -2.5682, HY 676377, KW17 2BL

5 MID HOWE BROCH & CAIRN ROUSAY, ORKNEY

Off the north-east of Mainland Orkney, a short ferry ride over the Eynhallow Sound, is a 4½-mile stretch of road so rich in remains that it has given the island the nickname of the Egypt of the North. This broch and cairn are two of the most impressive, and certainly the largest, prehistoric sites on Rousay; ideally, hire a bicycle and start here, heading back to the ferry via the other sites. Like the Broch of Gurness (see entry), Mid Howe stands above the ravages of the cold Orcadian sea, has a ground gallery and is surrounded a small settlement. As you walk through the stone doorway, you see the two chambers (thought to have been for guard dogs) either side, stairs leading up to the next level, and ahead a stone water tank, hearths and drystone walls. It all gives a real sense of what life must have been like here in the Iron Age. Gaps in the wall large enough to thrust spears through suggest this was a defensive tower. Next to it, housed in what looks like a large aircraft hangar, is the Mid Howe stalled cairn. It predates the broch by some centuries, built around 1,000 years before the Great Pyramid of Giza. It is a truly remarkable building, comprising a central passageway 23.6 metres long, divided into 12 stalls by large, flat flagstones, which you can view from walkways above. The remains of 25 individuals were found here, along with the bones of oxen, crows, buzzards, eagles and seabirds such as skua, cormorant and gannet.

From the ferry terminal (orkneyferries.co.uk, 01856 872044), follow the road inland as it bears L and then R to the B9064. Turn L and Trumland Farm Bicycle Hire is ¼ mile on L (KW17 2PU, 01856 821252) Follow the road W for 3¼ miles more to the bridge and small house at Westness. Cyclists and walkers can turn L down farm track then R, following track just over 1 mile to the large hangar; drivers continue 1¼ miles to parking spaces and signed path across fields to site.

59.1574, -3.1003813, HY371305, KW17 2PS

6 KNOWE CAIRNS & BLACKHAMMER
ROUSAY, ORKNEY

Knowe of Lairo, often missed, is a dilapidated but fascinating 'horned' cairn, where a 6-metre crawl leads to a chamber where the ceiling rises up above your head – bring a torch! Further along the road from is another stalled cairn like Mid Howe (see entry), the 22-metre Knowe of Yarso (59.1341, -3.0417). The bones of 29 people were found here, including 17 skulls, as well as pottery, arrowheads and stone tools and the bones of 36 reindeer. Knowe of Ramsay (59.1345, -3.0494) beyond it on OS maps, is now no more than a mound with a dip, but had 14 compartments. Blackhammer (59.1312, -3.0252) is a 13-metre cairn from around 3000BC, originally divided into seven stalls. The original roof would have been corbelled stone heaped with smaller stones, similar to the Grey Cairns of Camster (see Highlands); a modern concrete top with a skylight now preserves and displays it. You might think this would detract from the wonder, but if anything it enhances the atmosphere inside and can be a welcome escape from harsh Orcadian weather – unlike Mid Howe, you can walk inside the chamber here. Pottery, animal bones and the remains of two individuals were found within. Tracks to all the cairns can be very muddy!

On the B9064 heading E from Mid Howe (see entry) turn L at the red telephone box for a short walk to Lairo. Continue on road E for ¾ mile to parking spaces and a signed path L to Yarso (quite inland). A further ½ mile on is a layby and sign L for Blackhammer Tomb, just off the road to the NE via the path at the end.

59.1341, -3.0522, HY398279, KW17 2PT ▶🛈🚶

7 TAVERSOE TUICK
ROUSAY, ORKNEY

Less than a mile from the ferry is the double-decker tomb of Taversoe Tuick. The two levels of these chambered tombs now have a ladder running between them, which was absent from its original construction, so it is easy to access both. It is hard not to channel a little bit of Indiana Jones as you climb down to explore the dark chambers below, where human bones and a granite mace head were found. A unique feature of the tomb is a strange drain-like structure, which leads 5 metres toward a rock-cut chamber downhill. The only other two-storey Orkney tomb, the more ruinous, atmospheric Huntersquoy, can be found on the island of Eday (59.2240, -2.7680). We have no real evidence of why the tombs were stacked like this, but we do know islands were seen as holy places. Could it be that land here was in high demand? I would rather believe the two tombs hold different branches of a feuding family, tactfully separated from each other for all eternity.

Continue E from Blackhammer (see entry) for ¾ mile towards the ferry terminal to a gate L with information boards for RSPB nature reserve; follow the track, and the footpath to Taversoe Tuick is 230 metres on L.

59.1314, -3.0049, HY425276, KW17 2PU ▶↩🚶

8 BROCH OF GURNESS
MAINLAND, ORKNEY

Because it was hidden until the 1930s, this great Iron Age tower remains remarkably intact. Around the broch are the remains of ancient terraced houses, which would have stood under the protection of the broch. In the centre of the building there is a 4-metre-deep well, and many of the stone furnishings are clearly visible inside the large defensive walls. During the Iron Age the shores of Eynhallow Sound, the stretch of sea separating Mainland Orkney from the Isle of Rousay, were protected by eleven brochs: it is likely that this was an important route for Orkney during a time of burgeoning international trade. An amphora was found in the broch, which could have contained wine or olive oil, and within the kitchen midden two severed hands were found, still wearing a total of 5 bronze rings! Both the impressive size of the broch and the artefacts found there suggest those living here were high-status individuals. Eventually the Vikings took over the site, with evidence of a typical longhouse.

On the A966 in the NE, to the E of junction with B9057, take the turning opposite Evie Community School signposted Broch of Gurness. Follow the road as it bends L then R to the Historic Scotland car park and visitor centre.

59.1239, -3.0813, HY381268, KW17 2NH 🌊↩▶🏔

9

10

11

11

9 BRODGAR AREA
MAINLAND, ORKNEY

The Ring of Brodgar is the largest stone circle in Scotland, measuring 104 metres across, and still has its encircling henge, making it almost unique along with Avebury (see Wiltshire and Wessex). The Ring is thought to be the latest of the sites here. The older Stones of Stenness (58.9940, -3.2078) were once 12 in number, on a raised platform surrounded by a henge. Today, only three complete and two partial stones stand; one with a hole that was used for sealing oaths was destroyed by the landowner in 1814. What is thought to be a temple complex between these at the Ness of Brodgar (58.9971, -3.2149) only adds to the complexity of the area. Continuing work here has revealed the first evidence of painted decoration on Neolithic walls, shaped roof slates, and the bones of several hundred cattle that seem to have been slaughtered in a single event. The dig is open to visitors July–August (nessofbrodgar.co.uk for times). The roundhouses of the nearby Barnhouse Settlement (58.9959, -3.2064) give us insight into the size and shape of the homes of Neolithic farmers who made this fascinating region of Orkney their home, like a miniature Skara Brae (see entry). All these sites are free to visit, and can be reached from the car park by the Ring of Brodgar.

From Stromness docks take Ferry Road N to roundabout by petrol station, take R and follow to T-junction. Turn R onto with A965 and follow for 2 miles to crossroads shortly after Stenness. Turn L onto the B9055 signposted Bay of Skaill (B9056), and follow 1½ miles until you come to the Ring of Brodgar car park signed R. The Ness of Brodgar, Stones of Stenness and Barnhouse Settlement are all within 1-mile walking distance back along the road and signed L. Bus T11 from Stromness or Kirkwall to Stenness near Ring of Brodgar stop.

59.0014, -3.2295, HY294133, KW16 3JZ

10 MAESHOWE CHAMBERED CAIRN
MAINLAND, ORKNEY

Thought to have been built into an existing stone circle, Maeshowe is a passage grave design known only on Orkney. It is the finest of the seven examples, and may well be the last that was built. Its entry passage is only 1m high, but the beautifully crafted inner chamber walls are vaulted far over your head. The winter solstice sunset flooding down the passage lights up the rear wall, just as the solstice sunrise illuminates the similar tomb of Newgrange in Ireland. There is a charge for Maeshowe, with hourly tours departing by shuttle bus from the Visitor Centre at Stenness – booking is strongly recommended (KW16 3LB, 01856 851266).

As for the Brodgar area (see entry), but in Stenness turn R for Maeshowe Visitor Centre.

58.9966, -3.1881, HY294133, KW16 3HH

11 SKARA BRAE
MAINLAND, ORKNEY

During a February night in 1850, a ferocious storm ripped across Scotland. So powerful were the winds, they killed a number of people on the mainland, and on the treeless landscape of Orkney they tore away the earth at the Bay of Skaill. Under what was thought to be an irregular-shaped sand dune, locals found the roofless dwellings of Skara Brae, dating back to 4,500–5,000 years ago. First excavated in 1868, the site gave up a rich array of finds. There were at least ten structures over some 600 years of use, complete with stone furniture including box-beds, hearths, dressers, wall cupboards and tanks for water, possibly for keeping limpets for fish bait. One building seems to have been a workshop. There are interactive displays for all age groups and a reconstruction of one house with its stone furniture in use gives a real insight into Neolithic life. To the south of Skara Brae is the Broch of Borwick (59.0309, -3.3532) beautifully positioned close to towering sea stacks.

Follow the B9055 on from the Brodgar Area (see entry). Follow signs from the junction with the B9056 at East Aith, to the E of Loch of Skaill, taking the B9056 N and W across the edge of the loch to the Historic Scotland car park, visitor centre, café and shop. Bus T11 from Stromness or Kirkwall to Skara Brae Visitor Centre stop.

59.0487, -3.3417, HY231187, KW16 3LR

12 WIDEFORD HILL CHAMBERED CAIRN
MAINLAND, ORKNEY

An early example of its kind, built in 3500BC, Wideford Cairn is like a prototype for Maeshowe (see entry). It is a marvel of Neolithic ingenuity and engineering: the ground would have been levelled to build the tomb, which meant cutting into the very bedrock of Wideford Hill, and the drystone walling on the site shows a building technique that easily rivals Egyptian and Roman masonry. It is a good three-hour or 6-mile round walk from Kirkwall, with impressive views from the top once you have made the steep climb, and accessed through the roof. No human remains were found at Wideford, which led the Victorian archaeologist Flinders Petrie to believe the tomb had long since been emptied; the central chamber had been deliberately infilled. Nearby Cuween Hill chambered tomb, 3 miles to the west (58.9973, -3.1084), is quite a different story: along with remains of eight humans, the skulls of 24 dogs were found in the central chamber, a 5-metre crawl in. Archaeologists have several theories as to why the skulls were there: they may have been totem animals, sacrifices or burials of beloved companions. Bring a torch!

From Kirkwall High Street follow Glaitness Road, signposted Finstown, W for 2 miles. You'll pass a collection of houses on the L followed by a single house R. After the single house turn R to follow the road toward the transmitter towers. Head past barn-type buildings and follow track ¾ of the way up to small parking space with sign and follow the path 800m to cairn. Bus 437 from Kirkwall to Firth opp Lesliedale stop, weekdays only.

58.9919, -3.0301, HY409121, KW15 1TS 🏠🔲

13 DWARFIE STANE
HOY, ORKNEY

Legend has it that this huge sandstone block was once home to magical dwarf. Half-fairy, half-human with the gift of eternal youth, he made his living selling herbs and potions at exorbitant prices; a tradition it seems a few unscrupulous Orcadians still maintain! Rather than the home of a magical creature, the Dwarfie Stane is thought to be a Neolithic chambered tomb. A passage and two cells were carved out from the erratic, which

was deposited on Hoy during the ice age. Tombs like this are common in Southern Europe but rare in the north, and it is thought to be the only one of its kind in Scotland.

From the B9047 just S of Moaness, at the staggered crossroads, turn S following brown sign for Dwarfie Stane. After 1⅓ mile there is parking on the R. Cross the road and follow the path 400 metres S to the stone.

58.8844, -3.3143, HY243004, KW16 3NJ 🔲🔼🔽

14 ISBISTER CAIRN
SOUTH RONALDSAY, ORKNEY

This cairn is also called the Tomb of the Eagles, because when archaeologists began to sift through the deposits inside they found a large number of sea eagle bones – so many, they were led to believe the birds must have been important to the lives (or afterlives) of those buried there. However, there are also the bones of fish and other birds, and the tomb had been unattended for many centuries, so it may be the case that the eagles chose to hide within to devour their prey; indeed, the nearby Banks Cairn or Tomb of the Otters (58.7347, -2.9379) may have also been a hideout for wild animals to dine in peace. The tomb also housed a proliferation of human bones: 16,000 in total, belonging to at least 342 individuals. It appears the bodies were 'excarnated', or had the flesh removed, elsewhere before the bones were disarticulated and placed in the tomb. The individuals found seemed to have a short average life expectancy, of no more than 20 years, and of the 85 skulls found within the tomb, 16 showed significant trauma to the head. All of this leads experts to question whether the Neolithic was the peaceful time it is often thought to have been. There is a visitor centre with finds from the tomb (KW17 2RW, 01856 831339) and guided tours; it is a 1-mile walk to the tomb, taking in a Bronze Age burnt mound and building on the way, and the entrance is a low crawl.

Take the A961 over the bridge from Mainland Orkney onto South Ronaldsay, and follow S for 8¼ miles, almost to the bottom of the island, before turning L onto B9041. Turn R after ¾ mile at brown Tomb of the Eagles sign, and follow signs to the cairn.

58.7391, -2.9313, ND461838, KW17 2RW 🔼🔽🔳

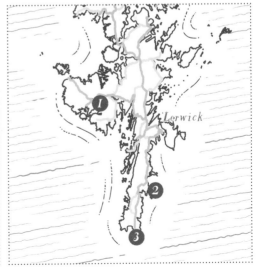

Nine Ladies, p148

INDEX

INDEX

Dun Borranish, p251

Photographs

Wild Ruins BC
The explorer's guide to Britain's
ancient sites

Words
Dave Hamilton

Photos
Dave Hamilton
Jon Taylor
and those credited

Editing and Proofing
Candida Frith-Macdonald
ProofProfessor

Design and Layout
Sue Gent
Amy Bolt
Tania Pascoe

Distribution
Central Books Ltd
Freshwater Road, Dagenham
RM8 1RX, United Kingdom
Tel +44 (0)208 525 8800
orders@centralbooks.com

Published by
Wild Things Publishing Ltd.
Freshford, Bath,
BA2 7WG, United Kingdom
www.wildthingspublishing.com

Copyright

Author acknowledgements

No book is written alone, and I would like to thank the following for their help. Firstly, my family; Liz, Doug and Lenny for the patience on another of my all-consuming projects. Jon Taylor and Richard Byles for their excellent photography and company. The incredible hard-working team of Dan and Tania at Wild Things Publishing. Thanks to all those who worked on the manuscript, including the fact-checking and prehistory chats with Stephen Keats, Vivienne Evans for her tireless reads of early drafts and Candida Frith-Macdonald for her very human editing approach. Thanks to all those who gave me somewhere to stay or met me en route, including my parents, Mark Bloomfield, Frag, Sarah and Willow, Scot, Gemma and family, Steve and Lucy, Chris and Karen, Paul and Mick, Matt and Leila and family, all the lads that came on Dan and Anthony's two 40th's bashes in Scotland and Wiltshire, Sasha, Ali and their kids, Vintage Vacations on the Isle of Wight for use of their 1950s caravan www.vintagevacations.co.uk, Rob Woodward (especially as he wasn't mentioned in the last book) and Tony, Ange and Albert. Thanks to Dominic Read-Jones, Rowan Muskin, Lionel Williams for drone shots and the promo video. Sue at Visit Isle of Wight and the people at Visit Isles of Scilly for help and advice. A final special thanks goes to all those people I met at the sites and all those who helped out in any way.

Health, Safety and Responsibility

Like any activity undertaken in the outdoors, particularly in remote and elevated areas, exploring ruins has risks and can be dangerous. Terrain, access and signage are subject to change and areas that were once safely and legally accessible may no longer be so. The author has gone to great lengths to ensure the accuracy of the information herein. He will not be held legally or financially responsible for any accident, injury, loss or inconvenience sustained as a result of the information or advice contained in this book. Exploring the locations described is undertaken entirely at your own risk.

Other books from Wild Things Publishing:

Scottish Bothy Bible
Bikepacking
France en Velo
Hidden Beaches Britain
Lost Lanes Southern England
Lost Lanes Wales
Lost Lanes west
Lost Lanes West Country
Only Planet
Wild Garden Weekends
Wild Ruins & Wild Ruins B.C.

Wild Guide - Devon, Cornwall
     and South West
Wild Guide - Lake District and
     Yorkshire Dales
Wild Guide - Southern and
     Eastern England
Wild Guide Wales and Marches
Wild Guide Scotland
Wild Guide - Scandinavia
     (Norway, Sweden, Iceland
     and Denmark)

Wild Guide Portugal
Wild Swimming Britain
Wild Swimming France
Wild Swimming Italy
Wild Swimming Spain
Wild Swimming Sydney
     Australia
Wild Swimming Walks
     Around London
Wild Swimming Walks
     Dartmoor and South Devon

hello@wildthingspublishing.com